The Spartan Drama of Plato's *Laws*

Political Theory for Today

Series Editor: Richard Avramenko, University of Wisconsin, Madison

Political Theory for Today seeks to bring the history of political thought out of the jargon-filled world of the academy into the everyday world of social and political life. The series brings the wisdom of texts and tradition of political philosophy to bear on salient issues of our time, especially issues pertaining to human freedom and responsibility, the relationship between individuals and the state, the moral implications of public policy, health and human flourishing, public and private virtues, and more. Great thinkers of the past have thought deeply about the human condition and their situations—books in Political Theory for Today build on that insight.

Recent titles in the series:

Tradition v. Rationalism: Voegelin, Oakeshott, Hayek, and Others, edited by Gene Callahan and Lee Trepanier
Democracy and Its Enemies: The American Struggle for the Enlightenment, by Paul N. Goldstene
Plato's Mythoi: The Political Soul's Drama Beyond, by Donald H. Roy
Eric Voegelin Today: Voegelin's Political Thought in the 21st Century, edited by Scott Robinson, Lee Trepanier, and David Whitney
Walk Away: When the Political Left Turns Right, edited by Lee Trepanier and Grant Havers
Idolizing the Idea: A Critical History of Modern Philosophy, by Wayne Cristaudo
The Spartan Drama of Plato's Laws, by Eli Friedland

The Spartan Drama of Plato's *Laws*

Eli Friedland

LEXINGTON BOOKS
Lanham • Boulder • New York • London

Published by Lexington Books
An imprint of The Rowman & Littlefield Publishing Group, Inc.
4501 Forbes Boulevard, Suite 200, Lanham, Maryland 20706
www.rowman.com

6 Tinworth Street, London SE11 5AL, United Kingdom

British Library Cataloguing in Publication Information Available

Library of Congress Cataloging-in-Publication Data Available
Library of Congress Control Number: 2020930511

ISBN 978-1-7936-0368-5 (cloth : alk. paper)
ISBN 978-1-7936-0369-2 (electronic)
ISBN 978-1-7936-0370-8 (pbk. : alk. paper)

For my mother who has always shown me what responsibility is;
for Charlotte, Léo, and Hector who show me what it is for;
and for my teachers with gratitude

Discors concordia fetibus apta est.
Ovid, *Metamorphoses*, 1.443

Contents

Acknowledgments

This book was undertaken with the generous funding of the Social Sciences and Humanities Research Council of Canada.

The debts and pleasures of gratitude that I have experienced and accrued in writing this book—and beforehand—are not, and should not be, repayable.

First and foremost, I want to thank my mother, Joan, the first and most important example of genuine responsibility in my life, and throughout my life. Amos, my brother, thank you for starting me on this path; Jess, my sister, thank you for taking it with me: you are both living examples for me. To all my brothers and sisters, and to all of my nieces and nephews, thank you. And not only because "every atom belonging to me as good belongs to you."

Travis Smith, thank you for your incredible generosity and rigor in your careful consideration of every word I wrote (and rewrote). Marlene Sokolon, thank you for keeping me grounded as I wrote this, and for pushing me to connect the dots. Horst Hutter, you are an inspiration to me. You changed my life when I walked into your classroom for the first time twelve years ago. Few moments in my life can match that one in magnitude. Christina Tarnopolsky, Mark Antaki, Geoff Sigalet, and Cam Cotton-O'Brien, what a blessing you have been for me. This book owes a very great deal to the many and varied conversations we have had over the years. Ryan Balot, your generous and thoughtful critique of this book has invigorated my thought. Thank you all.

I have also benefited greatly from the generous interrogation of chapters, as they took shape, from many readers, discussants, and conference participants, of whom I would thank in particular James Stoner, George Kateb, Nina Valiquette-Moreau, Alexandra Oprea, and Tiago Lier. I would like to thank as well one anonymous reviewer at Lexington Press, who provided invaluable feedback on my original manuscript. And I have been blessed with several extraordinary students in my Plato classes at Concordia University, whose insights led us down fruitful roads I had never even seen were there. Thank you.

Julie Blumer, Alex Roldan, Dónal Gill, Natalie Goulard, Eve Pankovitch, Mario Paquet, and Kathryn Rawlings, your impact on my life has been enormous, and your contributions to these pages subtle, massive, and innumerable. Thank you.

And, finally, to Hector, Léo, and Charlotte: you are the only way I have ever learned anything. For you, because of you, and through you, I know what gratitude is. Thank you.

Note on Texts and Translations

In what follows, references to Stephanus pagination (e.g., 803b, or 803b2) without a dialogue will always be to Plato's *Laws*. All other references to Platonic texts will contain the dialogue's name. Unless otherwise noted, all translations from Greek and Latin are my own; texts that I have translated are listed in my bibliography. For the *Laws*, I use Des Places and Diès's critical edition of the Greek text, *Les Lois*, in Platon, *Oeuvres Complètes* vols. 11–12 (Paris: Société d'Édition "Les Belles Lettres," 1956–1968) [Plato 1956–1968].

I have read and considered every English translation of the *Laws* that I am aware of, from Burges's *tour de force* 1859 literal translation (from which, I would add, I have learned a very great deal), through to Griffith's handsome 2016 Cambridge blue-book edition. Despite my admiration and gratitude for Burges's work, to my knowledge the best and only acceptable English translation of the *Laws* as a whole is Pangle's (1988 [first published 1980]), by a very wide margin.

Introduction

We almost all love badly, and the more we love, the worse we love. . . . We recklessly embark on the arduous journey of love that is [only] knowable by its end, the way we walk toward it, and the perilous steps along the path. . . .

—Marsilio Ficino to his friends Bernardo del Nero and Antonio Manetti

Allow me to make some broad and as yet unsubstantiated statements. Plato's *Laws* is a book about human nature and its place in the whole. Its scope in this respect is comprehensive, and it succeeds in its purpose. It is one of the most valuable books to which we have access, but accessing it is a difficult—indeed a very difficult—undertaking. It is likely the most important book on politics ever written.

In the *Laws*, with three characters, Plato seems to present virtually the full spectrum of human nature in its relationship with politics—or, to use the words he has his characters use, "political things." Yet it is certainly not lost on him that he has done so with three male characters, even though, and especially since, it is the contention within the *Laws* itself that a politics that lacks full female involvement is a paltry thing, capable at best of less than half the possible worthiness, and happiness, that a city in the best possible condition might attain. How are we to understand this? Is it sufficient to say that the nature of soul is not ultimately determined by gender, but by quality? To say today, as the Stranger says, that "my law would say exactly the same things about females as about men" (804d7–e1)?

Reflection upon the particulars of Plato's project may serve us, now, as a worthy guide into the conundrums of human nature and the politics that that nature, as a spectrum, both needs and despises. I submit that walking the long and slow way through the inexhaustibility of the *Laws*, step by step—and with all the wonders that open along the way—is not only the best but the

1

necessary means of accessing Plato's teaching in the *Laws*. I hope to have substantiated this submission in what follows, a brief overview of which may be in order.

OVERVIEW

In chapter 1, I give fresh consideration to the character I believe is the most often misunderstood in the *Laws*, Megillos. Megillos is a Spartan, the only Spartan character Plato wrote. How does he comport himself, and why? My interpretation suggests that Megillos is far more thoughtful and careful with what he says than is generally assumed, and with considerable consequences. He is troubled by what seems to be a lack of moderation in general among both Spartans and Cretans—and perhaps among all peoples—and he very subtly incites the Stranger to address this: while ostensibly rising to the defense of Sparta, and of Crete, he in fact deeply criticizes the excesses of one of Sparta's own colonies, Tarentum. He thereby more or less invites the Stranger to launch a broadside at an aspect of Sparta which, in antiquity, was reputed to be the major cause of that colony's existence to begin with: the all-pervasiveness of male homosexuality amongst Spartan men. Males consort-ing almost exclusively with males (socially and sexually, save for deliberate child-making purposes with wives who were otherwise neglected and left entirely to themselves), led—the story goes—to a proverbial lack of chaste-ness on the part of Spartan women (particularly with the subject and slave populations of Sparta) and thus to a massive cohort of "bastards" who were eventually sent away from the city to colonize Tarentum.

In chapter 2 I likewise examine the character of Kleinias—the Cretan statesman in the *Laws*—revealing a disposition that is far more dependent than the character himself realizes, a character whose very belief in his own independence disguises, to himself, his profound deference to—and affinities with—the people he holds to be his inferiors.

Chapter 3 takes this éxamination deeper, considering how the Athenian Stranger—often taken to be *the* philosophical character in the *Laws*—presents, with Megillos's subtle assistance, as an historical account that is in fact a mirror of Kleinias's soul, much to the latter's initial delight and eventu-al dismay.

In chapter 4 I turn to responsibility properly so called and ordinarily so called, illustrating the conflicts between the demands of necessity as they impose themselves on the Stranger and Megillos, and as they appear to Kleinias in the form of moral and political righteousness.

Finally, in chapters 5 and 6, we come full circle back to the concerns about sexual immoderation that are raised by Megillos at the outset of the *Laws*. I closely consider Plato's teaching on natural and conventional right as it emerges in the controversial discussion of sexuality, and particularly homosexuality, in Book 8 of the *Laws*. That discussion comes into a profoundly different light when the ramifications of *character* are brought to bear upon it, than it does when taken as a simple statement of Plato's "beliefs," or even when taken as a simple statement of his characters' beliefs. In particular, Megillos's opening concern with sexual immoderation, and his desire to correct that politically, meets with a questioning by the Stranger that Megillos in fact turns on himself, and that leads him to a realization about the scope of political things that he truly understands (i.e., comes to live). It is for Megillos's sake that the Stranger will make such a seemingly bizarre prognosis of the blissful moderation that will obtain if only the laws discussed about male homosexuality (forbidden) and monogamous marriage (mandatory) might come to pass (839a–c). It is Megillos—not Kleinias—who has, along his path, fallen victim to the delusion of a dream that is both exaggerated and clarified within that prognosis: the dream of righting the world based on his own experiences—which in this rare case are actually philosophical experiences, but that have not yet achieved the fruition of philosophy. Where Kleinias makes the mistake of believing that there is no real difference at all between himself and Megillos, Megillos makes the mistake of believing that only a difference of degree (if a great degree) separates him from a man like Kleinias, whereas the difference seems rather to be one of kind. It is in coming to understand and accept the abyss that divides him from a man like Kleinias that Megillos overcomes his potent desire to reform human desire—to overcome a desire that would lead both him and his city toward, or perhaps to, a Pyrrhic Robespierrianism whose ghastliness would be matched, measure for measure, by its uselessness.

I have engaged the philological debates concerning the Greek text at several points throughout this book. I have done so only where I considered it necessary to defending the text that is extant against unacceptably loose but influential modification, and I have largely confined these engagements to endnotes. Those endnotes are very often long and detailed, a consequence of debating two centuries of long and detailed arguments concerning the Greek manuscript tradition.

In addition, I have pointed out, at some very few points, corrections that I believe are necessary to the best existing English translations—by whole orders of magnitude—of the *Laws* and the *Republic*, Thomas Pangle's and Allan Bloom's, respectively. I have done so only rarely, and after long reflection, for both translations are simply superb. I use my own translations throughout, for the sake of a precision in particular passages that would render a broader translation unreadable, but my admiration for these two translators, and my debt to them, is enormous. That I offer actual corrections—and then very rarely—only to their translations is a mark of my great respect for their singular achievements in the extremely difficult task of translating Plato. There are, in my opinion, no other English translations of either the *Laws* or the *Republic* that are worthy of the careful attention and consideration necessary to suggesting minor corrections, nor for which minor rather than wholesale corrections could be reasonably expected to make a significant difference. I have defended those corrections that I do suggest, and I leave it to my reader to reflect on whether or not I have made my case.

What I have said about philology and translation will be best demonstrated and engaged throughout this book, but I must say something as well here about how I read Plato, and why. This requires more extensive discussion immediately, or what follows will surely obscure it. Every reader of Plato must, will or nil, make his or her own judgments, or form opinions, concerning accepted opinions about the whole and the parts of the dialogues. There are schools of thought or opinion, and there are recognized "sides," on virtually every major and minor general and specific quandary. I decline to take any of the conclusions thereof for granted, including—and especially—those that I agree with. I am aware that there are "methodological" issues that seem to be settled—or at least firmly delineated as terms in a debate—but I insist on working my own way through those issues, by reflecting on the Platonic contexts in which they arise. I do not believe that we "stand on the shoulders of giants"—nor do I believe that any of the true "giants" think that we could or ought to. I am therefore obliged to inflict upon my reader a brief "discourse on method."

How I Read Plato, and Why

My approach to Plato's *Laws* is derived from the Platonic dialogues themselves, and is an interpretive method employed by the greatest political thinkers throughout most of the history of Western political thought (the first clause is a *reason*, the second merely an interesting historical fact). In fact, its prominence has only waned briefly under the sway of a particularly hubristic period of nineteenth- and early-twentieth-century German and British philology, with authors such as Ast (1816), Hermann (1839), Burges (1854, Introduction), Zeller (1923), and in particular Wilamovitz-Möellendorf (1920), who were so sure that "the conquest of the ancient world by science was complete[]" (Wilamovitz-Möellendorf 1982, 105) that they could and should, as arbiters of this new science, correct Plato's "non-scientific" errors rather than understand him on his own terms;[1] continuing through the methodology of the twentieth- and twenty-first-century Tübingen school (Krämer 1972; Hösle 2008; etc.), which assumes that the dialogues contain only a general or shallow teaching, and that the true teaching of Plato is only accessible from exterior sources—from students who had access to his oral teaching; and a particularly reductionist period of Anglo-American "analytic philosophy" (Annas 1981; Reeve 2006; etc.) that focuses from the outset on the principal "doctrines" of Plato, assumed to be his principal interest, to the neglect of the larger dramatic context and "play of characters" (Blondell 2006) in the dialogues. John of Salisbury (1159 CE), citing and paraphrasing the great Aristotelian interpreter Bernard of Chartres and Augustine's incisive *De doctrina Christiana*, outlined the interpretive approach employed by most great readers of Plato very well in his *Metalogicon*:

> The meaning of words should be carefully analyzed, and one should diligently ascertain the precise force of each and every term, both in itself and in the given context. . . . The considerations prompting the speaker may be surmised from the occasion, the kind of person he is, and the sort of listeners he has, as well as from the place, the time, and various other pertinent circumstances that must be taken into account by one who seriously investigates [anything] that demands reflection. (1.19.850b; John of Salisbury 1955, 1991, trans. modified from McGarry's translation)

If I am to be accused of a "method," then, let it be a Salisburian one. This method is in particular focused on the Platonic texts as we have them, and very much away from myths about those texts that are substantiated (if that is the right word) only by a truly massive modern scholarly commentary that seems to me to have, by and large, erected Platonistic idols at the expense of careful attention to Plato—for example, the myth that Plato thought written (or recited) words were unreliable because unselective of and unresponsive to particular readers, while words spoken in conversation were trustworthy (Havelock 1982; Howse 2015), based on Socrates's discussion in the *Phaedrus* (relevant texts for rebuttal: 275d7, 277d2, 278a3–5; see also Sayre 1988); the myth that Plato thought true knowledge could only be derived from hypothesis-free universal principles, not particulars (Aristotle, ironically; Zeller, not); among others.

Despite and indeed because of this focus, I am brought back to such simplified interpretive or doctrinal myths about Plato by my very method, for my refusal to accept these myths as simply true, and my efforts to understand Plato's texts as we have them, lead me to the tentative conclusion that oversimplified doctrines are not merely collateral damage, so to speak, of Plato's own "method." As I will try to demonstrate, the two Dorian characters—Kleinias the Cretan and Megillos the Spartan—are deliberately illustrated by Plato as taking or developing two quite different conceptions from their discourse with the Athenian Stranger (and each other) that comprises the *Laws*: Kleinias takes an oversimplified myth of law and the laws, and his own position within them, from that discourse; Megillos develops a complex understanding of law and human nature within that discourse that both undermines such myths *for him*, and at the same time demonstrates for him precisely why such myths are necessary. Megillos's deeper understanding itself requires or makes possible a deeper appreciation of Kleinias's superficial "understanding." He would agree with Leo Strauss that "[t]here is no surer protection against the understanding of anything than taking for granted or otherwise despising the obvious and the surface. The problem inherent in the surface of things, and only in the surface of things, is the heart of things" (Strauss 1978, 13).

I will note briefly that the now fairly commonplace acceptance of a chronological division of the dialogues—according to when Plato is supposed to have written them—in no way informs my interpretation of the *Laws* (or any other Platonic writing). While I regard this hypothesis (associated principally with Vlastos [1991] now, but dating back at least to Ast [1816] if not to Schleiermacher) as almost surely specious (Nails [1993] treats this subject with both appropriate acuity and levity; Wieland [1982, ch. 5], with systematic solemnity), I cannot see what possible advantage there would be to allowing one's interpretation to be predetermined by it even if it was and could be proved to be completely true. For if it is true (regardless, in fact, if it is true), it is equally true that Plato himself did not advertise when or in what order he wrote the dialogues, whereas he saw fit to specify in some detail, *within* almost all of the dialogues, what the dramatic date of each was (Lampert 2010; Zuckert 2009). The *Laws* is commonly supposed to be Plato's last dialogue, which is unverifiable, though Aristotle attests that it was written "later" than the *Republic* (*Politics* 2.1264b26); and Plutarch, writing four hundred years after Plato lived (and quite possibly simply repeating what Aristotle said) notes that Plato was "older" when he wrote the *Laws* than when he wrote "in veiled and covert terms of opposition and identity" (*De Iside et Osiride* 48).

As for the assumption that the *Laws* was Plato's *last* dialogue, and unfinished, this rests, as far as external sources go, on a single highly dubious reference, whose sole source of authority seems to be that it is now "ancient"—and it is moreover quite clearly not trusted by its own author. That reference is a short passage—an aside, really—in Diogenes Laertius, in which Diogenes relates that "some say (*enioi phasin*) the *Laws* were transcribed/edited (*metegrapsen*) from wax tablets by Philip of Opus himself. And they say that the *Epinomis* is his [Philip's]" (III.37). Now, anyone who reads further will see that Diogenes himself gives no credence whatsoever to what "some say" here (see III. 34, 39, 40, 50–52 [where Diogenes clearly says that *he* believes the *Epinomis* to be Plato's, despite what "some say" in section 37], 62 [in which Diogenes lists the dialogues "agreed" to be spurious, and the *Epinomis* is not among them, nor is *any* of the canonical thirty-five dialogues]). Nor does Diogenes even explicitly say here that "some say" this occurred after Plato's death. But even *had* Diogenes believed (and said) that the *Laws* was the last, unfinished Platonic dialogue, we would have to remember that while Diogenes is "ancient" for us now, he was writing, at the *very* least, six hundred years after Plato lived. By way of analogy, this is like a historian writing about what "some say" in the early twenty-first century, without even attempting to adduce evidence, about the works of Nicolas of Cusa.

And what could it mean, on its own, even if we could verify for a fact that the *Laws* was Plato's last dialogue, and unfinished? We would still not know which parts were "finished" or "unfinished," for example, and we would still not know the role that Plato's own old age played in writing the dialogue. On the other hand it is clearly important that Plato stresses, again and again, *within the dialogue*, that the participants are very old men (634e, 712c, 770a, 819d, 821e). And it is important that the conversation takes place *after* the Peloponnesian War, and possibly even after Plato's lifetime, which is likewise indicated *within* the dialogue (*pace* Zuckert 2009, 53–54; see *Laws* 636b2–4, 695e4–5, 699d5–6). Given these internal facts, it is easy to see how the conjecture of Plato's old age as the author might have arisen, and indeed this conjecture seems plausible. But I fail to see how that conjecture is in any way helpful if imported from the outset, nor can I see how it adds anything even as a conclusion drawn from the text itself. Can any serious reader of the *Laws*, for example, think that *Plato* equated old age automatically and universally with increased (or decreased) wisdom?

I call attention to one thing, at least, that this means: *if* the order that Ast (1816) or Vlastos (1991) or whoever else suggests is correct for the time that Plato wrote each dialogue, *and* this somehow matters to the extent that they (or whoever else) claims it does and in every particular that he or she (or anyone else) claims it does, then one *still* has to account for the fact that at such and such a historical date that Plato chose *not* to openly disclose, Plato assigned a very specific dramatic date that he *did* choose to openly disclose. The latter as fact is not disposed of by belief in the former as a fact, and would not be disposed of even if, *per impossibile*, one knew it for a certain fact rather than simply believed it.

That Plato originally wrote some dialogues before others is almost certainly true (it is difficult to picture him writing the originals of all thirty-five at the same time). But what would have prevented him from "combing and curling and braiding them together in every way" (in other words, constantly reworking them all), as Dionysius of Halicarnassus suggested he did (*De comp. verborum* 25),[2] and as close reading seems to reveal over and over again (for a particularly glaring example, compare the lexical, thematic, and character affinities and tensions between the opening lines of the *Republic*, Book 1 of which is supposedly an "early" dialogue; with those of the *Symposium*, supposedly a "middle" dialogue)?[3]

One hazard of my own approach to the Platonic dialogues is that it tends to rely on the accuracy of an author's words being transmitted through centuries or even millennia of manuscript copying and recopying, a transmission whose reliability is uncertain at best, and simply nonexistent at worst. However, while this problem should not be underemphasized, it should not be overemphasized either, nor are all manuscript traditions created equal. The problems that plagued the highly dubious transmission of the Aristotelian corpus in important respects simply do not apply to the transmission of the Platonic corpus. Aristotle's ties to Macedon, for example, made the Lyceum the target of popular attacks in Athens during the period of Macedonian imperialism during and just after Aristotle's lifetime, and again after Theophrastus, who succeeded him as head of the Lyceum, died; and there is evidence that his school and library suffered extensive damage thereby (see Lord 1981 and Pangle 1987 for a full discussion). Thus at precisely the time in which an authoritative collection of the Aristotelian corpus could have been compiled and preserved by Aristotle himself and his actual students, physical assaults on the Lyceum most probably rendered such a collection collateral damage. The Academy did not face such attacks until its destruction by Sulla in 88 BCE (when the Lyceum was also destroyed, along with a great deal of Athens), by which time Plato's successors had had almost three hundred protected years in which the Platonic corpus could quite easily have been preserved intact, and any secret modification thereof—especially the addition of entire dialogues—would have required the participation of a great deal of people if not the school entire. Indeed the Academy, with some short breaks, in Athens and later in Alexandria, survived for one thousand years after Plato wrote, and seems to have been able to carefully protect the Platonic writings throughout the very period that saw the dispersal and/or destruction of Aristotle's. By the time Justinian closed the Alexandrian Academy in 529 CE, as Ilsetraut Hadot (1996) has persuasively argued (3–50), arrangements were already in place to move the Academy to Persia, from whence it returned safely to Alexandria in the tenth century—having left complete copies of the dialogues and letters of Plato that were already at the center of the Islamic and Judaic Renaissance in Arabia. There is in fact a spatially shifting, but unbroken and identifiable chain of careful manuscript preservation and transmission of the Platonic corpus (and equally careful study thereof) from the time it was written by Plato himself to the present day (see Klibansky's [1939] discussion of the Arabic, Byzantine, and Latin traditions of transmission, which tracks the transmission of the Platonic dialogues from Dionysius the Areopagite to Gemistus Plethon). Small wonder, then, that while more than half of the references to Aristotle by Cicero are to works no longer extant (sadly including all of his dialogues), there is not one Ciceronian reference to a Platonic work that we no longer have. The analogy drawn by scholars (many of them of the highest professional prominence, such as Ast [1816]; Zeller [1923]; and Gomperz [1902]) from the Aristotelian corpus's transmission, to that of the Platonic corpus, is, as Aristotle himself would describe it, mere enthymeme. Or, to borrow Bowen's (1988) succinct judgment, "Much of today's scholarship and its polemic consists only in the blind application of clever answers to a bad question" (51).

I am of course not suggesting that the transmission of the Platonic texts has yielded completely faithful copies of Plato's originals for us. My point is that the transmission of Plato's texts has been verifiably much much more reliable than the transmission of Aristotle's, and that any arguments that fundamentally rely on analogizing the two are specious (which is not to say that all arguments about the transmission and authenticity of Plato's texts would *necessarily* be specious). And as a matter of fact, the whole project of declaring at times up to *three-quarters* of the dialogues specious, and emending the Greek texts thereof based on supposedly faulty manuscript transmission (coupled with a hubristic certainty that the new, "scientific" philologists knew Plato better than Plato knew himself) relies precisely on such an analogy.

I think that addressing the manuscript tradition head-on is crucial to my approach. It is the one real substantial (as opposed to accidental because political) weakness in making even a provisional or conjectural assumption that every (or indeed, any) word of a text written 2,500 years ago matters to its interpretation. I am, implicitly or otherwise, making a claim about Plato's intention. That claim means accepting that the transmission of Plato's words is not completely reliable, but nevertheless not deeply unreliable either, and that careful interpretive study is the only way to determine whether what we have is valuable enough to warrant such study—that is, whether it is the work of an extraordinarily wise human being. What is more, this is a challenge to *any* methodology or approach to the Platonic texts. But whereas meticulous interpretation can validate the worthiness of a text and by extension itself as a "method" (though it cannot ultimately prove absolute "authenticity" or authorship of a text), other methodologies that import and rely on major assumptions from the outset (stylometry, developmentalism, strict historicist contextualism, etc.) can validate neither the text nor themselves in the face of this uncertainty. That is, most other methodologies have to pretend that this uncertainty does not exist in order to have any foundation at all.

Among the facets of the methods that I use is attention to historical context. I distance myself, however, from the Cambridge school represented prominently by Skinner (2002) and Pocock (1972), who insist that historical contextualization necessarily means historic*ist* contextualization. For both Skinner and Pocock, historical context not only informs, but *binds* a writer, and his or her thought and writing speaks necessarily only to his or her time, and can be informed solely by a hope to influence his or her contemporaries, as it is limited in its capacity both by the parochial context of all language, and the idiomatic and specialized nature of languages that emerge in specific contexts to discuss specific and contextually determined problems and solutions. I see no reason to believe *a priori*, however, that a philosopher could not both speak to his or her time, and at the same time—and indeed *by* doing so—speak to all time. It goes, or should go, without saying that this does not mean that all writers are philosophers, or that all or even most writers speak to all time. But some do, and there is a reason why Skinner focuses so much on Hobbes, and Pocock on Machiavelli, when the tenets of their own interpretive technique suggest that such focuses are erroneous.

We pay tribute to the authors of these texts by calling them *sui generis*. But this tribute does not mean that we consider them to have created their works *ex nihilo,* nor does it mean that we consider them infallible. The very idea of creation *ex nihilo* and infallibility is preposterous, and even the *bête noire* of the Cambridge school, Leo Strauss, cannot reasonably be accused of suggesting that such a creation has been performed by any human being. A work can be seminal and still born of its environment, just as an unusually wise or beautiful person can be born, and can only be born, from an environment and lineage that is not necessarily so apparently wise or beautiful. I don't see any contradiction in this, and it seems to me that it is only Skinner's insistence on an either/or distinction that makes us think there is. I find nothing compelling in such a distinction, and much to be distrusted. It seems rather to me that there are great works of thought, and that they are extraordinary products of the environments in which they were born.

Shakespeare is a great example. Shakespeare used mediums and a language that were already there, and that his audience could understand, but at the same time he permanently altered those mediums, that language, and perhaps also that audience. There is, for example, a remarkable difference between pre- and post-Shakespeare English, in terms of vocabulary (he invented almost two thousand words that are still in use today, almost as many words as Racine used in his entire oeuvre—see Bloom 1998, 423), semantic range, and adaptability. It is very hard for me to believe that Shakespeare did not purposely create his plays and sonnets both as timely and as timeless, and I don't see any contradiction in that. For over two and a half thousand years, Western writers have had examples of works that had or have already been revered for centuries or millennia, and the aspiration to create such a work might well attend the ability to do so. Inasmuch as this is so, that aspiration is in fact *part* of the work's parochial context. So when someone pays attention to the seminal, timeless quality of a masterpiece, that is not necessarily to dismiss the context of its creation (which is not to deny that people can and do dismiss this context, only that it is not an inherently necessary thing).

As for the "unity of Plato's thought" (Shorey 1903), there is nothing objectionable in principle about this, and as noted above I agree with Shorey that "developmental" labels, applied in order to separate Plato's "late" thought from his "early" thought (and elevate the former over the latter), are arbitrary evasions of the challenges Plato poses for his readers. And to be sure, my method at least provisionally assumes that Plato's thought was unified by an intention or intentions, rather than being confused or arbitrary. What it does not assume is that I as Plato's reader am in possession of the kind of knowledge or wisdom about his written works that would be necessary to decide which aspects thereof should be accepted and "unified" (for Shorey, this means predominantly "participation" in "transcendental ideas"), and which aspects discarded. Nor do I believe Shorey possessed such knowledge or wisdom, or demonstrated it.

And all of this is to say nothing of the most fundamental recognition, which is that Plato and Socrates and the Athenian Stranger are friends, and friends to themselves, but truth is a greater friend than any of them (*Phaedo* 91b–c; Aristotle, *Nicomachean Ethics* 1096a11–15; Roger Bacon, *Opus Maius* 1.5; Thomas Aquinas, *Sent. Lib. Eth.* 1.6.n4–5). That the famous Latin phrase used most often to indicate this—*Amicus Platon sed magis amica veritas* ("Plato is a friend, but truth is a greater friend")—first appears in literature in a letter written by Don Quixote (*Don Quixote* 2.51), indicates only that the sentiment can also be misused or misunderstood (comically and otherwise), or presented as misused or misunderstood, not that it is therefore untrue. It is not untrue.

In sum, my method, such as it is, is eclectic and flexible. As much as possible, I read Plato (and others) in order to challenge the presuppositions that attend reading a text, and being human. My method cannot be defined by a commitment other than the attempt to lay bare and engage commitments I am not aware of. I do not ever rely on *anyone's* interpretation as either a starting point or a general interpretive crutch thereafter. I have learned a great deal from reading Leo Strauss, for example, and many others, but at every point I have learned from them by being sent back to Plato's text to reread and rethink—I have not learned by taking anything on faith, no matter how much respect I have for any particular scholar. In what follows I certainly cite many authors, but when I do so in agreement it is because I agree with them in a particular respect based on my own reading and reflection, not ever because I am relying on their interpretation to obviate the need for my own. My approach is therefore not plagued by concerns about whether or not a particular commentator whom I cite intentionally or unintentionally misrepresents a text, or has a particular political agenda, prejudice of one sort or another, or deficient methodology. I believe that Plato would approve of this approach, which is necessarily that of a novitiate. Let my maxim be: better a dilettante with no preferred method at all than a Procrustes with a fatal penchant for methodological precision.

A final note: I remark throughout this book that the Socratic principle that "no one is willingly unjust" is simply true. It is. But I have by no means provided a sufficient defense for that insistence, and I have ensured that no argumentation I offer relies upon it. It is my intention to offer some partial substantiation for this claim, not depend upon it to substantiate my own arguments.

NOTES

1. As Pangle (1987) puts it, "Scholars came to be convinced that they had a new and superior understanding of what Plato could and could not have written at the same time that they succumbed to the delusion that they were in possession of a deeper understanding of the issues of philosophy than that held by Plato and the great mediaeval Platonists" (5).

2. Note that I am *not* accepting this as an assumption to be applied based on dubious external evidence. I cite this as an expression of a hypothesis that I consider plausible (not certain) and at least worth considering, based on my own Platonic investigations. See, for example, footnote below.

3. A representative sample phrase: at the outset of the *Republic*, Socrates says of Polemarchos: "*katidôn . . . porrôthen . . . ekeleuse . . . ton paida perimeinai e keleusai*" (327b2–3)—"catching sight [of us] from a distance . . . he ordered . . . his slave to order [us] to wait for him." In the *Symposium*, Apollodorus says of Glaukon (since this is the name of Plato's own brother, it is unlikely that he only accidentally uses the same name as the character in the *Republic*, though this is not the same character. This conceit thus mirrors and therefore evokes that of the two Socrateses' in the supposedly "later" *Sophist* and *Statesman*): "*katidôn . . . porrôthen . . . ekalese, kai paizôn hama tê klêsei . . . ou perimeneis?*" (172a3–5)—"catching sight [of me] from a distance, he called, playing with his call. . . . 'Won't you wait?'" What disappears in translation is very clear in the Greek: even as Plato writes that Glaukon was "playing with his call," *he himself* is "playing with" κελευω and καλεω, παις and παιζω, command and request; looking up and looking down (*katidôn* literally means "looking down," and colloquially, "catching sight of." That the literal meaning is clearly denied to Polemarchus by the dramatic action in the *Republic* is part of the opening irony of that dialogue. That it is clearly implied of Glaukon by the dramatic action of the *Symposium* is likewise part of that dialogue's opening irony). Even *if* Vlastos et al. are correct about their chronology of the dialogues' writing, what does it say about *Plato*'s intention that he crafted the *Symposium* to be in direct dialogue with the "earlier" Book 1 of the *Republic*, and also, in the same "middle" period, composed the rest of the *Republic* as a continuation of the "earlier" Book 1?

Chapter One

Megillos

"[The god Ammon] would rather there be the Lacedaimonian reverence of speech, than all the sacred offerings of the Greeks taken together."

—attributed to Ammon's prophet by Plato's Socrates in *Alcibiades II* 149b

The purpose of this first chapter is to carefully examine the character of Megillos in Plato's *Laws*, as he appears from the outset of the dialogue. There is, so far as I know, no such examination currently available, and the overwhelming neglect of this aspect of the work makes access to the complexities of the dialogue as a whole somewhat difficult. The commentary that follows does, I hope, partially illustrate why this is so.

I do not mean to suggest that Megillos has been wholly ignored. As I will discuss in what follows, his character and its part in the drama of the *Laws* has in fact received consideration by a very few careful commentators. But I do not think he has been given his due.

My commentary begins with two principles in mind. The first is that the two Dorian characters, Kleinias and Megillos, should not be homogenized unless the dialogue itself reveals otherwise. The second is that it should not be assumed at the outset that Megillos is the "slower" of the two. As I will try to show, by attending carefully to the opening of the text, the commonly asserted opposing positions to these principles only have any purchase if they are imported by the reader from the outset. Plato himself has crafted the Dorians as very different indeed, and Megillos reveals himself—subtly—to be remarkably thoughtful and astute. That this is not immediately apparent would seem to be part of the deliberately difficult work which Plato designed his dialogues to be. In both the *Republic* and the *Laws*, a "longer road" not taken by the characters within the dialogue is mentioned (*Republic* 435d, 504b; *Laws* 683b and cf. 727a). Yet one could say that this longer road is in fact accessible within those dialogues, provided that their readers transform them (and themselves) into arduous paths of reflection and especially self-reflection (the former not being possible without the latter).

To begin with, we should ask: on what grounds is it so "naturally" assumed that Megillos and Kleinias have essentially the same aptitudes, or that Megillos is the more traditional, less acute interlocutor among the two Dorians—if not an outright ignoramus? I am aware of only two commentators who explicitly suggest otherwise—Wilamowitz and Whitaker—but each does so in passing, and each in his own way does so backhandedly. Wilamowitz briefly notes that Megillos is the more "insightful" [or, "sensible"—*einsichtigere*] of the two, but he means only to damn by faint praise (Wilamowitz-Möllendorff 1920, 404; I will discuss Wilamowitz's comments further in chapter 5). And Whitaker (2004) mentions that Megillos seems to be the more "sophisticated" interlocutor [based on 680c–d, 804b, and 842a], but he makes no further comment concerning his observation, and otherwise homogenizes the two Dorians' views, even, it seems, on the rare occasions where he remarks that Megillos in particular is implicated in the conversation (e.g., ibid, 134–35, on a very crucial passage at 804b, in Book 8 of the *Laws*).[1]

Aside from these watery compliments for Megillos, the vast majority of modern commentators assume that the two Dorian characters are either identically incapable of reflection, or that Megillos is less capable thereof than Kleinias. Unfortunately for the sake of the argument, this assumption is most often simply undefended (England 1921, vol. I, 232–33; Morrow 1960, 32; Stalley 1983, 24, 31, and 174; Clark 2003, 6, 81, and 86; Görgemanns 1960, 79 and 100; etc.).[2] When it is, on rare occasion, defended, the defense leaves much to be desired. Thus Pangle (1988, 430–33). While not approaching a full analysis, Pangle is certainly more articulate and thoughtful than most (and I will engage his work on the *Laws* throughout), but in relegating Megillos to the position of "pedestrian check" and "typical citizen of the future regime," I believe he misses the subtleties of Megillos's character as shown in Book 1.[3] As I will try to show, what Pangle (394–95) interprets as weak argumentation that "has a crude rhetorical effectiveness" on Megillos's part, is in fact much more thoughtful than it appears.[4]

The most obvious probable starting point for the modern assumption of Megillos's ignorance would seem to be his quantitatively limited role in the discussion of the *Laws* (thus Nightingale 1993, 294). He is overshadowed by Kleinias's more vocal participation, and is thus seen as incapable of following the unfolding argument.

But this is ultimately to confuse quantity of discourse with quality of discourse (cf. 654c–d)—to say nothing of the fact that it does nothing to explain what he, as a Spartan, is doing there. If Megillos is simply meant to represent the more ignorant and obstinate aspect of traditionalism (and this common aspect of every "ism" must not be ignored), why does Plato assign this role to a Spartan, rather than a Cretan (and indeed, to the only Spartan character he ever created)? It would be easy to say that a Spartan statesman would naturally be present, given that Spartan colonists will be welcomed to the new city (707e–708a), and that previous Spartan colonies had abandoned Spartan ways (637b; cf. Xenophon, *Lac. Pol.* 14; Thucydides 1.77.6). But while this is a possible conceit for having a Spartan present,[5] it does not explain why that Spartan must necessarily be closed-minded or slow to learn (cf. Megillos's statements regarding his knowledge of poetry at 680d1 with Thucydides 1.84.1–4). If the Spartans, with these concerns in mind, had wished to send a rigid traditionalist, why did they send one of the only people in Lacedaimonia who was officially recognized as a friend of Athens (642b–d)?

Further to this point, it should be noted that Spartans, as well as others from the Peloponnese, are only to be welcomed to the colony (708a4–5)— they are not required in order to found it. Kleinias is under no obligation to appease Megillos with the regime or laws of that colony, because he does not *require* his support. Had Plato wanted to imply a necessity for such appease- ment, he could easily have made the third character another Cretan states- man, or made the new colony a joint Cretan/Spartan venture. It is telling that he pointedly did neither. Should he want to, Kleinias can tell Megillos, as he can the Athenian, to take a different sort of hike than the one they are taking, at any point in the conversation. But of course, he never does. Kleinias's motivations are his own, and if he defers to what *he* sees as Megillos's intransigent traditionalism, it is because *he* is so inclined. That is, this tells the reader something about Kleinias's character, not necessarily about Megillos's.

It should be noted as well that Plato's audience would by no means necessarily have taken Megillos's "laconic" way of speaking (and especially *not* speaking) as evidence of a slower intellect (cf. also, incidentally, Exodus 4:10; and *Pirkei Avot* 3:17).[6] In fact, the careful *listening* that it implied, together with the thought and attention involved in expressing oneself well with an extreme economy of words, suggested just the opposite to many in that audience—hence the proverbial "Laconic wit," or, as Socrates himself elsewhere discusses, Laconic philosophy (*Protagoras* 342a–343b).[7] In an- other context, Socrates speaks of Spartan reserve in speech as *euphêmia* (*Second Alcibiades* 149b3, mirrored and magnified in his description of the god's speech at b4–5)—literally, "speaking well," but in practice the silence or near-silence appropriately observed in divine rituals, the nonobservance of which is *blasphêmia*, from whence the English word "blasphemy" (cf. Soph- ocles, *Women of Trachis*, 178).[8] Aside from the modern (especially academ- ic) valorization of gaining attention at every opportunity (which Plato called "love of honor" [*philotimia*]), it is unclear why this should not to this day be a reasonable *prima facie* expectation. It is still less clear why the absence of desire for attention, coupled with the presence of careful listening, should *prima facie* indicate ignorance. Socrates himself, as Plato creates him, is often content to say virtually nothing, and to exclusively listen (cf. *Timaeus* and *Cleitophon* in their entireties); or to respond only because it is pointedly demanded of him (*Hippias Minor* 363a); and would have happily been absent from a discussion that clearly fascinated everyone else involved, had he not been specifically implored to participate (consider the inordinate length of this "persuasion" at the outset of the *Laches*, 178a–181c). Plato does not seem to have had a love of love of honor.[9]

So quantity of speech, at least within the context of the Platonic dialogues, does not stand as a criterion for judging the worth or impact thereof.[10] Nor does eagerness to speak (cf. *Crito* 49d; *Protagoras* 357e and context; *Hipparchus* 225b–c; *Alcibiades I* 134c; *Statesman* 206a–207e), or city of origin (*Laws* 951b). What is said (and not said—cf. *Hippias Minor* 369d and Lampert 2002, 244), to whom, how, and when, would seem to be the only criteria that the internal structures of the dialogues allow. It is these aspects of each thing said within them that allow the reader to think about *why* it is said (or not said). So it is to these aspects that we must attend in the *Laws*.

What Do We Know about Megillos?

Before we assume that *we* know about anything Megillos, it is worthwhile asking what the characters in the dialogue know about each other at the outset. Since we will only know these characters through their interactions with each other, it would be helpful to establish what they do (and do not) know of each other to begin with.

Our problem here is that, despite and because of the abrupt scene in which Plato has these strangers (*xenoi*) meet, we can do nothing of the sort. What we *can* do is learn something about the manner in which Plato wrote by grappling with this initial difficulty—a difficulty that is a difficulty precisely because at first it seems so easy.

Start with the "easy"—three strangers, an Athenian, a Spartan, and a Cretan—meet near Knossos, and the Athenian asks the Dorians (Sparta and Crete were Doric Greek cities) a question about the origin of their laws. The Athenian is called "Athenian" in the list of characters, and we find out where Megillos and Kleinias are from within the first few lines (624a4–5, 625a1), so we know where they are from. They call each other "stranger" (*xenos*— 624a1, a3), so they must be meeting for the first time. The opening scene is one of formal introduction between parties, some of whom belong to mutually hostile cities—who could miss the Athens/Sparta thing, for example?— with intention of good will all around: "it is safe to propose that the dialogue begins exactly where we have it" (Whitaker 2004, 13). "Easy." And even easier if it never comes up as a question at all (e.g., Stalley 1983, 5).

But easy it is not. For if their meeting is a complete coincidence, that coincidence begins before the dialogue proper of the *Laws*. In the first place, they have clearly already decided where they are going, together, by the time *we* are introduced to them (625a7–b2). Perhaps they are just pilgrims who happen to meet on a walk to the sacred cave and temple of Zeus's birth, on the day of the summer solstice (625b2, 683c5)? Stranger things have happened. But the Stranger knows Kleinias's name, and that he is from Knossos (629c3). And Kleinias knows that Megillos is from Lacedaimon (624a4–5), though it is unclear whether he or the Stranger knows his name, since neither Kleinias nor the Stranger calls Megillos by his name until after Megillos himself says it at 642c2 (Whitaker 2004, 13). All these difficulties present themselves precisely within the circumstances that give us the "easy" interpretation. We will later discover that Megillos knows himself to be the eldest of the three (712c8); and the Stranger knows himself to be the youngest (892d7). How do they know this?

Plato has in fact made it deliberately unclear to what extent the three men have earlier conversed, or even whether all earlier conversations took place between all three of them. What he *has* made deliberately clear, however, is that *some* earlier conversation(s) took place between or concerning them— while the other statements could be imagined, if some only barely, as being the result of guesswork based on appearance, without divine aid or prior introduction (or indication by someone else) the Stranger cannot possibly know Kleinias's name, nor is it at all likely that he would have any way of identifying Kleinias as from Knossos without knowing beforehand. And the journey that the three characters take, regardless of the possibility of it being a chance meeting of pilgrims, cannot possibly have been already decided upon without prior discussion, unless by a god. Note how early in the dialogue (its first few sentences) Plato chooses to make this clear, and then more or less drops it.

What Plato shows us here is that we don't know. This bears repeating: *we don't know*. And we can't. We move from certainty to uncertainty, and the way out of uncertainty, or perplexity, is not given and cannot be given by Plato as easily as the way into it. But it is there. It took some care to get us into uncertainty to begin with. It will take the same care and much more to extricate ourselves from it. Unlike the greatest things, lesser things can be known, but they require patience, diligence, and thought. They require reflection, and self-reflection. And they require admitting that we don't know, when we don't (*Apology* 21d).

We come back, then, to the manner in which Plato wrote, and his lesson on that manner here. Al-Farabi was correct: the at least two-part lesson is illustrated with great clarity at the beginning of the *Laws*, so long as one does not presume that Plato is a sober pedant (*Summary of the Laws*, Introduction). First, Plato seems to *want* his reader to fall into the easy assumption. Second, he then provides very subtle hints (which transform into not at all subtle hints as soon as one notices them) that provoke a careful reader to question that assumption, and to go back, reread, and reconsider. There may *be* no definitive solution to all the riddles, no ultimate dispelling of doubt. But that in itself may be an important lesson about laws, which "by nature" must be decided upon and established in the midst of great uncertainty, and are necessary just because of that uncertainty.

Which means that Plato, despite his obscurity, and indeed precisely because of his obscurity, has provided the most fitting and best introductions to the *Laws*: certainty that gives way, upon reflection, to perplexity. He indicates the "longer way" (*Republic* 435d, 504b; *Laws* 683b and cf. 727a) even though he also notes the way in the *Laws* which, as we hear, is "entirely long enough," with places to stop and rest (625b1–2). Who could resist the longer way?

That said, let us return to our original question: what do we know—what can we discern—about Megillos? Let us begin at the beginning.

It has been frequently noted that the first word of the *Laws* is "god" (*theos*) (Strauss 1975, 3; Pangle 1976, 1059; Voegelin 1977, 228; Stalley 1983, 166). Given its place, the immediate evocation for an Athenian listener would likely be Aeschylus's *Oresteia*, which also opens with this word (*Ag.* 1, though importantly there in the plural—*theous*), and which also relates the story of what can only be described as a political sea change. The auspices under which such changes can occur are, Plato suggests, always bound up in piety.

The question for which this is the first word is posed by an unnamed Athenian Stranger to Kleinias, a Cretan, and Megillos, a Spartan: "[A] god or some human being, Strangers, has taken the responsibility (in the sense of credit *or* blame—*aitian*) for setting down your laws?" (624a12).

However, the Greek has an ambiguity to it, an ambiguity also exploited by Plato in the first line of the *Minos*, one of the companion dialogues of (and in many ways the introduction to) the *Laws*. Because the second person dative pronoun *humin* (in the *Minos*, the first person *hêmin*) can be taken as either possessive or as indicating interest, the sentence might also be translated: "A god or some human, for you (i.e., according to you), strangers, is responsible for setting down the laws?" (cf. *Hippias Major* 281a1). Taken in this sense, the Stranger is asking for the personal opinions of Kleinias and Megillos about laws in general, not—or not only—what the Cretans and Lacedaimonians believe in general about their own laws.[11] The Cretans and Lacedaimonians seem to believe that a god is ultimately responsible for their laws. But does Kleinias himself believe this? Does Megillos?

The ambiguity of this sentence is crucial, and sets the tone for the rest of the *Laws*. In the very act of establishing his piety as a whole, the Stranger is also questioning piety, and specifically the piety of his interlocutors (not to mention asking the *Euthyphro* question—what *is* piety?).[12] And the subtle way in which he poses his question conceals its subversive aspect: only if Kleinias or Megillos is already questioning the veracity of the particular political interpretation of his religious beliefs with which he has grown, will either of them hear the question as a personal one (the same, perhaps, is true of Plato's readers—there is perhaps a reason that this ambiguity has not been explored in twentieth-century literature on the *Laws*).[13] Otherwise, the first and main sense will be the only audible one.

Kleinias takes the Stranger's question in the first and main sense, and responds with the "most just" answer: "[A] god, Stranger, [a] god" (624a3). Of course, "most just" and "*true*" are not identical (cf. 630d9, 664c1, and Strauss 1975, 3),[14] but Kleinias's interest at this point is the just. It remains to be seen whether that interest will, or can, advert to the true; or whether for Kleinias the just is and remains identical with, if not higher than, the true. What is more, the very basis upon which Kleinias has built his sense of justice (cf. 680e1–5) is about to become the seriously contended topic of the rest of Book 1 (and beyond), and his fondness for expressing his opinions in superlatives[15] will meet gentle but firm reproof (cf. for example 627d5, which we will have cause to consider shortly).

Such is our introduction to Kleinias.

"Among us," he continues, "it is Zeus, among the Lacedaimonians, where this man is from, I believe they say it is Apollo. Isn't that so?" (624a3–5). This brings the Spartan, Megillos, into the conversation, who responds in a most Spartan style: "Yes."

Importantly, Megillos's response does not necessarily reveal anything about what he believes personally, but affirms only what the Lacedaimonians believe or say in general—in the Platonic terms of the dialogue, what "the many" (*hoi polloi*) Lacedaimonians believe or say (cf. Herodotus 1.65). This is not an accident, as Plato will demonstrate almost immediately (633b1–2 and 5). When Kleinias brings Megillos into the conversation again—mere moments later—this time asking whether the latter supports him in his belief that any properly governed city must be primarily ordered toward defeating others in war (626b–c), Megillos once again answers only with what the Lacedaimonians believe, or are supposed to believe, in general: "How else would any Lacedaimonian answer, you divine man?" (626c4). Particularly given that he has just demonstrated a proverbially Spartan economy of words,[16] and that this very question draws attention to how (*pôs*) a Spartan would respond (as distinct from simply what [*ti*] he would say in response), this is not an unequivocal Yes. That is, "any Lacedaimonian" would generally just agree, and not answer with what is, for a Spartan, such a verbose reply. *How* would any Lacedaimonian respond? As briefly as possible. *What* would any (or almost any) Lacedaimonian say in response to Kleinias's question? "Yes." But Megillos's carefully worded response is a riddle whose surface *seems* to say Yes—if Yes is, as it is for Kleinias, the desired and expected response—but whose solution suggests hesitation at least. And so he can at one and the same time show Kleinias the political support he has demanded, and a careful listener, such as the Stranger proves to be, his hesitation to aver that what they are discussing is in fact true. [17]

Thus with the first two times he speaks, Megillos demonstrates his own capacity and willingness to speak differently to the Stranger than to Kleinias, even as he pays deference to the latter, and indeed with the very words with which he does so. He speaks, in other words, in the same manner that the Stranger did in the opening question of the *Laws*. Did Megillos perhaps hear the second, more subversive, sense of that initial question, the sense that Kleinias missed?

Stepping back a moment, we should note that between these first two times that Megillos speaks, Kleinias demonstrates something significant about his knowledge of the most prominent and influential of Greek poets, Homer, whose epics were *the* principal authority for Greek religion as a whole. Just after his opening question in the first line of the *Laws*, the Stranger had asked Kleinias if he says, "with Homer," that Minos (the celebrated founder and first king of Crete, who ruled from Knossos) had received oracles regarding lawgiving from his father (Zeus) "every ninth year." Kleinias replied, "So it is said by us" (624a7–b3)—he raised no objection about this characterization of what Homer said. Why does this matter?

It matters because behind the myth of Minos the lawgiver that the Stranger cites to Kleinias as being of Homeric origin (624a7–b3), lies a curiosity that is to the highest degree pertinent to everything that is to follow, and striking to anyone who actually knows the Homeric epics. That it is not striking at all to Kleinias tacitly demonstrates that he does not in fact know these epics. That curiosity is this: Homer in fact does not say, as the Stranger says he does, that Minos received oracles from his father (i.e., Zeus) every eight[18] years when they were together (*sunousian*), and used those oracles to guide the laws he gave to the Cretan cities. This story brings together aspects of Cretan beliefs (on which, see also my chapter 3), but Homer in fact says almost nothing of the sort. Homer *does* have his Odysseus say—in the midst, it should be noted, of a long and convoluted *lie*—that "Minos reigned, [who] at nine years old was great Zeus' beloved friend (*oaristês*)" (*Od.* 19.178–179). As Benardete (2000, 5–7) points out, when in the *Minos* Socrates tries to defend the same version of the myth that the Stranger presents here, he is forced to counter the prevailing, Ionian (Homer was an Ionian Greek), understanding of these lines, which was that Minos was Zeus's cupbearer, fellow drinker, and sexual plaything at a *symposium* when he was nine years old (*Minos* 319b–320b, especially 319e5–6).[19] The Stranger, in asking his question, was testing Kleinias's knowledge of Homer.

If those listening to the Stranger know their Homer and his reception, the themes of *symposia* and *paiderasteia*—soon to become serious subjects of debate—are already evoked and adumbrated here. Kleinias indicates here that he knows almost nothing about Homer, beyond the fact that the poet is an authority he is happy to appropriate for his own (and Crete's) beliefs. He will only later make explicit that he knows little about Homer (680c2–5). At this point, however, he is loath to sacrifice the support from an authority that he sees for his opinions, by confessing his ignorance.

Megillos, on the other hand, will later stress that he himself is quite familiar with Homer poems (680c6–7).[20] As we will see, Megillos will be strangely eager to assure the Stranger of his deep knowledge not just of Homer, but of poetry in general (cf. Benardete 2000, 99). For him and the Stranger, though not for Kleinias, the *contexts* of the Homeric references employed will be accessible, though unspoken, as will the alterations and absences in the Stranger's use thereof, and all these will form part of their tacit communication. But that will come later. For now we must note, as the Stranger and Megillos surely do here, that Kleinias—and only Kleinias—has, as it were, shown his hand.

Let us return to Megillos.

The third time he speaks (627d6–7) seems to be, as Strauss notes (1975, 5), "his first spontaneous utterance." But Strauss calling this a demonstration of "Megillos' agreement" (5) with what the Stranger has said is, while not incorrect, misleading.[21] In order to understand why this is so, we must note two key aspects of that utterance: (1) it is the first time Megillos speaks explicitly *for himself* (*hôs ge emoi sundokein*—"so it seems to *me*"); and (2) his "agreement" with the Stranger is highly qualified by the fact that it is phrased as a *dis*agreement with Kleinias's wholehearted agreement with the Stranger. Just before Megillos speaks, Kleinias had agreed with the Stranger that what the latter had said was *true*—or rather, tru*est* (*alêthestata*—627d5). Megillos agrees only that it was "*kalôs men oun*"—"finely (or nobly, or beautifully) [said] at any rate" (627d6–7). Whatever agreement with the Stranger is here evinced, it has been pointedly downgraded from agreement that what he said was the "truest" possible thing. As Pangle (1988) notes, Megillos is "reserved and cautious" here, not enthusiastic (391).

What Megillos is agreeing is *kalôs*, but not necessarily true (or truest, at any rate), is the following statement by the Stranger, concerning a situation in which, of many brothers born of the same parents, more became unjust and fewer just:

> It wouldn't be fitting for me and you (two) to hunt down whether that house-hold and the family itself as a whole ought to be declared inferior [or, weaker]

to itself when the bad are victorious, or superior [or, stronger] when they are inferior [or, weaker]. For it's not the speech of the many with respect to appropriateness (*euschêmosunês*) and inappropriateness (*aschêmosunês*) of words that we're examining now, but correctness and error—according to nature—about laws (627c8–d4).[22]

Why, according to Megillos, is this "finely said," but not necessarily true or truest?

In a manner of speaking, the reader who "examines" the literal meaning of the words used by the Stranger here, in addition to just their colloquial or commonplace significance, will see that Plato has basically put his cards on the table. Kleinias jumps at the opportunity to get out of the pickle he finds himself in after examining the literal meaning of the particular "speech of the many" (which is his speech as well) that he was so confident about when he first accepted and proclaimed it, just moments before: the phrase, "superior (*kreittôn*) to oneself"—and by extension, "inferior (*êttôn*) to oneself" (cf. *Rep.* 430e–431b, on these phrases as commonplace). When the Stranger had adopted the former as expressing Kleinias's original "victory (*nikan*) of oneself over oneself," Kleinias accepted this as identical without hesitation (626e2–4, e7–8, 627a3, a6–10). When the Stranger goes on to note that the many bad may prevail over—that is, "be superior to," in Kleinias's war-focused terms—the few good, Kleinias is eager to find a way to avoid an inescapable but repugnant conclusion that follows from his own logic.

In his eagerness, though, he then not only does not bother to examine the very words that the Stranger is using to give him his "out," but responds with another unexamined "speech of the many," or commonplace: "tru*est*." And this one is of even more doubtful literal significance. For if the word "true" (*alethes*) is meaningful, then the word *truest*, and indeed *truer*, is *ipso facto* meaningless: something is either true or it is not. On the other hand, if "true" means nothing, then *truest* (and *truer*) also necessarily means nothing in particular just because it can mean anything.[23] Either way, the word that Kleinias uses is, taken literally, meaningless. It reminds us of Hippias's bombastic, and highly imprecise, claim to be able to speak "more precisely than total precision" (*Hippias Major* 295a; cf. Sweet 1987, 354). And since the root of the word Kleinias uses is *the* philosophical desideratum. . . .

Rush, as Kleinias does, to agree with any way out of one's perplexity or confusion, and one will grasp at anything—even something that would, under examination, turn out to be meaningless. But it will seem like it is truer than true.

And people say Plato doesn't have a sense of humor.

Of course, it may be objected that the Stranger himself is shortly to use the word "truest" with respect to his equation of the most pleasant life with the best (664c1). We will return to this when we consider Kleinias's character with more careful precision in chapter 2, but for now we should note that the Stranger seems there to self-consciously adopt Kleinias's careless use of the word, without indicating anything but acceptance that Kleinias attaches significance to it (cf. 677e1–5 with 679c4).[24] The context speaks volumes: within a discussion of the effectiveness of persuasive myth, the Stranger says that "we" will be saying (*eroumen*) what is "truest" and also "better persuading those who need persuasion, speaking this way rather than another" when [we] say (*phaskontes*) that the gods say (*legesthai*) that the pleasant and the best life [which is the just life] are the same (664b7–c2). Kleinias is among those who need to be persuaded of this, since he had been not at all persuaded by the Stranger's original statement to the effect that the most unjust man was the unhappiest (661d–e), and indeed had once again deployed his favorite catchword[25] in announcing this, claiming that it was "truest" (*alêthestata*) that he was not persuaded by it (661e5). After then leading Kleinias through an argument to the same effect, and obtaining only grudging acquiescence from him (663d5, cf. b4–6), the Stranger had asked outright whether, true or not, "a lawgiver of even the slightest worth, who dared to lie (*pseudesthai*) to the young for the sake of the(ir) good, could ever lie (*epseusato*) with a more profitable lie (*pseudos*) than this one, and more capable of making everyone do everything just, not by force, but willingly" (663d6–e2). *This* is what the Stranger means by "truest" (cf. 716d–e, 881a).

I will return to Kleinias's character, and to the considerable implications of his character for the ensuing conversation (including necessitating its sometimes "relativistic" terms), in the next chapter. For now we return to Megillos, and the discussion of appropriateness of words, and correctness of law according to nature.

As we noted, Megillos does not affirm that what the Stranger said was "truest." Nor does he affirm that it is true. Instead, he acknowledges that it was "finely [said]." The Stranger had taken the opportunity to get Kleinias out of the confusion he had fallen into, by telling the two Dorians that the three of them ought not to be so literal and careful about the words they were using, since they were after something else entirely: what is correct and incorrect about laws according to nature. But his statement about the lack of need for careful attention to precise literal meaning is itself phrased very precisely, and in such a way that *its* precise literal meaning is highly significant. It will be a major part of the *Laws* to discern the "nature" of laws, and whether they must speak clearly, and be spoken of, with "one voice on one subject" (634e, 664a); or whether they may or must sometimes contain ambiguity. But regardless how or if that question is settled, there is reason to at least provisionally assume at the outset that neither superior lawmaking nor understanding permits of careless imprecision. Nevertheless, even in the case of very carefully, very precisely worded law, it may not be "fitting" to require careful and precise consideration or understanding of laws on the part of everyone subject to them. We cannot all be judges.

We may note, in this respect, that the word that I have fittingly translated as "appropriateness" in this passage is *euschêmosunês*, which literally means, "carefully formed"; the negative of which is *aschêmosunês*, or "unformed" (i.e., without design). Since Megillos has been, up to this point, using exclusively the "speech of the many" (though not with the same easy use that Kleinias has with such speeches), and since he has quite precisely been *very* carefully forming these speeches, he does not agree that it is true (or truest) that it is unfitting for him and the Stranger to carefully consider the care or lack thereof with which the characters are speaking. What the Stranger's statement amounts to is asking, very subtly, whether his interlocutors were deliberately speaking carefully—whether, that is, the ambiguities in their words are intentional. Kleinias's answer, because he does not even hear that there *is* a question, amounts to "No." Megillos's answer means "Yes."

What is more, the last part of the Stranger's statement has him assert that they are examining laws for what is correct and what is erroneous in them with a view "toward what is by nature" (*hêtis pot' estin phusei*).[26] It is Kleinias who had introduced the idea of nature, according to his opinion, in support of his opinion of Cretan law. He had both cited the nature of the terrain (625c10), and both the fact of cities, and of undeclared but perpetual war between them all, as occurring according to nature (626a5). It is to these claims that the Stranger responds, and Megillos agrees that what the Stranger says is finely or nobly spoken.

What Megillos *has* agreed with the Stranger about, and has demonstrated his agreement by the very subtlety of his disagreement with Kleinias, is that it is *not* fitting (*prepon*) that the three men be examining, at this exact point, the significance of the literal meaning of the "speech of the many." On this point Megillos is clearly in wholehearted agreement, both with the Stranger, and with Kleinias. But with each for different reasons.

Let us make one further observation. With the exception of two brief instances—once when Kleinias points out features of the Cretan landscape to both Megillos and the Stranger (625d1), and once when, as discussed above, Kleinias seeks support for his own opinion from Megillos's (626c3)—the entire conversation on the purpose of Cretan laws that precedes Megillos's "agreement" with the Stranger's statement on what is "fitting" has been entirely one-on-one between Kleinias and the Stranger (625c6, c9, e5, 626a5, b5–c1, d2–7, e1–2, 627a5, b3, c1). The instances in which either of them uses "we" within this one-on-one conversation are therefore almost certainly understood by the characters of the dialogue (and therefore meant to be understood by the dialogue's readers) to refer only to Kleinias and the Stranger. But at the outset of the statement we have been examining, the Stranger emphatically brings Megillos back in. Instead of saying, "It wouldn't be fitting for *us* (*hêmin*)"—which might, and indeed would likely be understood as meaning only Kleinias and the Stranger, given the conversation thus far—he says, "for *me* and for you [*plural*] (*emoi te kai humin*)." Megillos's response is not as spontaneous as it seems, nor is the inclusion or exclusion of one or another of the interlocutors, at any given point, in any way artless on either the Stranger's or Megillos's (or Plato's) part (cf. the emphatic inclusion, one by one, of all three at 629c3).[27] The Stranger has at this point heard enough from Kleinias to understand that Kleinias has not been particularly thoughtful about the catchwords (and watchwords) that govern his beliefs. So he tests him to see if he would rather remain being not particularly thoughtful about them, and indeed that is the case. But the Stranger deliberately draws Megillos into his test as well, and receives a very different response from him.

Shortly thereafter, the Stranger once again draws Megillos into his conversation with Kleinias, this time to confirm Megillos's familiarity with poetry. At 629b, the Stranger, after citing the Athenian cum Spartan poet Tyrtaeus (accurately in his direct quotation, slightly modified in his paraphrase thereafter), notes that Kleinias has "perhaps heard of" (*akêkoas pou*) this poem (cf. 680c2–5), whereas Megillos is, the Stranger believes, "surfeited (*diakorês*) with them" (629b3–5). Megillos assures him: "Entirely so" (*panu men oun*).

Beyond the overt confirmation of Megillos's knowledge of Tyrtaeus's poetry, there is a subtle indication of increasing familiarity and warmth in the language used by the Stranger with Megillos. Both Kleinias and Megillos are Doric Greeks, but whereas with his comment to the former the Stranger had remained within the Attic dialect (*akêkoas*—see above), with the latter he here—the first time he directly engages Megillos alone—uses a Doric inflection (*diakorês*, as opposed to *diakoros*).[28] This is especially striking, given that virtually the entire dialogue of the *Laws* is written by Plato in Attic Greek (Benardete 2000, 40–41). We know that Kleinias and Megillos are Dorians, but Doric inflections and dialect are very rare in the conversation Plato creates for them.

What is more, Megillos's strong confirmation that he is "surfeited" with the poems of Tyrtaeus is the first of three times in the *Laws* that he affirms or demonstrates a deep familiarity with a variety of poems that seems unusual for a Spartan. Every Spartan may be presumed to know or know of Tyrtaeus's poetry, but Megillos, as noted above, knows his Homer as well (680c6–d3). And perhaps more surprisingly, his knowledge of poetry seems also to extend to Athenian tragedy, which he intimates when he criticizes the behavior of Athenians and Tarentians at their Dionysias (celebrations of the god Dionysus, with theater and drunkenness entailed): Megillos attended those festivals (737b, cf. especially *eidon*—"*I* saw" at b3 and *etheasamên*— "*I* beheld" at b4; Megillos did not just *hear* about this—he was there).[29] He indicates this still further when the Stranger, in Book 8, overstates the case that tragic characters always immediately commit suicide if they engage in incest. Megillos—very diplomatically, it should be noted—declines to agree with him (838c9–d2).[30] The importance to the *Laws* as a whole of the subject there addressed, the sacred character of the prohibition against incest, cannot be overstated. Megillos's knowledge of Homer and tragedy—and the Stranger's awareness of this knowledge—will play an important role in the later discussion of incest, homosexuality, and law "according to nature." We will return to this in chapters 5 and 6.

This is the first overt instance of a stated difference between the two Dorians. It is Megillos who asserts the difference.

Reviewing the circumstances of Megillos's participation so far, we note that he has certainly not overtly distanced himself from the opinions of the "many" Lacedaimonians that he has related. But nor has he overtly identified with those opinions. In his next major exchange—his first as primary interlocutor—with the Stranger (633a–d), he will for the first time explicitly so identify (with the emphatic *egôge*—"*I*" stressed as such—at 633b1). The subject is the whole of virtue, as seen by the original Spartan lawgiver. We must note that at the outset of this exchange it is *not* how the laws laid down by Lycurgus actually play out in practice, but what Lycurgus's *intention* was with these laws (633a5, b2, 636a4–b1). What is significant in Megillos's list of institutionalized practices in Sparta is that while he seems to stress only the aspects thereof that involve endurance of suffering, he in fact first mentions hunting *outside* of this preoccupation (633b1–2—note that Megillos here emphatically speaks for himself [*egôge*] as well as his countrymen). And of all the examples he gives, it is the only activity for which he describes no corresponding goal. The conversation proceeds by three stages:

1. The Stranger asks first whether "we said (*phamen*)[31] that the common meals and gymnastics were invented/discovered (*exêurêsthai*)[32] by the lawgiver for [the purpose of] war?" (633a4–5; he has dropped the "weapons" mentioned at 625c7–e2—this is more important than it seems, as we will see in chapter 5). Megillos agrees, though he had not, as we have seen, added his voice to this assertion (nor had the Stranger—cf. 688a2–c1). The Stranger then asks what other "devices" the lawgiver had invented, in rank order (after these two), and with a view toward the whole of virtue—that is, not *only* war.

2. At this point Megillos makes clear that when he had earlier declined to specifically add his own voice to what the "Lacedaimonians" say, this was purposeful (this will become even more clear at 636a2–3).[33] He does so by now specifically adding his own voice to what the Lacedaimonians say. "Thirdly, *I* (*egôge*) and any Lacedaimonian would say that he discovered (*êure*) hunting" (633b1–2).[34] While it is tempting

to hear this, within the broader conversation, as Megillos mentioning just another means to war and education in suffering, he has precisely isolated it from both. The *fourth*, distinct group of practices that he will immediately talk about have to do with suffering hardships. The first two were "said" to have been focused on war, but the Stranger explicitly asked Megillos what practices *other* than those focused on war had been instituted by the lawgiver (thus the fourth group too is, in Megillos's opinion, not merely looking toward war). Moreover, Megillos does not himself say what hunting was designed to promote, nor does he link it only (or at all) with the Spartan initiation hunting ritual. To modern readers, the connection between hunting and erotics may not be evident, but it is certainly not lost on the Stranger: when he later "legislates" hunting (822d–24a), he is quite precisely concerned with the "erotic" and excessive enjoyment that should be expected to attend this activity. What is more, in Greek mythology, "sexual"[35] eroticism and hunting were mutually implicated in a tension built on both prohibition and indulgence (Barringer 2001, 125–28).[36] Megillos's silence concerning the purpose of hunting with regard to developing virtue is, perhaps, pregnant. It would seem that he too (i.e., not only the Stranger) is concerned with moderation (*sôphrosunê*).

3. The Stranger now asks for another practice legislated by Lycurgus. In response, Megillos for the first time says what *he* would focus on, without mentioning the Lacedaimonians (633b5–6). The sequence of his speech is therefore temporally: (i) what the Lacedaimonians say; (ii) what I *and* the Lacedaimonians say; (iii) what *I* say.[37] What *he* would focus on for the fourth practice is the array of experiences common to Spartan youths. Some of these, such as the *krupteia* (the secret murder of Helots) and thievery, were shameful for the Spartans (cf. Pangle 1988, 515n31), but Megillos is startlingly frank about their existence.[38] His focus, however, is exclusively on the effects of these institutions *for character*, not for larger political ends (and the *krupteia* at least, and to say the least, had such political ends). They educate Spartans in enduring pain, cold, heat, and extreme physical trials (633b–c) and, importantly, Megillos speaks of these also as somehow distinct from a war-focused sense of virtue. In fact, as will shortly become clear (though in a very polite way) it turns out that, according to him, *none* of the Spartan practices mentioned (common meals, gymnastics, hunting, and education through suffering)[39] were devised only with an eye to war and courage in war—it is likely that all were also finely devised for moderation as well (636a). Megillos, unlike Kleinias, does not confuse current habitual practices and beliefs with the original intentions of the lawgiver.

All this may of course seem like getting Megillos off on a technicality (or a series of technicalities). The point, however, is that Megillos speaks in such a careful way as to give one general impression, while another specific one is available only to a listener who is as careful as he is (such as the Stranger). The same cannot be said for Kleinias. In fact, when Kleinias is pressed for an overt admission of his opinion concerning whether any well-ruled city must be arranged mainly so as to defeat others in war, he gives it clearly and emphatically—"Entirely so" (626c3; cf. 628e2–5)—then solicits Megillos's support. As we have already seen, Megillos responds with what seems like support, but his words leave room for ambiguous interpretation (626c4–5).[40] He then distances himself further from Kleinias's opinion, until he finally says outright that the common meals and gymnastics of the Dorian regimes were "likely finely devised for both" *andreia* (courage, or manliness) and *sôphrosunê* (moderation) (636a2–3). In terms of the question directly asked by the Stranger (635e6–636a1), this is *different* than regimes organized predominantly or only for war. In other words, he seems to Kleinias to have agreed with him, and then to have reluctantly admitted their mutual error. But Megillos never actually said this error was mutual, and seems to have taken as much care to avoid *actually* doing so, as he did to *appear* to do so.

What Megillos has done (not for the last time—see, for example, chapter 3) is facilitate the discussion past an impasse that Kleinias could not get through on his own. Regardless of his willingness to discuss the Cretan laws, Kleinias could not admit that the lawgiver designed his laws without war and therefore courage in war as their principal or only object in view, nor that this would not be an inferior sort of law (628e2–5, 630d2–3, 635e1–2). The furthest he can go is acknowledging (*after* Megillos has acknowledged this— 633d) that "courage" must mean resisting not only pains, but especially pleasures (633e–634a), but he is unable to cite clear examples in Cretan Law (634c),[41] and is reticent to accept the consequences thereof even when he admits the necessity of its logic (635e).[42] Moreover, Kleinias's short-sightedness in this respect was closely linked to the narrowness of his reflection on the purposes of Dorian institutions. When the Stranger had asked him to suggest the original reasons for the common messes, gymnastic training, and weapons employed by the Cretans (625c), it did not occur to Kleinias to mention other Cretan institutions as well, nor can he extrapolate reasons for those mentioned by the Stranger beyond the immediate exigencies of adult men in battle. It does not occur to him, for example, that the immediate effects of forcing grown men to take common messes during a war could be substantially different than the variety of effects such messes might have over a lifetime, when they are mandatory daily activities from very early boyhood (beginning at seven years old, as they did in Sparta at least) until death. Indeed, Kleinias's argument rests on his assumption that the effects of a particular institution are both static in general, and essentially the same for males of all ages. By contrast, all of Megillos's examples of Spartan institutions bring the focus of the discussion—subtly—to their educative functions and effects on young and adolescent boys (both the *krupteia* and the exercises of survival by theft, for example, were only for such boys in Sparta—they were not engaged in by grown men). With these examples, Megillos opens the space for the philosophical and political quandary that may be fairly said to be the obsession of the *Laws*: the education of the young. And the Stranger, at least, does not mistake Megillos's subtlety in opening this space for a lack of intention to do so on his part.

Megillos facilitates the topic's pursuit by ostensibly taking up and defending Kleinias's opening position, though on behalf of Sparta (636e8–637a2, 638a1–2),[43] but then *admitting* the point that Kleinias would not (633d4, 634b7–c2, 636a2–3). He acts the conservative elder on whom Kleinias may rely to value tradition above all, but who in fact articulates *Kleinias's* reluctance to part with his traditional assumptions in a manner that allows the Stranger to assuage that reluctance.

This is a point to draw out. While there is certainly deception involved here, Megillos does not *trick* Kleinias into giving up his hostility against his will, as it were. Rather, he *articulates* the roots—emotional and reasonable[44]—of that hostility, in a way that obviates its most frequent expression: obdurate silence and refusal to entertain the alternative possibilities that in fact already inhere in the structure of one's own opinions. Megillos's articulate traditionalism permits examination—and persuasion—where Kleinias's passionate but obdurate[45] traditionalism would not. And actual persuasion is necessary here—this is not simply a conversation to be dominated while it lasts by rhetorical dexterity, or "won" through slippery forensic embellishment. If Kleinias comes away from the exchange feeling that he was trapped by superior but unscrupulous logicians or orators, not only will those orators have failed to gain anything but an ephemeral victory, but there is a significant likelihood that Kleinias will be suspicious of, if not hostile to, anything to do with their efforts. He must be persuaded, to use Rousseau's (2003) term, to develop new opinions of his own, having been guided to reflect upon and to question the opinions of which he is currently persuaded (*Du contrat social* 2.7). And because there are limits to how much, and which, of those current opinions may in fact be reflected upon and questioned by Kleinias, there are necessarily limits to real persuasion by or to new opinions. But because the former limits are not necessarily exactly as Kleinias believes them to be at the outset, he can be convinced or persuaded that they are broader than he, left to his own devices, would have believed.

Such persuasion is essentially what Megillos and the Stranger now attempt by way of introducing symposia as part of an education—or safeguard of education—in moderation. It may be helpful to once again proceed step by step.

To begin with, the Stranger attacks the *Cretans* specifically for their pervasive practices of *paederasteia* (homosexual and homosocial relationships between older men and boys and young men), and for manipulating divine myths to provide legitimacy for those practices (636b–e).[46] It should be noted that paederasteia was by no means practiced only in Crete (and Sparta), but was a fixture of many if not all Greek cities. But the Stranger singles out Crete as the originator of this practice, and its most complete proponent. That Megillos the Spartan, rather than Kleinias the Cretan, should respond to this charge is in itself somewhat remarkable.

Megillos begins with a strong assertion of the superiority of Spartan law and practices (636e–637a), and thereby shows Kleinias two things: (1) he, the eldest of the three discussants (712c8), is on Kleinias's "side" (i.e., the Doric side) against the youngest (892d7), the Athenian; and (2) he is patriotic (cf. also 638a1–2). Both of these may be expected to impress the old Cretan statesman. Having done this, he attacks the ritual drinking parties (note that he does not attack drinking per se—cf. *Minos* 320a; Xenophon, *Lac. Pol.* 5.2–6), which in his opinion are rather spuriously legitimized by the worship of Dionysus everywhere else in Greece (637b1–6). Since the Athenian is the only member of the present group who is from a city in which this practice occurs, this presents itself as an attack on the Athenian, in response to the Athenian's attack on Crete. Megillos strengthens this by criticizing what he had once seen among the Athenian's people (637b2–3), but then gives as his broadest example what he had seen in Sparta's own colony, Tarentum, at the Dionysia (637b3–5).[47]

Of course, both the myth of Minos and that of Ganymede, in Homer, would seem themselves to provide divine legitimacy for symposia, had the Stranger not specifically interpreted away the aspects thereof that would do so. But the Stranger seems to *want* the god Dionysus to be introduced into the conversation—a god who, it must be noted, is never mentioned by Homer in either of his epics.[48] He shows Megillos what he needs said *by Megillos*, by conspicuously leaving it out of his own account twice. And Megillos shows that he understands this not only by then saying it, but also by *doing the same thing himself* in doing so: the example he uses is what he has seen in the Spartan colony of Tarentum. Tarentum, as was widely known, was colonized by the vast number of children who were born of liaisons between (married) Spartan women and their Helot slaves (see Pangle 1988, 516n42; Strabo 6.3.2; Pausanius 10.10.6–8; Diod. Sic. 8.21).[49] Megillos *asks* for this fact to be noticed, by mentioning Sparta's colony—rather than only the Athenians he had already criticized (and virtually any other city in Greece would have served as an example as well)—and thereby leads the Stranger to the latter's criticism of Sparta's proverbially "loose" women (637c2).

This allows the Athenian to show his own patriotism, under the guise of which he is excused in Kleinias's eyes for insultingly mentioning the "looseness" of Spartan women (637c1–2)—a topic, it should be said, that Megillos could not patriotically have broached himself, but which he clearly pointed to by mentioning the very existence of Tarentum.

That this was deliberate on his part is reinforced by a rather singular exchange in Book 8: the one and only instance in the *Laws* in which Megillos voices his wholehearted approval of a law while acknowledging that Kleinias may differ (842a3–6). And Kleinias does indeed differ, deferring his answer (indefinitely, as it turns out, c7–9). What is being legislated are radically different laws and customs (different from Cretan and Spartan laws and customs) for the erotic interactions between women and men, and men and boys (see especially 841c4–842a2). What is more, it is once again Megillos who facilitates the entire discussion on this subject (837b–839d), and the Stranger deliberately asks him to do so (837d7–8).[50] We will return to this conversation in some detail in chapter 5, but for now we will provisionally suggest that Megillos wanted precisely the issues with which he was ostensibly "attacked" by the Stranger, raised and involved in the discussion. Kleinias, apparently, did not—and Megillos seems to have known it.[51] What initially appears to be an insulting exchange between Megillos and the Stranger in Book 1 seems on more careful study to be collusion, not hostility.[52]

But to Kleinias's eyes, Megillos and the Stranger have displayed clear evidence of one of the greatest political virtues, patriotism.[53] Moreover, he has also seen that Megillos is very much on his side, if needs be, against the impropriety of the Stranger. But this display of virtue and fraternity has also blinded pious Kleinias (for his piety, see especially 885e7–886a5) to the gross impiety that the Stranger has committed, and that Megillos has in fact seconded. To the Stranger's impious assertion that the Cretans invented divine beliefs for their own purposes, Megillos asserted that the Athenians (and other Greeks) had done the same. He did not in any way deny that stories about the divine (including Cretan stories) were human-originated, nor did he even attribute the myth of Ganymede to the greatest of human creators of divine myths, Homer—and such attribution would have been entirely accurate (*Il.* 20.232–5). Instead he hid his agreement with the Stranger on this issue in his *dis*agreement on another. It would appear that Megillos did in fact hear the subversive sense of the Stranger's question that opened the dialogue. It would also appear that he has now answered it. For unlike Kleinias, Megillos perceives that it cannot be simply true that existent laws have only a divine source: human beings necessarily impact the laws. But he says this in a way that Kleinias's focus, and therefore his understanding, will be directed elsewhere. Megillos has become the advocate and confidant of both Kleinias and the Stranger. He is the man in *stasis* whom both sides rightly trust (Benardete 2000, 17), the man who does not remain impartial, but takes *both* sides. That taking the Stranger's side as well is deceptive, to a certain degree, does not diminish his genuine advocacy for Kleinias's as well, nor does it mean he is engaged in deception *simpliciter*: Megillos largely shows (rather than tells) Kleinias how the latter's position is more open to the Stranger's than he thinks, or is habitually inclined to entertain.

This train of conversation opens up the discussion of symposia that will take up the rest of Book 1 (and bracket the discussion of education in Book 2). As we have already noted, Kleinias is highly reluctant to entertain such a discussion, even when he is forced to admit that there is some *prima facie* sense to the Stranger's initial comments on learning through experience to moderate—rather than simply flee—pleasures. Despite Kleinias's reluctance, Megillos consistently ensures that the discussion takes place, and in such a way as to be appealing to Kleinias's sensibilities and habituated character. The ways in which he does this vary, from expressions of patriotism and seeming hostility toward the Stranger (as we have seen), to at least one startling display of extreme respect and friendliness for him (642b–d). This latter, the third such instance in Book 1, once again follows a moment in which Kleinias is in a state of disbelief over one of the Stranger's proposals (the possibility that symposia might be beneficial for education—641c8–d2). Megillos now reveals that he and his family are the *proxenoi* (advocates) for Athenians in Sparta, and that Athens is, in a sense, a "second fatherland" for him. He also vouches, as a Spartan and Doric patriot, for the possibility of the Athenian's transpatriotic "true" goodness—a goodness not compelled by his city,[54] but in him "by his own nature" and by "divine share of fate" (cf. 951b).[55] In other words, he makes the strongest possible case for the Stranger that can at the same time remain politically feasible. Kleinias, having heard this, adds his own story concerning familial affinities for Athens (642d–643a). This, as the Stranger recognizes, marks the point at which they can approach the topics at hand with any reasonable hope of mutual understanding: "It seems likely that you are eager to take your parts and listen. And I am willing to take mine, though it's in no way easy to do—but it must be tried" (643a2–4). The journey they will take, as he now lays it out, is to start with education, and continue "until it reaches the god" (a7). They are now ready to begin.

Pangle (1988) is certainly correct that a "political philosopher who wishes to bring about fundamental changes is more likely to succeed if he appears to be not merely an old conservative, but a 'foreigner' in some sense" (396).[56] But he or she also requires welcome into the "host" culture which is to be the site of such change, and this welcome requires a different—much more self-effacing—political philosopher. To use examples that Pangle himself uses (396), though to change the context, Al-Farabi, Maimonides, and Marsilius of Padua (in the Islamic, Judaic, and Christian contexts, respectively) were such philosophers. And the analogy of *these* philosophers in the *Laws* is given in the character of Megillos, who is able to accomplish the difficult reconciliation of "foreigner" and "native," both in himself, and for the city and philosophy. From the position of genuine philosophy, a position attained and attainable only by a very few (and the author of this book does not pretend to be among them), "human affairs are worthy of no great seriousness" (803b2–3). But to make a place for philosophy within the city (cf. Plutarch, *Life of Nicias* 23.4), which is to say to pursue a *political* philosophy, "it is necessary to be serious about them" (803b3–4). Not fortunate (b4), but necessary.

Thus in order to understand the *Laws*, it is necessary to understand the unique role that Megillos plays throughout the dialogue. Moreover, it is also necessary to understand the play of characters in the *Laws* in order to understand how, as a whole, it is devoted to exploring how, and why, to reinvest politics with the higher purpose of the philosophical and soul-crafting life, if that higher purpose has been lost (cf. Al-Farabi, *Attainment of Happiness*, sec. 63, 47:6). To understand, that is, why it is today the timeliest of books.

At the outset of the *Laws*, the major theme is that the intentions of the lawgiver often (perhaps always) tend to get lost in the practices and habits that arise out of the laws he or she has devised. That this theme is also self-reflexive—the tendency also applies to the laws that are discussed in the *Laws* (cf. 962d)—is key to understanding why the laws (and *Laws*) must themselves educate their subjects (or some of their subjects) to revise and reshape the very laws that must maintain the *appearance* of immutability (cf. 879b with 709b–c; also 634e, 664a, 769a–771a, 802b–c, 960b–c; *Republic* 497c–d; *Statesman* 295b–296c; Aristotle, *Pol.* 1254b38–1255a1; and Lewis 1998, 3). Readings of the *Laws* that begin and end with the proposition that "Plato" believed he had discovered close-to-perfect laws that should never be altered (e.g., Klosko 1988, 82–83; Nightingale 1999b, 118–22, and 1993, 290–300; Morrow 1960, 570–71) quite profoundly miss the major opening (and in many ways governing) theme of the work.[57] While it is certainly true that law *qua* law must authoritatively establish a static version of the thought that originally informed it (653a–c, 656d–657b, 659d–660b, 663b–c, 965c–e[58])—which is to say, *doxa*, or "opinion"—it must also stimulate the activity of true thought, which in those to whom "nature" allows it, is anything but static (665c, 951b–c, 835c, 875c; cf. Aristotle, *Nic. Ethics* 1137b13–29, 1113a29–33; *Protrepticus* fr. 5).[59]

To put it perhaps too simply, for the moment, it is to these two levels that the characters of Kleinias and Megillos correspond. For Kleinias and the level of opinion, laws must have a single reasoning (*logos*) on any given subject—there can be only one, stable level of meaning. Likewise, "knowledge" is, for him, something attained and retained as a "known thing"—as something *explained* (cf. 957b; Aristotle, *Nic. Ethics* 1095a18–b22). For Megillos, laws simply *are* in constant motion, as is the world and the activity of true thought. The single *logos* with which law is obliged to speak, must contain within itself multiple *logoi*, only one of which engages the obedience that opinion simply *is*. Knowledge is, for him, a restless and unceasing activity that must be recognized as transitioning to *ignorance* when it comes to rest in the solidity and comfort of mere "known things" or explanations (cf. Aristotle *Nic. Ethics* 1104a4–10; Tarnopolsky 2011, 21). These two levels are constantly reflected in the discourse on law in the *Laws*: Kleinias consistently hears "one speech on one subject," and misses the different discourse that Megillos and the Stranger are engaged in (cf. 719c–d with 811c–12a; 961e; *Philebus* 52b6–d1).

And this is the way it must be, for the restlessness of thought by its nature threatens the stability—and the *desire* for stability—that opinion *is* (cf. 670c1–2). Megillos is aware of this, and carefully effaces himself: nothing he does overtly contests Kleinias's form of traditionalism (including, perhaps especially, his piety). Indeed, everything he says is calculated to support that traditionalism, even as it works to transform it.

It is that very desire to transform that must draw our attention—it certainly draws the Stranger's. We have some indication in the first book of the *Laws*, and the second, that Megillos is concerned about the immoderation—and especially the "sexual" immoderation—of the Spartans and perhaps the Dorian people as a whole. As we have seen, he subtly draws the Stranger's attention to precisely that, and agrees with the Stranger that moderation was necessarily a purpose for the Spartan lawgiver in giving his laws. Why he draws the Stranger's attention subtly but specifically to the erotic immoderation, and sexual segregation, of Sparta, however, is not yet fully clear, and we will have to return to this question as we attend carefully to Megillos's rare but pregnant participation in the conversation to follow in the *Laws*.

For the moment, though, it does not seem excessive to make a provisional suggestion: it may be that in Plato's political masterpiece, which he created both externally and internally to be studied over and over again (811b–12a, 890e–91a, 822d–23a, 858e–59a, 957d), the education of Megillos is no less important than the education of Kleinias, each according to his capacities. That this possibility as a possibility is not immediately apparent would in that case be a part of the education created by Plato for his reader. And experiencing that possibility appear would also then be a part of that most careful education, or of the safeguard (*sôtêria*) of that education (653a).

Before we rush to judgment about this, though, we must examine Kleinias's character as closely as we have Megillos's. Some, at least, of what I have suggested about Kleinias in this chapter might seem precipitous, as building precisely such an assumption about him into the story to begin with as I suggested was a mistake to do with Megillos. We must therefore give him his due, beginning at the beginning.

NOTES

1. Of this passage Whitaker (2004) writes that "the stranger's interlocutor*s* rebel" (134–35, my emphasis). But Megillos alone "rebels," which as we will see is of greater consequence than initially appears.

2. In the eleven essays, by eleven different authors, in the recent *Plato's* Laws: *A Critical Guide* (Bobonich ed., Cambridge 2010), I find not a single reference to Megillos that is not about "Kleinias and Megillos" as a homogenized pair (other than references to their respective home cities).

3. For example, while he notes that, in Book 1, the Stranger deliberately provokes Megillos's "attack on Athens" (636a–637b), Pangle (1988, 394–95) neglects to mention that Megillos then turns around and deliberately provokes, in the same manner, the Stranger's attack on Sparta (see 637b). So also Benardete 2000, 28.

4. Salem (2013, 53–55) offers an interpretation of Megillos as having a kind of "change of heart" or mind based on the Stranger's matching spirit (*thumos*) with spirit, and therefore being swayed by the Stranger's rhetoric. The assumption is the same as Pangle's: *even* Megillos succumbs to the Stranger's charm. According to Salem, both Kleinias and Megillos are "too ignorant of philosophy and perhaps too caught up in 'mortal nature' to make their way very far along that path" (58n10). Such an assumption makes an unprejudiced evaluation of Megillos's character (and also Kleinias's) difficult if not impossible. Lutz (2012, 54–89) pays unusual and careful attention to the interaction between Megillos and the Athenian Stranger, but that attention is still grounded in the assumption that Megillos is representative of the devoted or serious citizen, whose intellectual capacities and limits are wholly shaped by the apparent "awe" he feels for the law under which he lives and the assumptions about the character of the divine that that awe implies (see especially Lutz 2012, 82–83, 108). I do not entirely disagree with this assessment—I disagree only with the implication that such a formation should be assumed to prevent thoughtful reflection. This is, though, a significant and consequential disagreement.

5. Though compare 702b4–c2 and 723d8–e3, which suggest that Kleinias had thought the new colony a secret until that point. It is certainly not impossible that the seemingly amazing coincidence of this meeting of three old men is just that, a complete coincidence. Plato was under no illusion about what a huge amount of pure good fortune would be required for the *kairos* (critical moment of opportunity) necessary to even allow the possibility of such a political founding as is discussed in the *Laws* (cf. 709c5–9, 710c7–d3 and e7–9, 711e8–712a2, 879b2–3, 888e–889e; *Republic* 473c11–e4, especially the word *sumpesêi* at d2). However, Megillos at least is almost certainly in Crete in an official capacity (which does not necessarily mean that the drama of the *Laws* is reflective of that capacity). Spartans were—unlike Athenians—only allowed to travel abroad on official missions (Plutarch, *Lycurgus* 27.3; Xenophon, *Lac. Pol.* 14; Herodotus 1.67–8). It is possible that Kleinias has been led to believe that the new colony is a secret, by the powers that be in Knossos, who nevertheless solicited help from Sparta and/or Athens. It is, however, impossible to conclude anything about this coincidence with certainty—other than the fact that it *is* a huge coincidence, whether by chance or otherwise—which is surely a deliberate choice on Plato's part. We will have to narrow our speculations as we proceed.

6. Cf. also Nietzsche, *Human, All Too Human* I, preface §8: "in certain circumstances, as the old adage indicates, one *remains* a philosopher only by—being silent." The reference is to the medieval adage, "*si tacuisses, philosophus mansisses*," a paraphrase of Boethius, *Consolations of Philosophy* II §2, in which a false philosopher is exposed through his inability to remain silent. Nietzsche's comments in *Assorted Opinions and Maxims* (aphorism 127) are pertinent as well, among them this: "Something said briefly can be the fruit of much long thought. . . ."

7. Anticipating a little, one could well say that this passage contains a perfect description of Megillos in the *Laws*. The famous Socratic "irony" in the *Protagoras* is Platonic irony in the *Laws*.

8. Conversely, the awareness that a person could speak sweetly and clearly, and at the same time just be "babbling" (*akritomuthos*—literally: speaking without judgment), was quite prominently recognized since Homer at least (*Iliad* 2.246).

9. *Sic.* Cf. *Republic* 620c.

10. From the beginning of Greek literature, the potential weight of a single, quantitatively insignificant, statement has been evident. Consider the *Iliad* 1.184–187, and *Odyssey* 9.502–505. Without these lines, neither the *Iliad* nor the *Odyssey* exists.

11. The first line of the *Minos* (313a1), Socrates's question for his unnamed comrade, is: *ho nomos hêmin ti estin;*—"What is law, for us?" but also: "What is our law?" (Cf. Strauss 1968, 65–66). The author of the pseudo-Platonic dialogue *Peri Dikaiou* ("On Justice") demonstrates an understanding of Plato's deliberate exploitation of this ambiguity, by mimicking it in the first line his Socrates speaks, which questions what "the just" is—and whether it is worth talking about (372a1).

12. Cf. the order of the (pseudo?)-Platonic *Definitions* (or *Boundaries*) 411a1–4—not all spheres of thought begin with "god."

13. England (1921, vol. 1, 197), in his immense and practically authoritative commentary on the *Laws*, does not even mention this ambiguity.

14. I will frequently cite Strauss's *The Argument and the Action of Plato's Laws* (1975), as does any serious writer on the *Laws* since this "commentary's" publication. It should therefore be noted from the outset that simply reading a quoted page number from this work will often reveal little if anything in the first encounter (the present reference being an exception). Strauss is a very careful writer, and he deliberately mimics Plato in his commentary on Plato (like many great commentators—for example, Aristotle, Cicero, Al-Farabi, Maimonides). Very often, only critical reflection on the *Laws* itself, coupled with critical reflection on Strauss's commentary, allows the connections between the two to come to light.

15. It is on Kleinias's terms, for example, that the reader is introduced to the key themes of justice, truth, and the good, in the *Laws*—he is the first character to use each term in the dialogue: he is quite convinced that he knows what is "most just" (624a3 and b5), what "all the good things" in life are (626b5), what the "best" of victories is (626e3), and what the "truest" way of investigating conduct is (627d5).

16. For the proverbial "Laconic" style of minimal speech, see 641e6–7, 721e4–5; *Protagoras* 342e; Herodotus 3.46.1–2.

17. That someone can *say* something—and, in particular, say what the opinion of "the many" valorizes—while *believing* something else to be true, is a major and explicit theme of the *Laws*—cf. especially 655c–656a, where the theme comes to the forefront of the discussion. It is characteristic of Plato that he here presents this in one of its *base* uses.

18. Literally, "every ninth year," but the Greeks counted inclusively, so in modern English this means every eight years. It is, however, important to the Greek imagination that the ninth year is referred to here, given the importance of the number nine to ritual practices in ancient Greece (many temples had nine steps, the greatest sacrifice was nine times nine bulls, etc.).

19. It should be noted that nine years of age is by no means young for drinking wine in ancient Greece. Boys and girls were given wine to drink at some religious festivals, such as the Choës, at the age of three (Burkert 1983, 221n27).

20. He will also, at this point, subtly tell the Stranger that the latter's "Laconizing" of Homer was not lost on him. Homer, he says, wrote not of a Laconic, but of an Ionian way of life (680c7–d3). Which is to say that he caught the Stranger's evocation of the *symposium* at the outset of their conversation.

21. *Amicus Strauss, sed magis amica veritas.*

22. Cf. the very important resonances this whole passage has with 654e3–7, noting both the use of the word *schêma* ("design") there, which is the root of the words I have translated as "appropriateness" and "inappropriateness," and the virtually opposite sense the passage has to the present one. The Stranger will frequently deny that the discussion is concerned with words or "names," and almost always in connection with the very debate about the struggle in the soul that is at issue here (e.g., 644a6, 864a8–b1). Yet names are not unimportant (cf. 704a with 848d). We may at this point venture to say that names may mislead us if our aim is the discovery of the nature of human beings, nature being without names; but that names may be essential in the conduct of laws or conventions, conventions being highly reliant upon names. The significance of names is of inescapable importance to politics and thus to political philosophy, yet the philosophical consideration of names—the relationship between what a thing is

called and what it is or is not—comes perilously close to a sovereign contempt for politics by the very consideration of those significances. Our two greatest examples of meeting this particular challenge are the frivolity of Plato's *Cratylus* and the seriousness of Maimonides's *Guide*. The work of Hobbes as a whole might be called—indeed may be—a marriage of the two.

23. So far as I can see, there is one, and only one, way out of this conundrum of increased truth, or relative truth, which is the knowledge of a standpoint outside of the relativity that is generally experienced. So far as I know, the only writer to have proposed a non-self-contradictory explanation of such knowledge is Hegel, and it is most certainly not Hegel's contention that the standpoint by which all of history is understood as relative is itself relative. Indeed, for Hegel, it is only the achievement of "absolute" knowledge that opens on to the knowledge of history as relative. For this understanding, Hegel's *Phenomenology of Mind* and *The Science of Logic* must be carefully studied in their entireties.

24. With this rhetorical usage, the very rare phrase "*kai mala alêthês*" may be profitably compared. As Benardete notes, "The expression *kai mala alêthês* (very true) occurs four times in Plato—twice in the *Philebus* (29c4, 46d3), at *Euthydemus* 307b2 and at *Laws* 810d7—and apparently in no other Classical author. What the passages have in common is a sudden acknowledgement of the base or vulgar (cf. *Epinomis* 980d5)" (in Plato 2009, 143–44n23).

25. If I am not mistaken, Kleinias uses the word "truest" more than twenty times in the *Laws*. It is, moreover, virtually his first (627d5) and his last word (969d1), and always expresses his own personal opinion. The Stranger uses it considerably more sparingly—ten times—and always with reference to "the many" (an opinion *of* the many, an authoritative pronouncement rather than demonstrative argument *for* the many, etc.). Megillos uses it three times: the first in book 1 (642c), and the other two in rapid succession at the end of book 3 (701b, 702a). The two instances (701b and 702a taken together in the second) offer or affirm very narrow, but very strong, praise of Athens now and in time past; and both instances *immediately* precede the two most significant changes of heart that Kleinias undergoes with respect to the Athenian (642d–643a, 702b–d). As we will see, it is precisely Megillos's purpose to lead Kleinias in this direction, and he is remarkably attentive to Kleinias's predilections, verbal and otherwise, in order to facilitate this.

26. This is a very specifically worded phrase, with very important consequences. There is a very great difference between what is "by nature," and what is "according to nature." The phrase *hêtis pot' estin phusei* is unique in the *Laws* in pointing directly at this difference, by the awkwardness entailed in eliding it to the maximum possible degree.

27. Saunders (1976), criticizing Strauss for drawing the reader's attention to Megillos's "first spontaneous utterance," insists that, "Megillus merely echoes Kleinias's assent. So what? Even if this spontaneity serves to emphasize the Athenian's *caveat* about procedure, the point is utterly trivial, and has no significance whatsoever for interpretation" (240–41). As can be seen from my exposition above, I beg to differ. This is the first specific textual point that Saunders chooses to criticize, in his review of Strauss's *The Argument and the Action of Plato's* Laws, and his carelessness here is indicative of his carelessness in general in that review, and with the *Laws* in general. It is such dismissive carelessness that leads Saunders to characterize Strauss's book as "an utter disaster" and a "grievously misleading presentation of Plato's most important political work" (239). I beg to differ.

28. Benardete (2000, 40–41) is therefore incorrect that 642c is the first example of a Dorism other than *ô theie* at 626c6 (cf. England 1921, vol. I, 200 on this word—it is a Doric epithet expressed in Athenian dialect), though he is entirely correct to stress the implications for the *Laws* of dialectal difference in general, and his commentary thereof should be read with care. However, he is also incorrect that 642c2–3 "seems to be exclusively Laconic"—he is certainly correct that it is not common Attic usage, but its pedigree is Homeric, not Laconic (cf. *Iliad* 9.249–50; *Odyssey* 20.314 and 23.56); and regardless, Megillos is quoting directly what he heard the "many" say to him in Sparta—a "Laconism" is therefore to be expected.

29. This is the only classical reference that I am aware of to a Dionysia in Tarentum, though Cassius Dio, writing ca. 230 CE, also testifies in a rather vivid passage to a Tarentinian Dionysia in 282 BCE (*Hist. Rom.* 9.39.5). However, by the time Plato was writing, and as he has the Stranger himself attest (659b), theater had expanded well beyond its fifth century home in Athens. See Taplin 2001 for an overview of this increasing ubiquity of performance of

originally "Athenian" tragedy (i.e., most often composed by Athenians, but sometimes by foreign poets, for Athens first [48]) from the late fifth and throughout the fourth century. Taplin notes that during the fourth century, monumental theaters for the Dionysia were being built in nearly every major Greek city (36), and that extant vase-paintings from the period indicate that Athenian tragedies were popular in Tarentum *in particular*—despite the fact that it was a Spartan colony (41, 43).

30. Just as with his response "*kalôs men oun*" (617d6) that we considered earlier, Megillos's response to the Stranger at 838c9–d2 presents itself initially as agreement, but closer consideration reveals that that agreement is qualified in such a way as to express *dis*agreement in a key respect: his explicit agreement in one respect is so phrased as to be an explicit lack of explicit agreement in another. He begins, "you speak most correctly. . ." (*Orthotata legeis . . .*), exactly as he had spoken mere moments before, responding to a much broader solicitation or statement of agreement between himself and the Stranger (837e8, cf. 838b6). Here, however, he continues: "*to this extent . . .*" (*to ge tosouton . . .*), and then summarizes the Stranger's argument in general (cf. Strauss 1975, 120–21), while offering no agreement whatsoever about the Stranger's examples from Athenian tragedy. But it was about precisely those examples that the Stranger had inquired, and in asking whether Megillos concurred about his characterization of three tragic characters' immediate suicide following incest with their sisters, the Stranger had spoken as if he expected Megillos to be familiar with these examples (something he never does with Kleinias). What is more, with respect to his description of both the incestuous and the suicidal actions of the characters from Athenian tragedy ("Thyesteses" [plural], "certain" Oedipuses, and "certain" Makareuses—838c5–6), the Stranger mischaracterizes all but the last (on which see Pangle [1988, 532n13]), by describing the actions of "certain Makareuses" as if they were representative of all three. To say nothing of the self-reflexive irony involved here—two out of three characters discussing whether one out of three other characters is representative of all—that Megillos declines to agree with the Stranger's inaccurate if useful description of these characters would seem to indicate an intimate familiarity with Athenian tragedy. That he declines to agree in a very diplomatic and subtle manner would seem to indicate that he is in agreement with Stranger about the usefulness of his fiction, or lie. We will explore this more fully in chapter 6.

31. The verb *phêmi* does not mean "to agree," only "to say." To agree would be *sumphêmi*.

32. Cf. the Greek of *Minos* 315a4 and Herodotus 1.94.2–4.

33. Megillos is quite aware of the difference, it may be added, between saying something and praising another for saying it (686e1–2).

34. Here he mentions the activity in general, not the ritual. This mirrors his later "condemnation" of symposia, in which he mentions the ritual, not the activity of drinking in general.

35. A clinical term for which there exists no Greek equivalent. Obviously, any consideration of what *sophrosunê* is, for the Greeks, absolutely must leave such a clinical separation of the "things of Aphrodite" (*ta Aphrodisia*) behind.

36. All of this is not even to mention the metaphoric connection of hunting and philosophy throughout the Platonic dialogues (perhaps predominantly in the *Republic* and *Sophist*). "Hunting" is gestured to earlier in the *Laws*, by the Stranger, in just this context, but only suggestively (627c8–d1). Cf. also 654e and 728d.

37. One is tempted to infer here an analogous sequence to that of "most just" (624a3), "true and just" (630d9), "most true" (664c1).

38. *Pace* Benardete (2000, 26), I see no necessary embarrassment on Megillos's part when he mentions thievery.

39. Suffering is by no means connected only with developing endurance for war. The necessity of suffering for wisdom has a pedigree reaching back at least to Homer's *Odyssey* (as a whole). Cf. *Republic* 620c2–d2, 619c6–d5; Aeschylus, *Agamemnon* 176–83, *Eumenides* 523–24; Sophocles, *Oedipus at Colonus* 5–13; Ecclesiastes 1:18; Maimonides, *Guide of the Perplexed* 3. 21–24; John Keats, letter to George and Georgiana Keats, 14 February 1819 ("The Vale of Soul-making"); Nietzsche, *Beyond Good and Evil* aph. 188. This trope can also be seen in the Sumerian epic of *Gilgamesh*, the Indian *Ramayana* of Valmiki, and the Norse story of Odin, among many others.

40. It is important that the Stranger lets this ambiguity stand, and that he is aware of the ambiguity. When Kleinias later responds to him in an almost identical manner (673b–c), the Stranger forces Kleinias to say outright what he means. Kleinias does not indicate any ambiguity with his own statement there, but rather strongly confirms (*aristh' hupelabes*—"You have understood excellently" [the superlative quality of *aristos* is untranslatable here]) the Stranger's understanding that Kleinias obviously means he is in agreement with how Cretans and Spartans in general would respond to his question. There is no ambiguity possible in such a situation for Kleinias, and this itself indicates how deaf he also is to Megillos's earlier deliberately ambiguous use of an almost identical "rhetorical" question.

41. Megillos too claims to be unable to cite examples in Spartan law of resisting pleasure, with the "equal ease" (*isôs euporoiên*) with which he has discussed examples of resisting suffering in Spartan law, other than perhaps some "small ones" for which he could with "equal ease" (*isôs euporoiên*) do so (634b7–c2). But he has in fact already done so (consider both hunting and the "naked games" at 633b–c), and has moreover agreed—in his own voice (*oimai*)—that courage must fight against pleasure as well as pain (633d4). *Isôs* means both "equally" and "perhaps"—Megillos uses it in the *exact* same verbal phrase both when describing his ability to cite examples of resisting suffering in Spartan law, and when describing his ability to cite examples of resisting pleasure in Spartan law (*isôs euporoiên*—there is not the slightest difference even in verb conjugation). Plato did not want this to be unnoticed. Both times should be translated identically.

42. Pangle translates Kleinias's statement at 635e as beginning, "Offhand . . ."; Bury translates, "On the face of them [i.e., the arguments]. . ."; Saunders: " . . . at first blush." All these rightly indicate some hesitancy on Kleinias's part, but none of them quite gets just how hesitant Kleinias is here in the face of an argument that he cannot logically deny, but cannot dispositionally accept. What Kleinias says is: "*It seems to us* (*dokei . . . hêmin* [note that Kleinias again speaks for both himself and Megillos]), *somehow* (*pôs*), *anyway* (*ge*), that the argument is [well] spoken (*legomenou tou logou* [a direct response to the Stranger's "*legomenôn humin...dokei legesthai*" the line before—635d7–8]) . . ." (635e1). Kleinias is saying that he cannot see a way to refute the Stranger's argument—an argument that argues that to give in to pleasures is as cowardly as to give in to fears—but he does not agree with it ("Yeeessss, nicely said . . . but—"). Hence his next words (the *de* clause in a *men . . . de* ["On one hand . . . on the other"] sentence): " . . . but concerning such great matters, to be quickly and easily persuaded would be being youthful and thus (*mallon*) mindless" (e–3). Kleinias is *not* agreeing to the Stranger's argument in anything more than the barest words here. He is quite evidently resisting it.

43. Megillos is not "digging in his heels" here in opposition to a Kleinias who has already been convinced by the Stranger's arguments. At no point in the rest of this long (for Megillos) exchange with the Stranger here, does Megillos do anything other than agree with him—and agree emphatically (639a1, b3, b10–11, c7–d1, d4)—on every point. Indeed, Megillos "concedes" almost immediately that the fact of a "fight in speech" points to an inquiry that is not decided or decidable by one of the party's victory in war (638e3–639a1), despite having ostensibly taken the stance that victory in war is decisive *tout court* (638a1–2). If Megillos is "digging in his heels," he is doing so in what he himself knows to be sand that cannot hold them.

44. This distinction is strictly provisional. As one progresses through the *Laws*, such a distinction becomes increasingly dubious.

45. I am using this word in its etymological sense, from the Latin *obduratus*—"hardened." I do not at all mean the modern English connotation of hardened in *wrong*doing.

46. The Athenian opens the discussion with the most overt—though very diplomatic—reference to the Peloponnesian War in the *Laws* (636b2–4; cf. with Pangle 1988, 515n34). Zuckert (2009, 53–54) is incorrect that no such references exist in the *Laws*, and it seems important that all of the characters in the dialogue are intent on treating this subject only obliquely, and with extreme delicacy. The implications of 699d5–6 (Megillos's *ancestors* fought in the Persian Wars) and 695e4–5 (at the time of the conversation, there have already been several Persian kings after Xerxes) clearly indicate that the conversation related in the

Laws takes place after the Peloponnesian War, or at the *very* least (a least that would stretch the meaning of what is said here beyond any acceptable interpretation), during it.

47. It should be noted that this, together with the fact that he is currently in Crete, indicates that Megillos is unusually well traveled for a Spartan. Cf. 953c–d, 961a, and Herodotus 1.67–68.

48. He is of course mentioned in the "Homeric Hymns" (there are three such hymns devoted to him specifically), but Plato does not seem to treat these as genuinely Homeric in origin. As far as I know, he does not make reference to these hymns in any of his dialogues.

49. England (1921, vol. I, 233) questions with surprise whether Plato has here put "an argument for the Athenian into Megillus' mouth," but does not even consider whether Megillos might be aware of this.

50. The Stranger addresses Megillos as "friend" twice here (837d8 and e2–3), immediately following a discussion about the equivocal meanings of the word "friend" (837a–d). What does he mean *here* by this word?

51. As the Stranger also knows, at least by the time of the discussion in Book 8 (837e2–6; cf. with 659d–e, 665c, and 903b).

52. It should be noted that, in pursuing this line of conversation with the Stranger, Megillos has followed the Stranger's explicit suggestion that each blame "some aspect of the law of the others" (634c).

53. Pangle (1988, 395–96) notes that the Athenian deliberately provokes Megillos's attack, and assumes thereby the image of a patriot in the Dorians' eyes. He does not note that Megillos does precisely the same thing.

54. n.b. Megillos here makes a telling statement: people who are "good" because they are compelled to be so by their laws, are not "truly" (*alêthôs*) good, but "artificially" (*plastôs*) so. (642c8–d1; cf. 710a–b). And *only* (*monoi*) Athenians—that is, not Cretans or Spartans—can be good in a true way, though this is very very rare.

55. See Saunders's (1972) illuminating note on this passage (4–5).

56. Pangle uses a way of writing that seems to have affinities with both the Stranger's and Megillos's way of speaking. I doubt it is an accident that the passage cited above could just as well apply to Megillos, if not more so.

57. Nightingale (1999b, 118) cites 798a–b as essentially establishing "Plato's" belief in the permanence of his laws. But in this passage the Stranger speaks only of "some divine good fortune (*eutuchian*)" allowing laws to remain unchanged. The reality, however, as he makes pointedly clear, is that "no lawgiver is capable of ruling over fortune (*tuchês*) (879b1–2; cf. 948d). "Plato" could only believe in the permanent stability of "his" laws if he honestly believed that "divine good fortune" would accompany them for all time. Is there not a significant likelihood that he did *not* believe this was likely, and that the *Laws* anticipates this (cf. 751b–d, 752b, 757d–758a; not to mention the problems discussed and stressed at 769c–772d, with which cf. 779d)?

58. Cf. Saunders's (1972, 128–29) note on this passage.

59. Consider the important difference of Muses at 658e8–659a1: "*Almost* the noblest Muse is she who delights the best [*beltistous*—a word also used to describe the aristocratic class], and the sufficiently educated; but the nobl*est* is she who delights the one man distinguished in virtue and education."

Chapter Two

The Great Man in the City: Kleinias of Knossos

For we must needs, as rein, have law;
and a king who once perceived
the true city, or at least its tower.

—Dante, *Purgatory* 16.94–96

As with Megillos, when we first hear from Kleinias, he is not necessarily speaking in his own name. Instead, he is speaking for "we Cretans"—that is, what "we Cretans" believe is most just to say (or what it is most just to say that "we Cretans" believe) about the divine origin of their laws (624a2–5). There is, however, a subtle difference in the ways that the two Dorians say, or seem to say, "we." Kleinias, in his opening statement and elsewhere, uses the first person plural explicitly (*hêmin*; cf. also "*hêmeis . . . hoi Krêtes*"— "we Cretans" at 625a1). As we saw in the previous chapter, Megillos does not—it is implied, but only implied, in the answer he gives Kleinias.

What "we" say is not necessarily identical with what "I" say, but it can be. It is easy to imagine the more common case, in which the two are identical—in such a case it would not even occur to the speaker that what "we" say (we Cretans, we Catholics, we believers, for example) might *not* be what "I" say: what we say, I say and what I say, we say (note the different implications of the two statements, which within this mind-set often seem to the speaker to have the same logic). But a speaker may also say what "we" say in order to diplomatically reserve his own opinion—in this case, what "we" say is *not* what "I" say, though the speaker does not want to overtly draw attention to this distinction.[1] Which way does Kleinias mean this? And how can one tell?

He certainly seems, at the outset, to have the capacity to distinguish himself from "we Cretans." After all, he immediately offers an opinion on the nature of things that, so far as he is concerned, is not an opinion shared by those he calls the "mindless many" (625e5–6): namely, that "for every person, throughout life, there is endless war against all cities" (625e6–7), and that "every city is involved in undeclared war with every other city, by nature" (626a3–5),[2] with the result that "in public all are enemies (*polemioi*) of all, and in private each one is his own enemy" (626d7–9).

But let's not be too hasty about this. Does Kleinias here mean, by "the many," the many *among* the Cretans, as Pangle (1988, 382) suggests? Or does he mean the many non-Cretans as opposed to the few Cretans, or anyway the few older Cretans (635e1–3)? Or the few Dorians among the many non-Dorians? Kleinias certainly expresses no surprise when Megillos indicates that virtually *any* Spartan (not just "the few" among them) would agree with him (626c4–5), and he at no point in the *Laws* suggests that Cretans are, in his opinion, inferior to Spartans in general (indeed, he elides the two with some frequency when it comes to considering core beliefs and practices—cf. 660b1–4, 666d8–10, 673b5–9, which we will shortly have cause to consider further). It seems highly unlikely that he believes only an elite few Cretans understand what he accepts *all* Spartans comprehend as a matter of course, and therefore just as unlikely that he was distinguishing himself from "we Cretans" (or even "we Dorians") with his remarks about the "mindless many."[3]

Perhaps what Kleinias means, though, has nothing to do with particular peoples and fatherlands. Perhaps by the "many" he simply means the ruled rather than the rulers, always and everywhere. Certainly he has a lofty view of his role as an elder statesman, and the distinction between "the few" and the "many," which in fact everyone makes even if they do not articulate it as such, is in almost every case a distinction made relative to one's own specific "fewness," or to the "fewness" of another or others whose expertise or experience one recognizes and needs: for example, cobblers are "the few" compared to the "the many" who are not cobblers but need shoes, farmers are "the few" compared to the "many" who are not farmers but need food, generals are "the few" compared to the "the many" who are not generals but need victory in war, and expert dice players are "the few" compared to those who are not experts or who do not play (*Republic* 374b–d; cf. *Laches* 184d–185a).[4] Similarly, those who are particularly noble or beautiful or morally upstanding are "the few," and I might be particularly inclined to believe this if I consider myself to be among them. The distinction is so common, and so flexible, that we are not surprised that many citizens of ancient Athens (to say nothing of later examples) considered themselves to be among an elite "few" peoples who were distinguished by their very valorization of "the many" on principle. We must remember that Plato certainly did not invent the distinction between "the many" and "the few," nor did he originate the derisory connotations of the former. Rather, he attempted to change the criteria upon which that distinction is based.

It is therefore worthwhile, for our purposes, to consider the commonplace criteria with which Plato contended. Homer, for example, uses both that distinction and its connotations to describe the very difference that we have suggested Kleinias might mean: between rulers and the ruled, regardless of tribe or ethnicity (e.g., *Iliad* 2.91). In general, Homer's reliance on this distinction and especially its connotations of the subordinacy of "the many" is subtler than in Plato and later writers, and reveals itself largely when "the many" *accomplishes* something other than just being ruled. Thus "the many Achaean youths" whom Agamemnon rules are, in the context of saying this, simply "*polloi kouroi Achaiôn*" (*Iliad* 3.183; cf. 9.97–98); whereas when Ajax is surrounded on the battlefield and forced to withdraw by "the many Trojans," those Trojans are called "*hoi polloi te kai esthloi* [*Trôôn*]"—"the Trojans *both* many *and noble*" (*Il.* 5.624). Were Ajax to have been forced to withdraw by "the many" Trojans *simpliciter*, he would on Homer's terms have been a coward.

The distinction emerges in Homer as well in the contrast between the "people" (*demos*) and the "[heroic] man" (*anêr*). The most pointed example is in a passage the whole of which is illustrative of the distinction, the rebuke and beating of Thersites by Odysseus (*Il.* 2.198). The same passage, not coincidentally, contains the single direct statement in Homer on the "*rule* of many" (*polukoiraniê*), which is proclaimed by Odysseus to be axiomatically bad (*Il* 2.204: "*ouk agathon polukoiraniê*": "Rule of many is not good."). The sentiment is echoed precisely by Thucydides (6.72.4) and Xenophon (*Anabasis* 6.1.18), though the word used by both is *polyarchia* (n.b. Robert Dahl!). The word used is in each case a *hapax legomenon* for the author, and in Homer's case, it is the only extant use of the word at all, other than a few later authors who directly quote this very passage.[5] And in all three the context is rule during war. Needless to say, the context of *everything*, for Kleinias, is—at least initially—war.

Regardless if this suggestion is correct, it becomes quickly apparent that Kleinias's elitism is a vanity that conceals (from himself as well as, perhaps, others) his far more pedestrian nature, and his mistaken idea of himself as *not* part of the "many" that he looks down upon is in fact refuted by the very terms in which he states his supposedly "elite" understanding (cf. Heraclitus, DK aphorism B1). This understanding is grounded precisely in a "*logos* of the many" (627d2–3),[6] in the notion of "one's own victory over oneself" as opposed to being "weaker than oneself" (626e2–4; cf. *Republic* 430e–431a, *Laws* 863d6–11). This is a *logos* that Kleinias takes very literally, without having thought through its consequences—consequences which puzzle and distress him once the Stranger draws them out (627c1–2). Indeed, he is quite glad to be rid of those logical consequences when the Stranger suggests that they let them go (627d5), and almost immediately commits himself to a position that is essentially the opposite of what he had asserted earlier (628a4–c8).

He is, of course, not particularly comfortable with the consequences of that commitment either (628e2–5), which entail that Dorian legislation could not possibly have been intended to focus (only or predominantly) on victory in war. And this second instance of perplexity or confusion[7] causes a significant change in his speech: from describing his own "elite" opinion as against the "many," he now turns to stressing the commonness and communality of his beliefs, their origins, and their purpose. Having attempted to assert his "I" (625c9, e1, e5) as the proud explicator of the wisdom of his community as he saw it, and having grudgingly (note the switch to the impersonal—"*it is most necessary* to agree," not "*I* agree"—in his acceptance of the Stranger's arguments at 627c1–2) admitted failure in that regard, he withdraws into the shelter of the communal "we" (628e2–5, 629b6, 630d2).

The nature of what that "we" means to Kleinias thereafter can perhaps best be seen by considering whether or not he speaks *carefully* when he seems to elide his own opinion with others. Of the two types of "we"-sayers, the first that I mentioned—who does not even consider that there might *be* a distinction, at the level of fundamental values, between "we" and "I"—is *ipso facto* somewhat careless. The second *requires* a great deal of care in this regard.[8] How careful is Kleinias when he elides his opinion with others'?

A careful *reader* will begin to notice a pattern in Kleinias's way of speaking. For one, he speaks for both himself and Megillos with an amazing amount of confidence and frequency (Salem 2013, 50), though the reverse is never true.[9] What is more, he with equal confidence often assumes that what Cretans believe applies to Dorians in general—if Cretans believe something, so do Spartans, per Kleinias (660b, 666d, 673b). Which is to say, if *he* believes something, he also almost automatically believes that so do all Cretans and all Spartans (including Megillos).[10] If I am not mistaken, the only distinction that Kleinias notes between what Cretans and Spartans believe is that the former hold Zeus to be their patron, the latter Apollo. It falls to Megillos to interject on important points of disagreement or different practices—whether between he and Kleinias, or Crete and Sparta—Kleinias does not seem to be aware of these (e.g., 680c–d, 842a, 636e–637a).[11]

But if he is not aware of these points of difference, how can he reasonably be so sure about the many points of agreement that he assumes? It seems that Kleinias is rather careless indeed when he speaks of what "we" say and do. There is no other Cretan in the *Laws* with whom to assess his assertions about what Cretans believe in general, but it is surely indicative that he only *once* asks Megillos about what Spartans believe (again, see 624a2–5), and that one time on a matter of common knowledge; that is, his question is really just a statement—it does not *question* that common knowledge. He *never* asks Megillos what he believes personally. He is so sure that he knows that he is not interested in inquiring.[12] Is Kleinias's confidence dependent on his being, so far as he is concerned, a "we"?

Confidence in his own opinion seems to define Kleinias from the outset, not only concerning his knowledge of others' opinions, but also with respect to existentially definitional concepts. It is on Kleinias's terms, for example, that the reader is introduced to the key themes of justice, truth, and the good, in the *Laws*—he is the first character to use each term in the dialogue: he knows what is "most just" (624a3 and b5), what "all the good things" in life are (626b5), what the "best" of victories is (626e3), and what the "truest" way of investigating conduct is (627d5).

It is not a coincidence that Plato has Kleinias not only use all of these terms first, but also use the superlative in each case: *most* just, *all* the good things, *best* of victories, tru*est* way of investigating. Kleinias seems very comfortable with his knowledge of what these words mean; he is sure of his knowledge. But is *sureness* of knowledge, knowledge? Is "political courage," as Socrates calls it in the *Republic* (430c2), courage properly so called (*Republic* 430c4–6; *Laws* 708d6–7)? What kind of knowledge *is* a knowledge that stops questioning itself, and comes to rest in certainty and satisfaction (*Ion* 532b–533c, 542b)? While Kleinias is the first to pronounce upon these key terms, it seems unwise to grant that he thereby knows what these words mean, beyond their expression of a place of comfortable and unquestioning repose of thought: in Platonic terms, *opinion*. The *words* used by most people and those used by fewer are the same. But they can mean very different things (cf. Hobbes [1994, 28 and 489] on the "common" definition of "courage" as against his own definition in *Leviathan* 6.16–17 and R&C 2 [Curley, ed.]). To take but one example, the continuous struggle *within* each person, which Kleinias is so sure of (626d)—and his awareness of this is an obvious surprise to the Stranger (626e)—is not the same struggle that the Stranger holds to be constitutive of what a person is (644c–d).

What is more, there is something revealing in Kleinias's early and unguarded description of "all the good things" that a people has. In war, he says, "all the good things of the vanquished become the victors'" (626b3–4). It would be difficult if not ridiculous to suggest that Kleinias may be thinking of, say, wisdom or moderation as "good things" here. For him, "good" things are transferable, by force if necessary (and perhaps preferably); that is, the things that are "good" are material possessions (cf. 913b–c).[13] Even more, this appropriation of "good things" by victors in war is here presented by Kleinias as *the* grounding reason that he believes any "well-governed *polis* is necessarily ordered so as to vanquish the other *poleis* in war" (626b7–c3). It is not courage (no matter its meaning) *per se*, nor victory *per se* that is revered by Kleinias, though he deceives himself and others that it is. It is wealth and gain that Kleinias reveres.

This of course does not fit with the picture Kleinias presents of himself, and seems to actually *have* of himself. He is, for example, quick enough to join the Stranger in condemning love of wealth as destructive of noble dispositions (705b7–8; cf. 644a2–b5), when he hears that condemnation expressed with cool and abstract—to speak anachronistically, clinical—detachment. But it is highly indicative that when he later hears what he experiences as the Stranger's heated indignation at this love, he becomes ashamed and angry (832a7–b9).[14] (As readers, we will have to carefully consider whether the Stranger's indignation there is *real* indignation, which we will return to in chapters 4 and 5; what is important for the moment is that Kleinias certainly *believes* that indignation to be genuine.) That Kleinias agrees that love of wealth is destructive of virtue does not mean that he is not a lover of wealth—this is in fact a prime example of what the Stranger says is called "the greatest ignorance" (688e–689c): opining (genuinely) that something is bad or ignoble, but wanting it anyway (cf. *Protagoras* 352b–c, 357d–e, 358b–c).

Plato is of course well aware that someone who criticizes or even condemns "love of gain" can nevertheless be a "lover of gain" him- or herself. In the *Hipparchus* (whose second title—whether by Plato or someone else—is "The Lover of Gain"), Socrates has as his interlocutor an unnamed fellow citizen who opens the dialogue by vehemently condemning lovers of gain (*Hip.* 225a–b), but who proves to be just such a one himself (*Hip.* 231c–232c). As Socrates astutely notices, his comrade's condemnation arises, perhaps, not out of a principled disgust at devoting one's life to monetary profit, but at having been cheated out of such a monetary profit by a more capable lover of gain than he (see Socrates's seemingly innocuous comment at *Hip.* 225b10). The comrade does not *know himself,* something that is perhaps true of most, if not all, characters in—and readers of—the Platonic dialogues, and seems to be true of Kleinias in this respect as well.[15] As Pangle (1988, 413–14) puts it, "Kleinias's virtue is grounded in shame, a shame riddled with suppressed longings for pleasure, wealth, and tyranny."

Do the other interlocutors understand this about Kleinias? Our examination of Megillos suggests that he is an extremely attentive observer, and it should be noted that, as a Spartan, he is very likely intimately familiar with the kind of hypocrisy Kleinias displays. Spartans were legally prohibited from possessing gold and silver, and much public display was made of this "virtuous" despising of money, but it was notorious that in fact most Spartans privately hoarded as much of such wealth as they could in their homes (*Alcibiades Major* 122e–123a). Whether this is true of Megillos is not yet clear, but we may venture at the least that he is less likely than some others to trust a mere declaration of virtue in this regard.

The Stranger, for his part, gives every indication—though subtly—that he understands Kleinias very well. He seems in fact to be aware of this aspect of Kleinias's character from the very moment that the latter betrays it with his statement about winning "all the good things" from others in battle (compare his subtle castigation at 632c7–d1 with Kleinias's initial praise of victory in war and reticence to change his mind, 626b1–4 and 628e2–5). The Stranger's "selection" (i.e., modification) of authoritative poems, in Book 1, is indicative of this. Note how, just after Kleinias's statement, he specifically highlights as most important—except for courage in battle—for Kleinias, the quality of wealth in Tyrtaeus's poem (with his "paraphrase": "even were he the wealthiest human being"—629b1), though it is not at all highlighted as most important in that poem by Tyrtaeus.[16] He then specifically chooses a passage from Theognis (630a5–6) that suggests—or seems to—that virtue and wealth are of comparable importance: "a trustworthy man is equal in value / to gold and silver . . . in savage civil war." Needless to say, neither of the Stranger's "quotations" reflects what either poem is really about. In other words, in his attempt to influence Kleinias to think more broadly about virtue than only about courage in war, he modifies the work of poets whom Cretans, and therefore Kleinias, respect, in order to appeal—at this early stage[17]—both to what Kleinias *overtly* values (warlike courage) and what he *covertly* values (wealth). The Stranger knows his man.[18]

There is a deliberate interpretive difficulty worked into the drama of the *Laws* from the outset. Kleinias distances himself from "the many" Cretans almost immediately (625e5–7), while Megillos seems to immediately encourage being identified with "the many" Spartans (624a6, 626c4–5). Plato, however, leaves it to his reader to decide whether or not this initial appearance is reflective of the way things are, and it would seem that virtually the reverse is the case here. Kleinias's elitism disguises *from him* that he belongs to the "many" that he holds in such disdain, and Megillos's seeming self-identification with "the many" is part of a political-philosophical effort that actually shows him to be a rarer type indeed.

But this does not mean that Kleinias is entirely closed to reflection or to the possibility of learning and therefore desiring differently or more nobly. In comparison to the Stranger and Megillos, from our point of view, he is sure to appear as slow, narrow-minded, and obstinate. But he is not more than ordinarily so on any of these counts. The fact of his political power may lead him to believe that he is possessed of an extraordinary insight that "the many" lack, but this belief itself is the result of a very ordinary assumption that "the many" make: that the few rulers are separate in kind, or at least by very great degree, from the many ruled. Kleinias "naturally" believes that his insight has led to his power, and not that that power has led to his belief in his particular insight (cf. *Charmides* 162c1–3 with 163d1–3, noting the ambiguity of *archomenou*, which means both "begin" and "rule").

However, that Kleinias has not before now questioned the opinions he holds dear does not mean that he is entirely incapable, with the proper guidance, of questioning them to some degree—and some opinions to a greater degree than others (630d8, 632d8, 635a6–b1, 635e1–3, 842a4–9; Al-Farabi, *Summary* 1.7). As we saw with respect to his opinions and passions concerning the pursuit of wealth, he is not wholly unaware that as a human being he does not live up to his own standard of virtue. To use Galen's terms, he is, in a way, blind to himself, and may in important respects never be anything less, but he can be led to understand that he *is* blind (Galen, *Aff. dig.* 1.2; *Laws* 731e–732a). He is not one of those "blind men who persistently deny that they are blind," or whose "obstinate cupidity has extinguished the light of reason" (Dante, *Mon.* 3.3.4 and 8; cf. *Bereshit Rabbah* 28.8 and 30.9 on the righteousness of Noah as drastically inferior to the righteousness of Moses and of Samuel). What is more, he can accept, in principle, that the discord within himself (and others) is a greater problem than what he casually and perfunctorily calls the "mindlessness of the many" (689a1–689e3, especially 689c1–3 and c7–d4). We may say that Kleinias illustrates, in his character, the minimal requirements necessary, in a political ruler, for any feasible political shift toward orientation by wisdom or philosophy. Inasmuch as this is so, Kleinias is indeed extraordinary, for the conjunction of the ambition necessary to the political founding of a new regime (Pangle 1988, 414), and the capacity and willingness to be brought to question some of the very opinions that inspired and define political ambition as such, is rare indeed (cf. Parens 1995, 118 and 49–50, citing Al-Farabi, *Summary* 6.2–3; Pangle 1988, 382).

Yet as we saw in our discussion of Megillos, Kleinias's self-questioning is limited, and at key points, on subjects that marshal basic and major drives within him, he runs into an impasse. Regardless of whether he is able to or feels compelled to acquiesce to the logic of an argument that points toward, say, punishment of crime as nonretributive, his desire and sense of honor rebel, for it is "abhorred in [his] imagination." His "gorge rises at it" (*Hamlet* 5.1.176–7). His passions and his reason are not in concord (653b), which is not surprising. As the Stranger says, "lucky is the one to whom [concord] comes even in old age" (653a8–9).

These impasses focus around four general pleasures, which we may here describe as the things of Ares, the things of Aphrodite, the things of Ploutos, and the things of Nemesis: war, sex (and specifically, *paederasteia*), wealth, and vengeance. And the pleasures that Kleinias has experienced in, and anticipates from, war (Al-Farabi, *Summary* 1.9) will—despite the initial interrogation and problematization they undergo at the beginning of the *Laws*—turn out to be the least of the Stranger's concerns, and of Megillos. Indeed, they are susceptible at the outset to that interrogation precisely because they are not a fundamental problem as such for any of the interlocutors, and Kleinias's devotion to other pleasures demonstrates, by that very devotion, that his unexamined (un-self-examined) commitment to war as the central principle of law is not—as we have seen—what he habitually believes it to be. The impasse that he originally runs into with respect to considering the centrality of war to law (which as we saw in chapter 1 is an impasse that Megillos guides him through) results from his pride in the knowledge he was so sure of, not from a challenge to his deepest and unchangeable desires.

Nor is war as such a particular political problem for the discussion of the city and the human being in the *Laws*. War is not central to Magnesia, but this does not mean that it is to be displaced in anything other than the Cretan imagination (which of course is a considerable rearrangement on its own): it never was central in practice. It is certainly true that the Stranger will expound at some length on the merits of the city that is, in principle, directed toward defensive rather than opportunistic and offensive bellicosity (828d–829a). And the "war games" regularly engaged in by the citizens of Magnesia will likely have at least some impact with respect to turning the sacrificial aspects of war inward, and thereby mitigating the extent of the sacrificial drive while satisfying its needs (829a–c and e, 830d–831b, 865a–b; cf. Burkert 1983, 297). But they will also contribute to Magnesia having the largest and most trained standing army in Crete, if not in Hellas, and moreover one that is in consonance with itself (cf. 686b2–3). Needless to say, it would be a more than ordinary honor to conquer this army, or to try. And that army would likely also be felt as a more than ordinary threat by every other city in the area, and beyond—including the colony's mother-city, Knossos (Benardete 2000, 234). It is unlikely that other cities and men would ignore this possibility of honor and glory to be had, or assuage their fears by trusting in the "defensive ethos" of this army. It is instead considerably more likely that Magnesia would be under more or less constant attack from other cities and alliances, even if it did attain and preserve its purely defensive martial purposes—thus the "whole city" (women and men—829e4–5), must be "useful for the true contest [it engages in] *throughout life (dia biou)*" (831a1–3). In the end, it is no surprise that for all practical purposes, the place of war in the city remains essentially normal (i.e., highly significant) except for that place being open to the understanding of insightful citizens and visitors (942a–943a). As Benardete (2000) succinctly points out, "there are to be gods of war but none of peace in Magnesia" (237; citing 943c6). Victory in war is no longer taken by Kleinias to be *the* goal of law, but there is no expectation that war will be less frequently practiced thereby, or victory in it less necessary.

In fact, the very discussion of the supervised symposium in speech that leads the initial discussion from Kleinias's focus on courage (*andreia*) in war (against other cities, other citizens, and oneself) to moderation (*sôphrosunê*)[19] in pleasure, is marked, as Taki (2003, 51) notes, by a pronounced parallel between the Cretan or Spartan common mess (*syssition*) of armed warriors under a single disciplining commander, and the common drinking party under a single disciplining commander (640b, 641a–b). Taki (2003) argues that this parallel leads to the Dorians and the Stranger essentially speaking at cross-purposes with each other, with the Stranger arguing for a "peace-centered" symposium in which *sôphrosunê* emerges as higher than *andreia* in the hierarchy of "goods," and the Dorians agreeing to a "war-centered" interpretation of the symposium as a test of endurance and self-mastery, in which *andreia* remains supreme (52–53).

Aside from the conflation of the two Dorians into one general type, which Taki simply assumes, there is an unsupported reliance on another unsupportable assumption in this interpretation, which is that the difference between war-centered and peace-centered arguments is what is at issue here. In fact, the peace in which the Stranger says once, and at the outset, that the symposium occurs (640b6–8) is clearly the civil peace that Kleinias has already agreed is necessary and desirable even for a city devoted to war (627e–628d). The Stranger is not demonstrating to Kleinias that devotion to war and courage must be replaced by devotion to peace and moderation, but that Kleinias's devotion to victory in war and resistance to pain is already—unbeknownst to Kleinias—fully compatible with appreciation of peace and resistance of pleasure. What Kleinias understands, and is not wrong to understand, is that the symposium that the Stranger discusses is not a replacement of the *sysstition*, but an upgrade (cf. 842b2–9).

Yet there is indeed a distinction that Kleinias does not understand here, that does indicate cross-purposes in the dialogue between Kleinias (though not Megillos) and the Stranger, but that undermines Taki's focus on the "logic" of the argument alone. This is the experiential difference between, on the one hand, the image of *sôphrosunê* as restraint and self-restraint of inordinate and unreflective desire for pleasure; and, on the other, *sôphrosunê* lived as a natural disposition in which one's desire for pleasure accords with one's *phronêsis*, or prudent wisdom (628c11–d4 and context, 710a2–6; *Republic* 408d–409e; Strauss 1975, 23–25; Rowe 2010, 37–46; Benardete 2000, 259). In other words, it is the difference between the drunken revellers and the symposiarch—between citizens as such and lawgivers as such (cf. 637d1–3; 716c1–d4 and context; 865a3–b2; and 933e6–934c2 with Benardete 2000, 325 [especially on Plato's use of the obsolete "*sôphronistus*" at 934a1]; Maimonides, *Guide of the Perplexed* 3.34). The pleasures of war and the pleasures of peace, of enmity and of friendship, of food and of drink, are not divided by type into good and bad or positive and negative pleasures. They are *all* included in this distinction.[20] It is *this* distinction that Kleinias remains blind to (643d5 and context, 648e6–7, 661c8–662a8; consider the reluctance of Kleinias's agreement at 663d5, 664b1–2, and 664c3),[21] but that Megillos understands (642c8–d1, 687e5–9).[22] As Lutz (2012) notes, precisely because for Kleinias "justice seems to be noble and even choice-worthy," his candid refusal to agree that the just life is the happy life "shows that even if reason were to *counsel* the citizen what is just, the passions might resist guidance" (71, emphasis added). "Might" is, to say the least, a gentle understatement here.

Kleinias is, then, left with an understanding about the place of war in the city that is substantially correct, and that satisfies him; and at the same time is blind to the more important place—or indeed existence—of *sôphrosunê* and therefore of the lawgiver. To put it another way, he would, in this respect, be capable of accepting as a citizen what he would be incapable of providing for as a legislator. The separation of the two is experientially fairly easy here for Kleinias, which is the major point of this ostensibly difficult beginning, and he emerges from this trial "superior to himself." The consequences of that self-mastery will not be as easy for Kleinias to bear.

But it is not enough to merely illustrate this difference between the image of a virtue and virtue as such, for in leaving them separate we would ultimately only be chasing *two* different images of virtue, while laboring (or playing) under the Kleinian illusion that we had isolated the true from the false. Here the purpose of precisely a symposium—a drinking party—in speech comes into focus. For, as Strauss (1975) puts it,

> Wise men would not need wine in order to become able to make reasonable changes; they are flexible because they are wise. Yet they would need wine for the opposite reason: in order to participate fully in the "symphony" of the city, a "symphony" not possible in the medium of wisdom (cf. *Crito* 49d1–5); their mind must lose something—we do not know how much—of its clarity. Wine thus creates harmony between the few wise and the many unwise, the rulers and the ruled, and such harmony is moderation in the highest sense of the word (33).[23]

"True moderation" as such cannot exist, because it would by that fact alone lack moderation. By preserving the absolute distinction between the few moderate and the many immoderate (as Rowe 2010 does), we merely replicate Kleinias's immoderate and unwise distinction between the illusion he has of himself as being of the "few," and the "mindless many" (cf. 773c8–d4).[24] It is the very ascent to "moderation in the highest sense of the word" that compels the lawgiver to redescend, or is itself that *katabasis*, or *Untergang*. Moderation as such is by its nature a practice, but what can be grasped in thought alone about this practice cannot as such enter practice. Yet this problem, which has come to light in and because of the symposium in speech, cannot be resolved in or by speech alone: as a "thought experiment" arising from and considering the practical or experiential consequences—that is, misunderstandings, deterioration and habituations thereto—of the intentions of laws, it cannot, as a "model," possibly yield its own *experiential* consequences (Benardete 2000, 27)—in the way, for example, that *discussion* of that symposium as a "model" yields experiential consequences *of discussion*. As Wieland notes, this problem is permanently mirrored in the idea of supervision or "audits" of the law's magistrates (945b–948b), and the fact of the actual auditors to whom this task is assigned, and by whom it is hoped that responsibility will be taken. And this mirror is itself mirrored in the "nocturnal council" discussed near the end of the *Laws*:

> If an upstanding human being who had political knowledge existed, he would need no laws at all (875c). Knowledge is not subordinate to law. Law is needed only because such a human being cannot be systematically educated into existence. Were he to appear at some time, he would do so as the rare exception via divine dispensation. Nevertheless, the *figure* of an upstanding human being who has political knowledge remains a model for praxis in the society of law. This is also reflected in the rules concerning the supervision or "audits" of the magistrates. Standards about the actual exercise of these audits are barely to be found. In their stead there will be detailed regulations for the procedure of selecting those who are to be entrusted with the relevant office (945b ff.). The regulations relating to the composition of the nocturnal council, and the way in which it should care for the law (961a ff.), likewise belong in this context. (Wieland 1982, 34; my translation, emphasis added)

The mirror is not one of exact replication, or replication by reversal, but of permutation—a kind of subtle carnival mirror, or a mirror peered into at various levels of sobriety. "Political knowledge" is not pie-in-the-sky knowledge, but is knowledge also of how and when to effect the best political regime that is humanly possible at a particular place and time: it is this political "aspect" of knowledge, particularly in an upstanding person (or, perhaps as only available to an upstanding person), that Wieland rightly denies as anything other than the extremely rare exception. And a "figure" (*Figur*) is not a "form" but an image.

Needless to say, the charge laid against the perfect symposium as a "model" is leveled within and by the *Laws* itself, and applies *mutatis mutandis* to the *Laws* itself. Polybius and Machiavelli were not wrong to accuse Plato— by name or otherwise—of leaving, in his work, only "imagined republics or principalities that have never been seen or known to exist in truth" (Machiavelli, *Prince*, ch. 15); nor were they wrong to refuse to admit the Platonic regime to "the contest" with the regimes of Sparta, Rome, or Carthage, for example, for this would be "like erecting a statue to compete with living, breathing men" (Polybius 6.47.7–10). That such accusations and refusals would encourage some readers to turn away from Plato, and toward Machiavelli or Polybius in their search for a *book*, or model, on which to rely, was an irony surely not lost on either Machiavelli or Polybius. Neither *The Prince* nor Polybius's "History" can escape these charges any more than Plato's works can.

The reason for this is that the essential shortcoming, in this respect, of Plato's work—including the *Laws*—is not an inadequacy of propositional content or doctrine that might be rectified by, say, an explicit *discussion* of "effectual truth" rather than truth "as such." The essential shortcoming is inherent in the problem of effectual truth *as such*: no book—not even an instruction manual—can escape being composed of propositions and gestures that can at best point beyond themselves to what Wieland (1982) calls "non-propositional knowledge" (224–35). Not even the best book—the highest combination of "written and painted thoughts"—can elaborate a set of propositions that is equivalent, or automatically leads, to the nonpropositional knowledge which it gestures at as the necessary complement to and "fulfilling" of—thus *not* replacement of—those propositions (Friedland 2013, 237–42). As the mediaeval biblical commentator Nicholas of Lyra put it (citing a maxim that was already a thousand or so years old at the time):

> *Littera gesta docet*
> *Quid credas allegoria.*
> *Moralis quid agas:*
> *Quo tendas anagogia.* [25]

> [The letter teaches the gesture
> The allegory, what you should believe.
> The moral, what you should do:
> The anagoge, where you should strive to go.]

This is, clearly, not a new manner of approaching a text.

What an author *can* do in a book with these necessary shortcomings—which, just because they are necessary in the most ironclad sense, are therefore not "shortcomings" at all, and are instead simply the natural conditions and opportunities of writing and speaking at all—is point to them (*Phaedrus* 275d7, 277d2, 278a3–5; Sayre 1988). [26] With the glaring "flaw" in the very presentation of the symposium-in-speech, Plato does just that. And by unceremoniously having the Stranger drop the subject (673e–674c), *never* to return to it, he asks his reader to consider carefully the purpose of the symposium-in-speech to begin with.

From this self-critical presentation of what a model or *paradeigma* unavoidably is, and therefore of what the *Laws* unavoidably is, Plato turns to the gymnastics of the model proper—which at its most basic level is a model *for Kleinias*: its history, the immediate conditions of its existence, its institutions, its intentions, its constitution, its beliefs, and its failures. It is with this deepening of the model that the relative seamlessness of Kleinias's "conversion" to the importance of moderation, or to two-sided courage, begins to show its seams. But as our reflections on the moderation of the lawgiver indicated, it cannot be allowed to fall apart. Indeed, the seams must remain strong, and be strengthened, by the points at which they near breaking, and we can see both this and the limits of Kleinias's character only when they threaten to rip asunder. In Book 9, during the Stranger's argument concerning penalty, leniency, and mitigating circumstances (and lack thereof) for temple robbers, traitors, fomenters of civil war, and thieves, they do just that. It behoves us to have a look at this now, by way of contrast with the initial presentation of Kleinias. For the presentation of his character is no longer so evident. It emerges, in the deepened model, in more intricate interplay with delicate and highly sensitive subjects, careful interlocutors, and hidden motives. And the fact that character emerges or shows itself only in this way is in fact a lesson of the deeper model. How do Kleinias's various motives merge with each other in a way that is seamless *for him*? What are the ramifications of the conflict between desires he hides from himself and others, and the picture of himself that he presents to himself and others? What are the ramifications of the fact that he is, in many ways, blind to that conflict?

The Athenian Stranger begins his discussion of penalties for lawbreakers in Book 9 with the crimes against the very existence of the political community. As he moves through the most serious crimes (temple robbery, treason, and inciting civil war—i.e., three variations of civil apostasy), he prescribes a single penalty: death. These crimes strike at the foundations of any political order (884a6–885a1), and regardless of personal responsibility, their perpetrators must be removed permanently (cf. 958c). To these penalties, Kleinias agrees (853a–856e). However, we will soon see that his reasons for desiring such penalties are not the same as the Athenian's.

The fourth crime that the Athenian turns to is theft by one citizen from another person (i.e., *not* from a sacred place in the way that a temple is a sacred place), and the penalty he assigns for it is clearly inspired by his maxim that "no one unjust is ever willingly unjust"[27]—we aim at what we think is "good"; we are often wrong about that; when we are correct we often err (*hamartanomen*); and regardless, we are largely driven by the chaotic conflicts that our souls are composed of (904c): that is, no one has an inherent faculty of "will" (a concept that Greek would not even be able to express for almost a millennium after Plato),[28] with which to order these conflicts, and which alone would make (and allow) him or her to be "responsible" in any sense whatsoever. The penalty for theft (and, we now see, for other crimes, even the most heinous) is not intended as a retributive *punishment*. Those who steal will repay twice the amount stolen—whether great or small (857a–b).

This suggestion meets with strenuous objection from Kleinias (857b), who is suddenly aware that the Athenian's penalties have no interest in retribution. He demands to know why crimes that vary should not have varying punishments.[29]

To this clearly petty objection, however, the Athenian replies: "Well done, Kleinias! I was almost being carried away when you hit me, waking me up and reminding me of the things I was thinking about earlier: that nothing concerning law-giving has in any way whatsoever been completely cultivated, as can be said from what's just come up" (857b9–c4). This is, in other words, a frank declaration that neither god nor man has ever fully realized the possibilities inherent in giving laws. It is not at all coincidental that the Stranger now speaks the word "philosophy" for the first time in the entire dialogue (857d2), though ever so carefully, nor is it surprising that Kleinias is confused (857e2).

How did this happen? Why did theft, simply understood, follow the three capital crimes? The robbery of temples is capital because it is such a flagrant violation of the sacred, not because it is theft simply (cf. 864d1–2, 884a6–885a1). Strauss's (1975) (somewhat disingenuous; i.e., deliberately misleading) suggestion is that the initial rubric is not capital crime, but crimes against the city, of which individual murder is not one (128). But individual murder, and even wounding, *is* considered a crime against the city in the *Laws* (878c5–d4).

What is more, the Stranger does not in fact come back to theft, after the long digression entailed by Kleinias's objection. He *says* he will return to where they left off, but he does not do so—nor does he ever mention theft simply in his "recapitulation" of where they had "left off" (864c10–d3). In fact, theft will turn out to be a civil crime, not addressed again until a brief mention at the beginning of Book 10, and not comprehensively addressed until Book 11 (and see also, in particular, 941b–942a in Book 12). The Stranger's mention of theft, in the "natural" order of the laws, seems to make no sense at all.

But it does make sense. The Stranger has introduced his radical reconsideration of justice under the very rubric that is the most threatening to it, and to all forms of justice. He has appealed to the love of money—by mentioning a threat thereto—very specifically in order to have *precisely* it be the aegis under which his philosophical principle of justice be shepherded into the city, and there remain. The most common and debilitating vice (cf. especially 831c–832b, 870a–c) is the most useful guardian for the most uncommon judicial contemplation. The Stranger entrusts his philosophical insight not to the best guardian, but to the guardian that will last—and the love of money will last as long as humans do. The Stranger turns this unfortunate aspect of humanity to good purpose.

Tying this principle to theft also makes sense for another reason. There is simply no way that the conversation between these three old men will be remembered verbatim by all of its participants, nor is everything discussed to be automatically included in the legislation to come (858b–c; cf. the lengthy discussion of the manifold and unavoidable difficulties which force legislation to compromise—often substantially—with existing circumstances, at 704a–712a and 745e–746d; also 736b5–6 with 636a4–5). In order to ensure that this principle not only finds favor particularly with Kleinias but will also be remembered by him as fundamental, it must be presented in a way that is specifically memorable to him. As Kleinias has let slip earlier (661d–662a, and especially 832a–b), his acknowledgment that "love of money" is base and harmful (705a–b) does not mean that he does not share in that love himself (cf. his response at 922d4–9 with 729a2–b2; also the Stranger's subtle castigation at 632c7–d1 with Kleinias's initial praise of victory in war and his reticence to change his mind, 626b1–4 and 628e2–5). He seems to know that he *should* not, but he nevertheless, like so many, does[30]—he is, in the Stranger's terms, in "the greatest ignorance" about this desire (688e–689a, 691a, 696c; cf. 654c–d, 655e–656d). And as with most law-abiding "lovers of gain" (*philokerdeis*), the punishment of theft is important for him because he imagines his own wealth being stolen; in his memory, the principle that "no one is willingly unjust" will be tied to *increasing* the revenge on thieves, not the *mitigation* of penalties for homicide that the Stranger uses it for. One can be reasonably sure that this so important conversation will number among the "notes" that Kleinias is taking (*Epinomis* 980d3–4), however much his understanding thereof is limited.

There are, however, consequences to this "greatest ignorance" that are not remotely met by the mere introduction of a principle, nor remediable in any significant sense at all. Indeed it may be wondered whether Plato does not mean by "greatest" ignorance, in this sense, simply most intractable: most distant from, and hostile to, wisdom, not by degree—however great—but by its nature as an abyss. The Stranger, with Megillos's assistance, will be compelled to at least partially reveal to Kleinias both the fact and the nature of that abyss, an undertaking which they approach with the greatest care, and as a choice between Scylla and Charybdis. How they do so, and why, will be illustrated in chapter 3.

NOTES

1. Likewise the distinction between what "*is* said" (i.e., in general by many or most people) and what "*I* say" (cf. 720a6–8 and b5–6, where this distinction is made explicit by the Stranger). The distinction, or its possibility, can appear in other ways of speaking as well. For example, at the outset of the *Hippias Major*, Socrates's speech makes a threefold distinction between what is "public" (*ta dêmosia*), what is "common" (*ta koina*—i.e., "shared"), and what is "private" (*ta idia*), whereas Hippias makes only the distinction between what is "common" and what is "private" (*Hippias Major* 281b6, c1, d1–2, 282b3–4, b6, c2–4). This becomes a major theme within the dialogue, dramatized in many permutations (cf., for example, 300b–304e, especially 300e2–6 and 303a4–11), and the dialogue as a whole is itself a self-reflexive dramatization thereof.

2. Benardete (2000, 7–8) seems to suggest that Kleinias understands the implications of the telling difference between "*everyone* against all cities" and "*all cities* against all cities." But if, for Kleinias, everyone is first and foremost a *citizen* of a city, then the first statement merely indicates that he imagines everyone as a *soldier* for his city, in endless war against all other cities. He speaks something of profound import, but without realizing it—"he multiplieth words without knowledge" (Job 35:16). *Plato* certainly understands the implications of what he writes here, but that does not mean that his invented character does (cf. *Charmides* 162b8–11). The difference is essential.

3. Let us keep in mind, though, that Plato has created the character Kleinias as a human being, not a caricature. *We* may be clarifying here what is not necessarily clear *to him*—he may well not have a clear or consistent idea of what *he* means by "the mindless many," though he surely has at least a nebulous reckoning thereof. For example, he seems to feel that youths in general are foolish (635e1–3), but he might well have a vague and perhaps not entirely con- scious feeling that Cretan youths are not among the "mindless many" in the way that, for example, Athenian youths—or Athenians in general—are. This feeling might also vary accord- ing to the topic he is considering: piety versus geometry, for example. It may also not be clear to the *other* characters in the *Laws* what Kleinias means, at this early point, by "the many"—in fact, this probably isn't clear at all to Megillos and the Stranger here. Megillos, for example, might be chiding rather than apparently agreeing with Kleinias on the latter's elitism when he asks, "How would *any* Lacedaimonian answer otherwise?"

4. Robert Walser ([1902] 2015) offers a delightful and discerning portrait, with respect to art and artists: "The masses are indiscriminating, and this is only a broader reflection of the lack of discernment among the educated. With both, one finds soundness of judgment quite bitterly absent in matters of art, above all, and this is hardly surprising when you consider how unschooled our artists are. Flighty as the viewers of art may be, the artists are generally even worse. What's it to me? It's not my duty to establish order here; probably there'll never be any. Among both connoisseurs of art and the artists themselves, one finds splendid exceptions: for the most part quiet, unostentatious figures who are not much spoken of and make it clear that they have no intention of becoming influential. They know quite well how much new error, how little progress derive from influence" (15).

5. It would therefore seem that Homer, Thucydides, and Xenophon each recognize a need to directly address the possibility of the "rule of many," but are reticent to even mention it any more than is absolutely necessary. One may surmise that they do not want to suggest this possibility to anyone to whom it has not occurred already.

6. This is the Stranger's description of Kleinias's *logos*, which Kleinias accepts. Note the subtle reproof, therefore, of the latter by the former. "*Logos*—or speech—of the many" is a literal translation of a phrase that colloquially means, ironically enough, a colloquialism, or commonplace (cf. Nietzsche, *Beyond Good and Evil* 37).

7. There is a difference, indeed a great difference, between perplexity and confusion, though this difference is not always easy to discern. Maimonides, for example, certainly did not write a Guide of the *Confused*.

8. Cf. 633a4–5 with 688a2–c1.

9. 635e, 639e–640a (cf. what Megillos says at 637b), 644b, 653c, 661e–662a, 664b and d–e, 672c, 674c, 678b, 679d, 689c, among *many* others—these examples are from the first three Books alone. Consider also *Epinomis* 974c and 979e—even if this dialogue is spuriously attributed to Plato (and I do not think it is), it is still instructive that its author notices and highlights this aspect of Kleinias's personality.

Meyer (2015), in her translation and commentary of *Laws* Books 1 and 2 for Oxford's prestigious Clarendon series, suggests that *both* Kleinias and Megillos "typically repl[y] on behalf of both [of them]" (78). I certainly agree with her regarding Kleinias, but the only two instances she cites as examples of Megillos doing so (626c3 and 636e5) actually demonstrate the opposite, for *him*. Meyer's first example, 626c3, is clearly inapposite (at a minimum—see chapter 1), as it is Megillos's response to a pointed question from Kleinias asking whether Megillos agrees with him on a specific point. How can Megillos possibly be answering for both himself and Kleinias such a case? Her second example, however, is not only inapposite, but explicitly refutes her contention. At 636e5, Megillos does indeed say something like, "*we* are at a loss to say anything, etc." (to cite Meyer's own fairly loose translation [32]; my emphasis). But this is obviously a description of what he has just *observed* of Kleinias's own reticence to agree completely with the Stranger, and Kleinias's *expressed* struggle for words in this respect (630d8, 634c3–4, 635e1–3), given that Megillos *immediately* clarifies—in the *very next words of the same sentence* (note especially the *mên . . . de . . . de* construction)—that he is quite specifically *not* speaking for Kleinias here. Meyer (2015) translates Megillos's single sentence as three sentences (32); then, as support for her assertion, she cites the Greek text that, in her own translation, is the basis for only about half of only the first of those three sentences. Who has ever heard of such a thing? The *single* sentence that Megillos actually says here is this: "The things said, Stranger, are in some ways fine; and while we are certainly (*ou mên . . . ge*) struggling to find the words (literally: nothing but speechlessness is seizing us [*all' aphasia . . . hêmas lambanei*]) needed to respond to them, nevertheless (*de*), to *me* at least (*emoige*) the order to flee pleasures, [given] by the lawgiver for Lacedaimon, seems correct, though (*de*) concerning the laws of Knossos, *this man* (*hode*), should he wish, will come to their aid" (636e4–8). It is simply absurd to say, as Meyer says, that this is an instance of Megillos speaking on Kleinias's behalf: the passage in question is an exceptionally clear demonstration of precisely the opposite. Megillos explicitly *refuses* to speak for Kleinias here. 776c, unmentioned by Meyer, on the other hand, would at first glance offer support to her assertion. Megillos speaks there, however, of what "we" *learn* (*manthanomen*), and not, as the existing English translations suggest, what "we" *understand*. "We" as in we *Spartans*, not "we" as in Megillos and Kleinias. Of course, Megillos's locution obviously allows Kleinias to feel that he, and Cretans in general, are being spoken for as well, and what Megillos says certainly does apply to Cretans in general as well. This is not unintentional. One may mention in respect to this passage that *oiketês* (domestic servant) is very close to *oiketis* (mistress of a house) in speech. And in deed. The plural of *oiketês* (used frequently by the Stranger here) is *oiketai*, which is grammatically feminine, and refers as much to the women and children of a household as it does to the domestic servants of a household. This is not unintentional. The elision, and distinction, between *oiketai* and *douloi* (slaves) in this passage is crucial, and preserves a distinction in Cretan law (known to us through the extant Gortyn Code—though of course this is not a Knossian code) between a *Foikeus* (domestic servant) and a *dolos* (slave).

10. Consider in this respect Kleinias's statement to the Stranger in Book 2: "Best of men, you're having a conversation with Cretan*s* (*Krêsin*) and Lacedaimonian*s* (*Lakedaimoniois*)" (673b5). Kleinias elides himself and Megillos very easily with the multitude of Cretans and Spartans in general, perhaps without even being aware of it.

11. Cf. also 837e.

12. One of the very few times that Kleinias stresses that he is speaking only for himself actually supports this claim: In Book 10 (891a) he stresses that a lengthy argument is, in the current situation (arguing against atheism) very much to be welcomed if it works, though he cannot speak for Megillos in this regard. Now he seems to have in mind a consideration for his Spartan comrade in not asserting the latter's agreement, given the proverbially laconic style of speech among the Spartans. But he has forgotten that Megillos had earlier *explicitly* distanced himself from this typically Spartan style, in favor of *better* arguments—much as Kleinias is now doing (721e–722a, 683b–c). Kleinias's perception of Megillos—which is undisturbed by questioning—is a caricature of a Spartan that he has in his mind. As we have seen, Megillos is very far indeed from being a caricature of a Spartan, and it is indicative of something discreet in his own character that he is nevertheless willing—perhaps even eager—to let Kleinias, *though not the Stranger*, continue to see him as one.

13. They probably also include, as Pangle (1988, 382) suggests, "selfish security and glory," though it would be a stretch to limit Kleinias's "good things" to these. If one did, one would have to limit his conception of war to those that take place between adversaries that already "possess" such security and glory, so that it might be said that these possessions had passed from one to the other. Kleinias's conception of war, however, is much more global than this would allow (626d7–9). This is not to say that Kleinias is not considering the glory and (potential) security that attend victory in war here—he almost certainly is—only that the way in which he speaks includes acquiring the "good things" of the vanquished no matter what glory or security they formerly had.

14. I agree with England (1921, vol. 2, 332–33), Saunders (1972, 70–71), Pangle (1988, 532n6), and Burnet (*ad loc.*) that the disputed lines in 832a–b belong to Kleinias. There is no reason to disregard the fact that *all* of the manuscripts attribute the key interjections at 832a11–b3 and b5–6 to him, despite the objections of Wilamowitz, Apelt, Hermann, and Burges. While manuscript traditions are of course fraught with problems (the earliest MS of the *Laws*—Paris A—dates to almost two millennia after Plato wrote), there is not one extant manuscript that attributes any of these lines to Megillos (as the objectors insist they ought to be), and it makes perfect dramatic sense for Kleinias to reveal just how personally he has taken the Stranger's castigation of the love of money here. Wilamowitz usefully summarizes (and supports, in his authoritative way) the objections, all of which rest on a supposed dramatic inconsistency (Wilamowitz-Möllendorff 1920, 403–4). I see no compelling reason whatsoever to agree. Kleinias is irritated by the Stranger's disgust because he is personally offended by it, and therefore angrily cuts the Stranger short. In his shame, he betrays his true nature and disposition. Cf. 650b6–9, and see chapter 5 for a detailed rebuttal.

15. This key aspect of the dialogues is most succinctly and thematically treated in the *Lovers*, or *Rivals* (in the discussion as a whole, and in the character of the self-styled "philosophical" lover whom Socrates engages in that discussion).

16. Wealth is the fourth "good thing" mentioned of eight in Tyrtaeus's poem. See Tyrtaeus, poem IX, in *Poetae lyrici Graeci*, ed. Bergk, Leipzig, 1854; vol. III: 310–12.

17. The Stranger's first attempts are designed to *appeal* to Kleinias much more than to try to directly or immediately change his mind (cf. Xenophon, *Memorabilia* 4.6.15 on the necessity to first create "listeners who agree" [*akouontas homologountas*]). Thus after his "paraphrase" of Tyrtaeus noted above, he tells Kleinias that Tyrtaeus "speaks of almost all [the good things]" in his poem (629b2). It is of obvious importance that intelligence, prudence, moderation, and justice are certainly not mentioned by Tyrtaeus when he "speaks of almost all the good things." Tyrtaeus speaks of seven "good things" in comparison with an eighth, courage in war, in the following order: size and strength, speed, beauty, wealth, kingship, mellifluous (*meilichogêrun*) speech, and fame (cf. 631c–d with Tyrtaeus's poem in Bergk, ed. 310–311).

18. Kleinias gives several other indications, throughout the *Laws*, that his love of wealth is a large and permanent part of who he is. Compare, for example, Kleinias's response at 922d4–9 with 729a2–b2; and his initial response to the Stranger's description of a luxurious upbringing, 694b8.

19. Moderation as Kleinias imagines it, that is (648e6–7; cf. 710a3–b3).

20. Follon (2003, 190) is not wrong to say that "toute la législation des *Lois* est orientée vers cette fin suprême: *l'amitié et la paix entre les citoyens*" (emphasis in original). But this does not even pretend to address the "moderation" of particular friendship that the law*giver* must live (consider 681a–d).

21. Meyer sees Kleinias's "grudging response" at 663d5, but interprets 664b1–2 as a demonstration of his "lack of facility in argument," and 664c3 as a "surprising concession," that indicates either that Kleinias interprets the Stranger's claim "in the light of his own, Dorian, conception of excellence" (which is also Taki's argument), or that "perhaps the argument at 663c–d has been more convincing than his response at 663d5 would appear to indicate" (Meyer 2015, 275, 278, 280). Meyer does not seem to even consider that Kleinias's agreement in all three instances is continually reluctant, even though she highlights the word used by the Dorian in the last instance, *sunchôrêteon*—"It must be conceded . . . " Instead, she assumes from the outset that Kleinias is devoted to the logic of the Stranger's argument alone, and must eventually be fully persuaded by it, whether through understanding or misunderstanding thereof. Meyer therefore ignores the very theme from which the argument began, and toward which it is building: "the greatest ignorance," in which one's reasoning and one's desires are at odds (653a–c, 689a–c).

22. Taki (2003) cites 687e5–9 in order to suggest that "the Dorians . . . might perhaps have come to understand the systematic difference" that Taki insists is there (53). Taki himself has missed the real difference illustrated by the symposium in speech, and therefore misunderstands what Megillos—*not* "the Dorians"—shows he understands in Book 3.

23. Cf. 627e3–628a3 (n.b. *triton de pou dikastên pros aretên* at e3–4 [Des Places's translation, *ad loc.*, obscures the "third" place of this judge completely]) with 631c5–8 (n.b. *triton an*

eiê dikaiosunê at c8). The passage in the *Crito* that Strauss asks his reader to compare with his statement (a statement, we should note, that is separated by some curious punctuation from what follows in the sentence, and therefore both is and is not joined to it) is in the context of Socrates's insistence, to Crito, that "one must not return injustice for injustice, nor do evil to anyone, no matter what one has suffered" (49c8–10). Socrates then cautions Crito: "Crito, in agreeing to this, do not agree to something against your own opinion: I know that there are only some few who believe this or will believe it. For those who believe this, and those who do not, there is no deliberation in common (*koinê boulê*), but instead they must necessarily despise each other when they perceive the deliberated purposes (*bouleumata*) of each other" (49d1–5). Strauss's double use of "symphony," in quotes, points to the Greek word *symphônia*, or "consonance."

24. Cf. Aristotle, *De meteorologia* 339a11–b2, especially a37–b2; *De Caelo* 305a31–3; Peter of Auvergne, *Quaestiones supra librum De caelo* 2, qu. 38.52–73. Consider Mariana's statement to Isabella in *Measure for Measure* V, i. 436–9: "I'll speak all: / They say, best men are moulded out of faults; / And, for the most, become much more the better/ For being a little bad."

25. *Postilla super totam Bibliam*, First Prologue, folio 3. I thank Horst Hutter for introducing me to this beautiful mediaeval synopsis of reading. Cf. Aristotle, *Physics* 193b13–18.

26. In case it does not go without saying, I obviously include in this what I am writing here, and anywhere.

27. The idea that no one is willingly *un*just occurs so many times throughout the Platonic dialogues that it is easy to miss the question in what we might call the flip side of this *logos*: is anyone, with the *possible* exception of Socrates himself, ever willingly *just*? The closest Socrates ever comes to addressing this question explicitly is in his final words to the jurors at his trial (*Apology of Socrates* 41c8–42a5), and the suggestion there is that the answer may well be No (see especially 41d3–8). At the least, in Socrates's opinion, it is No concerning *all* of the jurors: by their condemnation, those who voted for the death penalty *un*willingly and *un*intentionally granted Socrates what he is confident is "better" (*beltion*) for him—to die and be free of *pragmata* (things, matters, affairs); by implication, the intention of those who did *not* condemn him was to grant what *they* believed to be better (more just?), but despite their "good" intentions, they did not know *how* to be just concerning Socrates. All of this is of course complicated by the final three sentences that Socrates speaks there. In the first two (41e1–42a2), he instructs those who condemned him (and curiously enough, *not* those who would have acquitted him) how they might actually be just to both himself and his sons: act toward his sons in the same way that they have just finished condemning Socrates for acting toward themselves. And in the last sentence, and in at least *seeming* contradiction (though it is important that it is not in fact a contradiction) to what he has just said about it being "clear" to him (*moi dêlon*) that it is "better" (*beltion*) that he die now, he tells them that no one can know which of them "goes to a better thing [*ameinon pragma*]"—he being put to death, or they living—"except/unless the god [does]." It is not humanly knowable whether death or life is better for any of us, and all of our conceptions of justice necessarily occur within this extreme and unavoidable limitation of our knowledge (cf. *Laches* 195c7–196a3). In fact, it is not humanly knowable if there even *is* death (note that Socrates specifically does not say that he goes to "death," which would be *thanatos*, but to "dying" or "being put to death" [*apothanoumenôn*]. Everything beyond, and including, that moment is radically unknowable). It is even to be doubted whether "the god" can know this—there is a deliberate ambiguity in Socrates's last statement here. Scholars are divided as to whether he says "*plên ê*" or "*plên ei tôi theôi*," but it does not really matter how it is *written*—the dialogues were written to be *listened* to, and both sound identical to the ear. The first implies that the god *does* know; the second that the god *might*.

28. An insightful and persuasive argument is made for this by Albrecht Dihle (1982), in his *The Theory of the Will in Classical Antiquity*. Useful (and persuasive) correctives are supplied by Schlabach 1994; and Kahn 1988, 234–59—it should be noted that both corrective efforts suggest *later* dates than Dihle (who focuses on Augustine's project) for the modern (especially Christian) conception of "will."

29. At 856b–c, the Stranger proclaims the sentence of death for tyrants, fomenters of civil war, and magistrates and citizens who do not oppose the former, in Magnesia. Immediately

afterward, he absolves all children of such criminals of both blame and retribution, except where three consecutive generations of fathers have been condemned to death. The children of such are to be repatriated to the city of origin of their forefathers, and their household in Magnesia taken by a lucky citizen's lucky child, chosen through a system of nomination, lot, and Delphic selection (856d–e). After the Stranger expounds the whole of this, Kleinias says: "Beautifully [said, or done]" (*kalôs*—856e4). Benardete (2000, 263) interprets Kleinias's response as perhaps a "gentle echo" of "Leontius's 'Oh beautiful sight!'" in the *Republic* (439e6–440a3). I thank James Stoner for pointing out to me that the refusal of attainder and corruption of blood could, on the other hand, be what Kleinias is thinking of when he says "Beautifully." I would suggest that Kleinias is responding to both the punishment *and* the forbearance, and that the combination of retribution and magnanimity is what is "beautifully done" here, for him.

30. To address both Kleinias's limited memory in particular, and also his position as a "lover of money," consider the "worthy titles to rule" (discussed in Book 3 at 690a–c), which he completely forgets in Book 4 ("What titles?"—714e2). He seems to forget they were even mentioned—is this perhaps because the Stranger does not list *wealth* as a worthy title to rule? It should be noted that in Book 11, concerning the civil law based fundamentally around private money and property, the Stranger only once addresses Megillos (and that one time with Kleinias, on the subject of proper judgment concerning all crimes—934c). By contrast, he addresses Kleinias six times by name in Book 11 (918c; 922b, c, and e; 923c; and 926a).

Chapter Three

What Is Political Philosophy?

Every phenomenon, whether it arises [directly] from what is essential, or from an action [that is not], must inevitably possess a nature peculiar to both its essence and the accidental conditions that attach themselves to it.

—Ibn Khaldun, *Book of Lessons*, Introduction

Stranger: So then, with a test and no great danger, or the opposite way?

Kleinias: Everyone would . . . agree to the test.

[. . .]

Stranger: This gymnastic then, my friend, would be wonderfully easy compared to the ones we now have, whether for one person, or a few, or as many as someone might ever want [to test].

—*Laws* 648b4–d1

Armed with an examination of the very different characters of Megillos and Kleinias, the reader of the *Laws* is likely to approach the strange account of political origins in Book 3 with more than usual caution, and rightly so. For it no longer seems so easily evident that Megillos "resembles, much more than does Kleinias, a typical citizen of the future regime that is to be founded," and is thus "a pedestrian check on both the philosopher and the founder who is open to philosophy," as Pangle (1988) suggests (430–31). Nor is it tenable to believe, with Benardete (2000), that Megillos "believes that one could not look elsewhere than at laws and regimes that preserve or destroy beautiful and great things" (107; citing 686b8–c3).[1] What is more, the internal dramatic consistency of the Stranger's ultimate focus on Sparta, rather than Crete, in his mythological narrative, demands our renewed attention, for we have seen that in the foregoing discussion (in Books 1 and 2) Megillos has allowed the Stranger to perceive his questioning and criticism of the original intentions and current practices of the Spartan regime at a fundamental level, even as he maintains his image as a staunch and unquestioning Spartan patriot, on Kleinias's terms, for Kleinias. Strauss's (1975) assertion that "Megillos . . . is none too pleased at the implied criticism of Dorian institutions" in Book 3 (43) may accurately reflect Megillos's deliberate positioning of himself with a view to what he wants Kleinias to perceive about him, but it misses the mark with respect to what Megillos actually questions and criticizes on his own and with the Stranger (Strauss does not cite specific passages here, but he is referring, I believe, to 685a1, a5, 686d5, and e1–2).[2]

The One-Eyed Man is King

Book 3 more or less begins with an account of what one might be tempted to call, anachronistically, "the state of nature." The Stranger imagines for his interlocutors a postpolitical world, in which mountain-living survivors of a cataclysmic flood (and their descendants for countless generations) live more simply, courageously, moderately, and justly than contemporary human beings, in peaceful family-communities governed by the eldest man (or woman?) of the multigenerational family. It comes as something of a surprise when, after completing a rough sketch of these communities, he suggests that it was of just such communities that Homer spoke when he describes the households of the Cyclopes, in the *Odyssey*.

To begin with, it is crucial that the Stranger is quite explicit that his account of postpolitical human life is suppositional, with its particular focus on a diluvial cataclysm a seemingly arbitrary choice among other possibilities that include "plagues and many other things" (677a5; cf. "one out of many" at a8, and "disasters" at 680d8; Cicero, *De officiis* 2.16). It is Kleinias who ignores this—and who is in fact incapable of not ignoring it. It is Kleinias who answers (for himself, and Megillos, and in fact "everyone") that "without a doubt such a thing is entirely trustworthy for everyone" (677a7), whereas the Stranger had asked only whether he and Megillos "believe there is *some* (*tina*) truth to the ancient accounts" of disasters (677a1–2; cf. 681a5 with b8). Kleinias already believes these accounts about antiquity completely, which as we will shortly see, matters a great deal. His response is comprised of eight words in Greek. Three of those eight words are *pan* and its derivatives—*panu* ("completely"), *pan* (here: "entirely"), and *panti* ("for everyone"); and two more are particles added to *panu* to strengthen its force—*panu men oun* ("without a doubt," "certainly"). In other words, five of his eight words serve to emphasize how utterly he believes in the other three: *pithanon to toiouton*—"such a thing is trustworthy." There is an extraordinary emphasis here on how wholly credible these ancient accounts are to Kleinias and, he believes, to everyone (nor is this an isolated incident of such trust, for Kleinias—see, for example, 782d2–3, and consider 840b3–5).

What is more, it is Kleinias who eagerly leaps to connect the Stranger's general hypothesis about an ancient past to the myths about his own time that he believes (of Daedalus, Orpheus, etc.), myths which he tellingly takes as true accounts as well. It is Kleinias who thereby abandons the hypothetical character of the Stranger's discourse (677d1–6).[3] The hypothetical account persuades and captivates his imagination, and establishes itself in him as a true account, because it provides a plausible connection between beliefs that he already holds to be true; that is, a temporal sequence between the destructions of antiquity, and the inventions of the arts. We should recall that a proclivity toward easily accepting an account—and an authority—that provides a connection or justification for his already entrenched beliefs was one of the first things that Kleinias revealed about himself in the *Laws*, just as it was also one of the first things the Stranger tested in him—and in testing him on this, at the same time tested his familiarity with Homer. For when at the outset of Book 1, the Stranger asked Kleinias if he says, "with Homer," that Minos had received oracles regarding lawgiving from his father (Zeus) "every ninth year," Kleinias replied, "So it is said by us" (624a7–b3). As we noted in chapter 1, Homer (or rather, his Odysseus) in fact says nothing at all about lawgiving oracles, to say nothing of other problems presented by the Stranger's version (*Od.* 19.178–9; cf. *Il* 13.450). But the Stranger's version authoritatively explains the connection between the divine providence of the Cretan laws, and the mortal Minos's role as the Cretan lawgiver, so Kleinias is eager to accept it not only as true (both in fact and in Homer), but indeed as an accurate gloss of what he and other Cretans *already* say.[4]

I am, up to this point, in general agreement with Sallis (2013) that the Stranger therefore takes his cue from Kleinias's list of inventors, in Book 3; but *pace* Sallis, he does so in order to illustrate what the lack of specific arts—what Sallis calls "useful *technai*"—implies for the account of the time between the cataclysmic flood and the relatively contemporary invention of the arts. Kleinias had identified six men who were, for him, inventors or discoverers of the arts: Daedalus, Orpheus, Palamedes, Marsyas, Olympos, and Amphion (677d). According to Kleinias, these men "brought these arts to sight" (Ast, England: these arts were revealed *to* these men; England 1921, *ad loc.*), where before they had "not come to be" (677d2–3): these men were not merely epitomes of artistic perfection, but were also the *first* human beings to discover the art at all. Briefly:

Daedalus was not only the inventor *per se*, but even in Homer is associated most frequently with finely wrought armor (the armor and shield of Achilles, for example, are called *daidala*) (*Il.* 18.612, 19.13 and 19, etc.).

Orpheus was a great musician (of the lyre), but also closely connected with the founding of Dionysian worship, as well as with Apollo. To say nothing of Nietzsche's interpretation of tragedy (which is a good deal subtler and more insightful, on Platonic terms, than a casual reading of Nietzsche—and Plato—suggests), Dionysus and Apollo as a pair have been emphasized as the patrons and leaders of education throughout the previous two Books of the *Laws*.

Palamedes was said to have invented the alphabet and therefore written language. He rivaled polytropic Odysseus in scheming and trickery, and was undone by his own invention—the written word—when Odysseus avenged himself by planting false evidence of Palamedes's treachery in his tent, in the form of a letter (Hyginus, *Fabulae* 105; cf. *Apology of Socrates* 41b).

Marsyas and Olympos were also musicians (of the aulos), and lovers. Marsyas challenged Apollo to a contest of wisdom or musical skill (*peri sophias*), according to Xenophon, and was flayed alive by him when he lost (*Anabasis* 1.2.8; cited in Strauss [1975, 39]). About Olympos, little aside from his connection to Marsyas is known. As Benardete (2002) notes, "the flute nomes of Marsyas and Olympus . . . according to both Socrates and Alcibiades, reveal those who are in need of gods" (83n17; citing *Minos* 318b4–c1 and *Symposium* 215c2–6).

Amphion, another great musician (of the lyre), was closely associated with the invention of city walls, having moved stones for the walls of Thebes with his music (for the above references, see also Pangle 521n2, and references given there).

Taken together, then, it is remarkable just how much music itself figures into Kleinias's "pantheon" of inventors, and if one sets aside the importance of music for—and as—law (see Valiquette 2013), one can see how Sallis (2013) might have arrived at his conclusion that "the inventiveness of the seven figures, the revelations that they bring to humanity, has little to do with the useful *technai* by which the needs of the city are served" (80). But while it is ultimately Sallis's point, and rightfully so, that music is of great importance indeed for the city (83–85; cf. Cicero, *De legibus* 2.38–39), he is mistaken to pass over the "useful *technai*" that are in fact evoked by Kleinias here, and are important *to him*. For the following "arts" are thus indicated by Kleinias to be unknown before "yesterday or the day before, so to speak" (677d): armor and the accoutrements of war, mystery religions (specifically of Apollo and Dionysus), education, written language, deceit, wisdom, hubris, and city walls. In joining the "music" of Marsyas and Olympos, Kleinias seems to suggest that the "art" of homosexuality is also due to modern "progress" (see my chapter 5).

Kleinias's list of artists is also marked by his rejection of another artist—and a Cretan artist at that—from this particular list (Sallis [2013, 80] does not note, and seems to see no consequence of, this rejection). After Kleinias lists the inventors (and by extension, inventions) that he fully believes in, and believes in as relatively new, the Stranger asks him why he has left out his "friend" who is much closer in time and place to Kleinias (642d–643a). Kleinias responds: "*Surely* you're not (*môn*) talking about Epimenides!" (677d9). *Môn* ("*surely* you're not . . .") is a strong word—the sense is: I'm very serious. Why are you making a joke about this?[5]

The *inventions* to which Kleinias had alluded with his list of inventors are all quite real (armor, alphabet, etc.), though the *inventors* he believes were real almost surely are not. But while Kleinias clearly believes that Epimenides was a real person (and unlike the other six, he may have been), to accept the *legend* of Epimenides—who supposedly invented a way to live without eating at all (England 1921, *ad loc.*; citing Plutarch, *Banquet of the Seven Sages* 157d–158c)—would be to accept something that is patently unreal, or essentially magic, regardless if the person associated with it was real or not. Kleinias, as we have seen in chapters 1 and 2, all too easily elides his own opinion with what "the Cretans" believe. But he does not follow them so far as to believe in magic, and the Stranger seizes the opportunity to demonstrate to Kleinias that Kleinias's own opinion and the opinion of (at least some) other Cretans are not identical in this respect. Such piecemeal efforts are at the very heart of the *Laws*, and this one is successful (cf. Kleinias's emphatic response at 679d1, in which he answers for both himself and Megillos, with no mention of "we Cretans").

What the Stranger proceeds to do is develop an image for Kleinias of the consequences of *Kleinias's* assumptions. None of the arts in Kleinias's list is therefore permitted to exist in the early-postflood human world, though the "art" of Epimenides, by which there would no hunger, is (in a nonmagical permutation). The Stranger banishes from that world only what Kleinias is sure did *not* exist prior to the invention of the arts he believes in, and allows or depends upon every other urgent human necessity being fulfilled. Human beings at that time were "well provided (*êuporoun*) with clothing, bedding, dwellings, and implements for use with fire and without fire" (679a4–6). About the existence and provenance of fire itself for human beings, the Stranger says not a word. This is to say nothing of his lack of mention of the theft of fire by Prometheus (cf. Strauss 1975, 40), and Prometheus's claim that Zeus wished to destroy the human race in order to seed a new one.[6] Molding (pottery) and weaving (the first requires fire, the second does not), the Stranger says, are essentially innate capacities of human beings, having been given to human beings by "[a] god" (679a6–b3). There is clear indication that this gift was given long before this particular "cycle," for it is said to be a gift that provides (*porizein*) for human beings "whenever" they are in such difficulty (*aporia*) (b1–2).

The Stranger's account is full of holes, and he in fact subtly highlights them. It is implausible, except to someone who is filling those holes him or herself, or who does not notice them. Kleinias is just such a person.

What the Stranger proceeds to do, then, is attempt to get Kleinias to reflect on these conditions from within them. He understands how human beings within such conditions would understand *themselves*, and gives an image of that understanding to Kleinias. Aware of the latter's unfamiliarity with poetry in general, he uses a model that, to someone like Megillos (and Plato's reader) who is familiar with poetry, will seem as grotesque as it seems innocent to Kleinias: the Cyclopes. He takes one of the "hardest cases" as his test case.

Even the most cursory exposure to Homer will mean that the Stranger's listener will picture a savage and inhospitable monster that eats human flesh (and who is therefore, if imagined as human—as he is in the Stranger's account—a cannibal) and, as the Stranger's discourse progresses, lives in incestuous isolation from others of its kind (on which more in chapter 6). But lacking that exposure, the Cyclopes as a model for Kleinias's assumptions about human nature can be seen from within. And from within, the Cyclopes are exactly as the Stranger describes them: innocent, foreclosed to awareness of consequences, good, just, courageous, moderate, unwarlike (though not without aggression), and without deceit or anticipation of deceit (679b–c). Unaware that they lack wisdom, they cannot possibly judge what they hold to be just or true from a different perspective than their lived belief in them. They cannot judge the just and the true by another standard because their belief in them *is* their standard (not unlike Kleinias himself). The "irony" of using the Cyclopes as a model to illustrate this is in one respect that there is no irony to it at all. They *are* innocent. The Stranger reveals that his model is the Cyclopes only after describing their innocence (680b). It is here that the Stranger, with Megillos's tacit assistance, begins to lay the imaginative groundwork for the true principle that "no one is willingly unjust."

The other irony is that what is missing entirely in the communities of the Cyclopes is missing almost entirely in every city and almost every individual. That we number among such individuals is illustrated to us by our very impulse to revulsion and condemnation when we hear the word "Cyclops," rather than understanding immediately that they—and every other "evil" person or thing—are innocent, and that no one is willingly unjust. That Kleinias's own lack of reflection about things he believes strongly in is a mirror of the one-eyed (or half-blind), cave-dwelling "Cyclopes" is illustrated at the end of the discussion about the Cyclopes. It will be helpful to consider that passage, keeping in mind Dunshirn's (2010) insightful hypothesis on "autoreferentiality" as a constant in Plato's dialogues (59; see fuller discussion in chapter 6).

Just before turning to Megillos, and pointedly asking him to take over as interlocutor (682e4–6), the Stranger drives this point home by undermining the very foundation of his "argument" about origins, while leaving Kleinias blissfully, and innocently, unaware. We recall how emphatically and immediately Kleinias declared his (and "everyone's") belief in the "entire" truth of the ancient accounts of cataclysms. Yet just before the Stranger ends their discussion of the consequences of those accounts, he stresses the likelihood that the settling of cities close to rivers, which must have happened a "vast amount of time" after the flood, indicates that "a terrible forgetting of the disaster" had come upon the descendants of the flood survivors by that time (682b9–c1; cf. Strauss [1975, 41–42]). To this, Kleinias emphatically agrees (682c4–5). What, then, is the provenance of the "ancient accounts" that he so completely believes in (and believes that everyone completely believes in), according to him? More important than answering this now- (and perhaps then-) unanswerable question is noting that Kleinias himself does not ask it, or even seem to know there is such a question. The contradiction between his initial assumptions and the consequences that he agrees follow from those assumptions is not evident to him.

Cusher (2011) suggests that "the texts in which these *logoi* are to be found are those of the poets: evidence will be cited presently, for instance, from the poems of both Hesiod and Homer" (281). But, to say nothing of the fact that written "texts" are not specified as the sources of these accounts (and that not only would such texts, if they existed, be open to the same question that Kleinias's belief is open to; but one would have to wonder how a man like Kleinias, who makes it clear that he—and Cretans in general—has almost no exposure to poetry, would have been so convinced by them), no such evidence for this is in fact cited presently, either by the Stranger in the *Laws* or by Cusher in his article. Nor is such evidence to be found in either Homer or Hesiod, nor in fact in any extant ancient Greek source before Plato himself. The extant stories of floods that *dramatically* predate Plato, such as those of Ogyges and Deucalion, were *written* centuries after Plato's time, by authors such as Ovid and Pausanius, who had access to both Plato's work and the Bible. Cusher has missed the deliberate affinities that Plato illustrates between how Kleinias, on the one hand, and the "primitive" human beings of the myth (that Kleinias believes in), on the other, believe things to be "most true," *just because they have heard it said.*

Cusher also recognizes (correctly) that Kleinias is a man who admires the tyrannical life as the best human life. Based on this, he suggests that the Cyclopean myth somehow tempers that admiration (and desire) by convincing him that the human condition is other than simply "perpetual conflict" (Cusher 2011, 292–93). Yet on what basis would we expect that myth to moderate the tyrannical impulse in Kleinias, or in anyone in whom it exists? It seems in fact that precisely the opposite is the case: the myth appeals to Kleinias because it *justifies*, in his imagination, tyrannical power as the correct desideratum according to nature. That myth, after all, proclaims the absolute rule of one man over the rest of the community (called the "flock" and the "herd") to be "the most just of all the monarchies"! And the image of the majority of human beings as sheeplike in fact shows them as *more* susceptible to tyranny than Kleinias's earlier image of them as largely war-like. The taming of Kleinias's admiration and desire in this respect—what taming, that is, that turns out to be in any way feasible—has not yet begun. The Stranger is focused here on winning an eager disciple, not on a "voyage to Syracuse." The appeal that Kleinias feels for the particular power of *written* law comes to light here, and is delicately tested by the Stranger. But the net with which the Stranger leads Kleinias to ensnare his own tyrannical drive, a net woven of the appeal of written law (cf. 890c1–3 with 890e4–891a8— these obviously crucial passages on written law are strangely not even mentioned by Cusher in his article on "the Origins of Written Law" [2011]; note that it is in exactly these passages that Megillos steps in to speak, though he has not for a very long time, and will not again until the very end of the *Laws*), is as yet and for all practical purposes a net unwoven and a trap unset. And if the Stranger is not as hasty about this as we would perhaps like him to be, then that is as much cause to reflect on our own expectations of politics as it is to reflect on whether his caution is over-cautious or judicious. Any good trapper or hunter knows that success requires not only general knowledge of an animal's general nature, but also specific—or precise—knowledge of specific predilections, drives, and perceptions. He or she must understand the animal as the animal understands itself. Such knowledge can only become possible with delicately adapted testing, as the example of the Stranger's testing of Kleinias about Epimenides illustrates very well, and as later examples will further attest (see chapters 4 and 5).

What the Stranger *has* succeeded in showing Kleinias, though, is the image of human "nature" that results from drawing out the consequences of the absence of the specific technological "progresses" that Kleinias himself holds to be very recent (relatively speaking). And that image demonstrates to Kleinias—and again, it is important that this demonstration derives from, and closely adheres to, his own terms—that the easy assumption he had earlier made about the permanent condition of war in human nature had been abstracted by him solely from his own contemporary and immediate circumstances.

This by way of suggesting that serious students of Hobbes, Locke, and Rousseau (to name a few of the early major figures who kicked off "modernity") are missing an essential part of those philosophers' *combined* effort, if those students do not also come to understand how carefully and deliberately they took up Plato, with each contributing and considering a successive piece of an examination (and its permutations) that in the *Laws* is presented complete.

What Megillos observes, and Kleinias is blind to, is that Kleinias mirrors almost exactly the ease with which, in the unfolding of the Stranger's myth, the "early" humans of the Cyclopean communities believe whatever is said of gods and human beings to be "most true," and cannot help but believe to be most true, and live accordingly (679c4, 6–7). And while the Stranger or Megillos might if they wished disabuse him of the particular mistake he makes with respect to the myth of Book 3, they could do little or nothing about his lack of capacity to discriminate between a "likely" account (likely for him, that is) and a true account in general. Kleinias is a man, and a politically powerful one at that, whose watchword and authority is tradition, but who is at the same time completely unreliable as a preserver and safeguard of any true tradition. For his criterion, if criterion it be, for accepting something as true or not—and it is no accident that Plato illustrates this with the example of a myth about ancient ancestors, for a man who believes that his own devotion to ancestral tradition is impeccable—is its appeal to his imagination, not to its truth or untruth, or its goodness or badness.

One might of course argue that the situation with Kleinias as a political ruler is not so dire. After all, he is being convinced not just by anyone, but by a philosopher. Should rulers not be open to such convincing?

The philosopher, however, is not using anything like philosophical argumentation with and for Kleinias. He is appealing to Kleinias's imagination and desires, and if he chose to tell an ignoble lie, Kleinias would have no standard by which to judge it other than his desires. Ignoble lies are of course legion (679c4–5). How likely is he to meet only philosophers who are committed to a long process of leading him toward fulfilling his highest capacity for reflection, and to supplementing what is nevertheless lacking with noble dreams beyond his ken? The Stranger's blatant arbitrariness in choosing to focus on a global flood rather than any "other disasters," after having expressly mentioned other disasters (plagues are mentioned, but volcanic eruptions, massive fires, and earthquakes also come to mind—cf. *Timaeus* 22a–e—as does the effect of sustained and sweeping attacks of marauding Dorian pirate-warriors [682e, 685d–e]),[7] are intended to remind us of this, to say nothing of the "surprise" at 680b, when the Stranger relates his purportedly idyllic postpolitical community to that of Homer's Cyclopes.[8]

One may think of this in particular with respect to Kleinias's disposition toward war, and particularly his focus on "victory" rather than "rule" and rule over oneself. The Stranger describes for him a kind of "rule" without victory—this is the essence of his Cyclopean story. He appeals to Kleinias's admiration for tyrannical rule in order to drive a preliminary wedge between it and the victory in war that Kleinias is convinced entails, and alone entails, it (cf. Meyer's discussion of the Stranger's locutionary shift to "rule" instead of "victory" over oneself at 644b6–7; Meyer 2015, 168–71).[9]

Sparta

Such is the circumstance that leads the Stranger and *Megillos* to begin again, one may say (682e8, 683b5–6). And what Megillos has observed *of* Kleinias in the preceding lesson *for* Kleinias is very different indeed than what Kleinias has observed—and especially *not* observed—of himself.

When the Stranger says to Megillos that they have returned, "as if according to a god," to the point at which they left off before digressing about music and drunken events, he is referring to the point in Book 1 in which he had stressed that their whole conversation was "not about the other people, but about vice [or: badness] and also virtue of the lawgivers themselves" (637c8–d2). Only having stressed this did he next say: "So let us speak further concerning the whole of drunkenness. For this practice is no small thing, nor does it belong to an inferior *lawgiver* to thoroughly understand it" (d3–5). The Stranger does not qualify his statement about having returned to this beginning: he does not say that they have "almost" returned to that beginning, for example.[10] But he does not say that this return is "as if according to nature" (cf. 682e10 with a2; Strauss [1975, 42]), for, to say the least, nature does not look back. Nor does he say this of the point at which they saw or imagined the first lawgivers—the lawgivers of urgent necessity—arise (681c–d), but only after the "coming to be" of "the figure (*schêma*) of a regime in which *all* forms and experiences (*pathêmata*) of regimes and cities coincide (*sumpiptei*)" (681d8–9—note the stress on both passive occurrence and on fortuitous coincidence of such occurences).[11] In the *Republic*, this regime-figure is called democracy, and Socrates explicitly attaches an almost identical importance—for the lawgiver—as the Stranger implicitly does here, to the city in which such a regime exists (*Rep.* 557d2–7). The true, and therefore complete, virtue and vice of the lawgiver cannot come to light in a situation of mere necessity. It can only come to the light of thought and knowledge once the full range of human possibility is experienced in mind and in deed; that is, in essence and in accident.

Why does the Stranger turn to Megillos, then, once Kleinias has revealed how easily he believes and affirms the Stranger's discourse on postpolitical human beings? It makes sense that he would do so, given the turn to the subject of Sparta—but why turn to the subject of Sparta at all?

To begin with, it is important to note that what is explicitly called the "myth" of Sparta is equally a myth about all Dorians (i.e., including Cretan Dorians)—the myth specifically gives an account of the origin of the name "Dorian," with the invention of "Dorieus," the man who the Stranger says organized the exiled post-Troy Achaeans to reclaim their homes from usurpers (682e, 683a7–8). In fact, it is just after the Stranger introduces this character, and the origins of the Dorians, that he specifically solicits Megillos's participation, saying, "And after all it's you, O Lacedaimonians, who tell the myth and finish everything that happened after that" (682e4–6). And Megillos answers, "Indeed" (e7). The Stranger then makes his statement about their having returned, "as if according to a god," to the point of their conversation before they digressed about drunkenness, and asks if they should discuss again, from the beginning so to speak, what has and has not been nobly established, which laws preserve what is preserved and which destroy what is destroyed, and what kinds of changes make cities happy (682e–683b). Megillos very resoundingly replies in the affirmative (683b–c).

Pangle (1988) suggests that Megillos's enthusiasm here is a result of his being seduced by the Stranger's seeming promise of a poetic ennobling and reshaping of Spartan history. He writes:

> Megillus's response to the Athenian's proposal that they begin anew is the most enthusiastic he will be heard to utter. And it is not difficult to see why. The Athenian has not only proposed a new beginning that promises to do justice to Sparta; in addition, he has woven together a new version of Homeric history that obscures the role of that embarrassing Spartan, Helen, and that transforms the Dorian invaders into the direct descendants of the heroes who triumphed at Troy. He has made Homer no longer "alien" to Dorian culture (cf. 680c–d). For the first time, Megillus is in a position to see solid advantages in the idea of a city founded on a new poetry that blends and reworks the traditional epic models. (430)

I respectfully disagree. For one, even *if* Megillos is in fact at all concerned about "that embarrassing Spartan, Helen" (on which, see below), at the point of his enthusiastic response to the Stranger, there has been no hint that she is to be excised from the new Dorian heritage. In fact, since the Stranger has only said that the soon-to-be Dorians were those soldiers driven into exile by the youths at home who revolted against them, which youths also caused "very many deaths and slaughters," the fate of Agamemnon (killed by Aegisthus, with the help of Agamemnon's wife, upon his return from Troy—*Od.* 11.405–34) would seem to be linked to the *Dorian* cause. Why would Megillos assume, *at this point*, that the Stranger's myth would end up including those Dorians unseating Agamemnon's brother, Menelaus, and thus also his wife, Helen?

Moreover, why would Megillos be concerned about Helen in the first place, if Homer is, *before* the myth that is promised by the Stranger, "'alien' to Dorian culture" (and thus Dorian Sparta)? If Homer is alien to Dorians, then so is Helen. And why should we assume that Megillos is so interested in Homer *not* being alien to the Dorians? He has demonstrated that he is well versed in Homer, but has expressed nothing that indicates a desire for contemporary Spartans (or Dorians in general) to be brought within the precincts of those epics. As a matter of fact, he has specifically said that the whole "way of life" (*bios*) (and not just certain events, for example) that Homer presents is *not* Laconian (680c7–d1).

It should be recalled here that whatever the Stranger is proposing to Megillos with his initial invention of Dorieus, and thus the description of Dorians as exiled Achaeans who returned to defeat their usurpers, he is asking Megillos to confirm what Megillos certainly *knows* to be the Stranger's invention, and *in front of Kleinias*. As Pangle (1988) notes, there is no other extant mention of either element of the myth proposed here, either before or after Plato (522n12). Nor is there any reason to agree with Weil (1959) that "history" in the *Laws* (as opposed to other Platonic dialogues) "suddenly distances itself from legend," and that therefore Plato either (1) must have had a source to which we are no longer privy; or (2) introduced a character into the "historical" past because he logically would have needed to exist (33, 52, 84–5; my translation). To say nothing of the complete circularity of such an argument, it also ignores the context of the Stranger's mention of Dorieus and the exiled Achaeans, and the fact that that mention directly follows what is an explicitly legendary account: that of the Cyclopes. The logic that the *Stranger*, not Plato directly, introduces into the "historical" past in that account has everything to do, as we have seen, with the assumptions of his interlocutor Kleinias, and the unexamined opinions and proclivities from which those assumptions proceed.

It also follows, within that legendary account, an instance in which Megillos has quite clearly refrained from drawing attention to the *prima facie* disjunction between the Stranger's description of the Cyclopes, and Homer's. The Stranger had implied, in citing Homer, that Homer agreed with his description of the "first regime" (680b–c). Kleinias admitted that he was not familiar with Homer, but found the verses he has heard "very urbane" (680c2–5), whereupon Megillos asserted his own knowledge of Homer and other "foreign poets," and proclaimed Homer a "good witness" to the Stranger's account—while gently correcting the urbanity (literally: "city-ness") that Kleinias sees in Homer to the "savagery" (literally: "field-ness") of the Cyclopes (c6–d3). The Stranger, accepting Megillos's support, then subtly downgrades Homer from a "good witness" to someone who "bears witness" to his account (d4). In other words, Megillos has understood what the Stranger is constructing with his myth, for Kleinias, and has demonstrated his willingness to lend the authority that he—as the patriotic and traditional fellow older Dorian—has in Kleinias's eyes, to the Stranger's efforts. The Stranger can and does count on exactly that for his continuation of the myth—and its purposes—that brings in the Dorian Spartans, and Megillos once again comes through for him. Needless to say, Megillos's authority vouching for the specifically Spartan aspect of the myth is all the more trustworthy in Kleinias's eyes.

As Nightingale (1999a) rightly draws our attention to, the Stranger says, and repeats, quite explicitly that the purpose of the "myth" is not for the sake of that myth, but for the sake of its pertinence to lawgiving (300–301; citing 683a–c, 683e–684a, 699d–e). All cities are necessarily spoken of and discussed by their citizens, by their founders, and by others: all cities are "cities in speech." It is particularly important to examine the continuities and discontinuities between aspects of the myth of the Spartan Dorians that the Stranger, with Megillos's help, constructs. One major conceivable discontinuity lies in the Stranger's naming the Spartan Dorians "the sons of Heracles," as against "the sons of Pelops" (685d7).[12] Another, perhaps the most pronounced, is the Stranger's assertion that the Achaeans were defeated in battle by the Dorians, who were thus believed to "prevail in virtue" over the army that sacked Troy (685d8–e3). How are the Dorians both *part of* the army that sacked Troy, and believed to prevail in virtue *over* that army?

The apparent contradiction resolves itself if we recall that this is almost exactly how Kleinias described a city, neighborhood, household, or man gaining a "victory by itself over itself" in the war of all against all in public, and each against himself in private (626d). It is not at all difficult to picture how *he* envisions a battle between two different camps within the Greek army that sacked Troy: not only is the victorious camp "superior to" the losing camp, but the army is thereby "superior to itself"—the victor in the civil war *within* the army that sacked Troy, is *greater* than the army that sacked Troy. The Stranger replaces Kleinias's earlier "superior to" with "better rulers than" (685d7–8)—which bespeaks his agenda—but otherwise retains the exact terms that Kleinias had used at the outset of the *Laws* (626d, 627a): "winning victory" (*nikaô*—685e1–2) and "inferior to" (*'êttaomai*—e2)—terms that the Stranger has preserved (and in doing so questioned) ever since Kleinias first introduced them (627b, 633d–e, 635d, 645b, 650a). *Pace* Strauss (1975), the Stranger does *not* "retract[] his earlier suggestion about the Dorians' autochthony" (44).[13] Rather, he and Megillos establish that autochthony in *Kleinias*'s imagination, and on Kleinias's *own terms*. In doing so, they introduce a subtle but crucial shift in those terms that Kleinias accepts, likely because he does not at first perceive it: from victory for the sake of acquisition, the Stranger and Megillos move to victory for the sake of rule. This shift, of course, actually undermines the fundamental thrust of Kleinias's assumptions about victory, for while victory in war may indeed lead directly to the acquisition by the victor of the defeated party's "goods" (as Kleinias defines them—see 626b), it clearly does not lead so directly or always to *good* rule (cf. Kleinias's remark at 627a). Indeed, in the myth of Sparta that the Stranger creates, and Megillos lends his Spartan authority to, it is precisely the *lack* of good rule following the Dorian victory that deprived the ensuing Peloponnesian confederacy (Argos, Messene, and Sparta) of its enormous potential for victory in external war (686b3–4), and committed it instead to endless civil war. And that lack of good rule, the Stranger insists— and Kleinias now *agrees*—is not the result of a lack of courage or ability in war, but of ignorance, of what the Stranger says is "justly called the greatest ignorance": lack of "consonance" with oneself (689a–c, cf. 686b3). As Strauss (1975) notes, in agreeing to this, "Kleinias . . . apostrophizes [the Stranger] for the first time as friend" (46; the reference is to 689c4). It is important that he does not merely reluctantly assent to a logic he cannot deny here (as he did, for example, at 628e and then 663c–e; cf. 661d–662a), but warmly embraces the lesson that he has derived from the Stranger's myth. The Stranger had earlier explicitly advocated, *to Kleinias*, the use of a "prof- itable lie" and myth to persuade people of truths they are unable to believe on the basis of arguments alone (663d6–664a8). What Kleinias does not realize, and is not intended to realize, is that the Stranger, with Megillos's assistance, has done precisely that *with him*. And in doing so, not only did the Stranger not hide the fact that his account was a myth, but he stressed it from the outset (682a8, e5, 683d3).

The Stranger, with Megillos's assistance, has brought Kleinias from and *through* his earlier (and long-held) opinion that law's principal or only con- cern is with victory and acquisition, to the recognition that law's fundamental quandary concerns rule and ignorance. That this does not automatically mean that wisdom as such becomes the essential desideratum for Kleinias does not prevent him from agreeing that "the lawgiver should try to create as much prudence (*phronêsis*) as possible in the city, and remove ignorance to the highest degree" (688e6–8). Moreover, he also emphatically agrees that what is justly called wisdom—the consonance of one's desires with one's opinion of what is noble and good—should be honored and praised in the city, with the "noblest and greatest consonance [being] most justly called the greatest wisdom" (689d–e).[14]

We should recall that when the Stranger had earlier advocated the use of a "profitable lie," it was in direct response to Kleinias's *own* firmly expressed lack of consonance with himself about justice in general: Kleinias believes that injustice is ignoble and shameful, but not unpleasant for the man who unjustly fulfills his every desire—Kleinias "likes and embraces what seems *to him* to be base and unjust" (689a6–7). For him, a man who unjustly acquired whatever he desires would be happy, even though that man was also fully aware that what he did was ignoble (660e–662a). The myth of Dorian Sparta, whose primary "lesson" is conveying the consequences of lack of consonance between one's desires and one's opinions about what is noble, is tailored quite precisely to address Kleinias's own failings.

Having accomplished this, that myth is then dropped without ceremony (693d), though its lesson is retained. The Stranger makes one more passing reference to that myth during his brief "recap" of the discussion they have had thus far, at the end of Book 3 (702a2–3), and that is all. When, in Book 4, he turns again to antiquity for a myth with which to illustrate the city in which a god "is truly master of those who have intellect" (713a3–4), he evokes the rule of Kronos in a mythical time long before the mythical flood that leads up to the myth of Sparta in Book 3 (713b–714a). The myth of Sparta will not be mentioned again in the *Laws*.

Empire

The Stranger has been "writing" his accounts and myth ever larger in order to let Kleinias see more clearly and more fully on his own terms—his terms being a politics of victory and acquisition, which must ever expand—the aspects of the quandary his own disposition (the regime of *his* soul) raises (702a7–b1): from the family-clan of the Cyclopes; to the first city in the foothills that protects itself (and is at war); to the city on the plain (or: by the sea—702a4) that is one among many cities (and is at war), and then to the Spartan confederacy of three cities divided against itself (and is at war). Finally, he writes in letters as large as possible, using the old empires of Athens and Persia (at war with each other) to draw out as distinctly as possible the aspectual differences between the two "mothers of all regimes" or almost all regimes (city, and soul): freedom and monarchy (693d–e) or, what is almost the same thing, slavery and freedom (694a).

These are, again, the aspects that in Kleinias's own lack of consonance with himself, are held apart in his imagination. On the one hand, his own opinion of what is just and noble is to him like a monarch to which he can only be a slave when he obeys it; on the other, he imagines fulfilling his ignoble and unjust desires as freedom itself, and this freedom as happiness. The Stranger mirrors Kleinias's images of these aspects as distinct, if not mutually exclusive, for him by first suggesting that it is "correct to say" that Persia is the fullest example of monarchy, and Athens the fullest example of freedom (693d–e). He writes in big letters what is written small in Kleinias, so that Kleinias may look into his own soul. As Socrates puts it in the *Republic*:

> If someone had, for example, ordered men who don't see very sharply to read little letters from afar and then someone had the thought that the same letters are somewhere else also, but bigger and in a bigger place, I suppose it would look like a godsend to be able to consider the littler ones after having read these first, if, of course, they do happen to be the same. (*Rep.* 368d2–7; trans. Bloom)

The Stranger's point in finally writing in or looking at bigger letters in a bigger place, though, is that neither freedom nor monarchy (or slavery), taken to an extreme that excludes the other, is appealing to Kleinias (cf. especially 699e, 701e). *Both* must be present in any one regime if it is to allow for "freedom, friendship, and prudence" (693d8–e1; cf. 694b6–7 and 701d8–9, where "prudence" [*phronêsis*] is replaced with "intellect," or "mind" [*nous*]). When the Stranger attempts to substitute "moderation" for "freedom" as the lawgiver's third goal, Kleinias insists that he first discuss the goal of freedom, and it is unlikely that returning to moderation is his heart's desire (693b6–d1; cf. especially his response at 694d9). Megillos once again steps in to have the conversation that Kleinias would rather avoid, and to "reluctantly" admit to the consequences that Kleinias would rather look away from (696b–702a). That conversation and admission, and the prudence and moderation with which they proceed, entice Kleinias finally to trust the Stranger and Megillos enough to reveal his mandate from Crete and Knossos, which is to found, together with nine other Cretans, the laws of a new colony.

This does not mean, however, that Kleinias has somehow experienced a "conversion" to moderation or to philosophy. Far from it. What he has experienced is a variegated but systematic and, within the horizons of his own imagination, complete exposure to the consequences of his fundamental opinions and proclivities. He has seen, as it were, all of history written on his own terms, and he does not like what he sees. He does not acquiesce unwillingly to a logic he cannot deny but is persuaded by (as he does, for example, in Books 1 and 2)—he is *convinced* by the myths and accounts of the Stranger (and Megillos). (Cf. *inter alia* Rousseau, *Julie, ou la nouvelle Héloïse* 5.5; Hume, *An Inquiry Concerning Human Understanding* 12.1n.) This is why it was so important for the Stranger to stick doggedly to Kleinias's own assumptions and opinions, and why he needed Megillos to step in to vouch for his myths or to finish arguments—again, on Kleinias's own terms—that Kleinias was, or would have been, otherwise hesitant to entertain himself. And this is why the Stranger took Kleinias's initial steadfast belief in the nature of things as all against all, and each against each—which is merely the "noble" political version of Kleinias's inconsonant disposition that believes justice to be noble, but injustice to lead at least potentially to happiness— from the level of the city (with which Kleinias began) to the neighborhood, from the neighborhood to the household, and from the household to the man (626c–e); then took his opinion back through the family, then the single city, then the many cities, then the many cities as one city, and finally through vast empires. For Kleinias believes that victory and acquisition are the purpose of the city and man, so he had to be led to the point where victory and acquisition could no longer be imagined *by him* to solve the quandaries entailed by his disposition and opinions: beyond the family and the city to the vast empires of Persia and Athens, and to the *immanent* failure of those empires. Only as such could this would-be legislator, in his pride, be brought to finally realize and be convinced of the immanent self-defeat of his own disposition and opinions, and to turn, shaken and therefore somewhat wiser, to a true legislator for guidance—to "something true, with respect to virtue, among shadows" (*Meno* 100a6–7; cf. Pascal, *Pensées* no. 331).

"Q.E.D."

The structure and content of the Stranger's myths, then, are designed to demonstrate to Kleinias, with Megillos's subtle and able assistance, what he was unable to see or accept, and did not want to see or accept, from argument alone. Thus Book 3 of the *Laws*, at first sight so seemingly bizarre and incongruous, in fact follows a strict logic from which it never deviates: the logic of Kleinias's opinions and of his dispositional comportment toward those opinions. This logic remains concealed, and is intended to remain concealed, so long as the vast differences between the two Dorian characters remain unnoticed. And it is fitting that this part of the *Laws* as a whole should present such an exceedingly odd face to its reader, for it mirrors the soul of a man without any internal consonance, who is therefore moved hither and thither by forces he is not even aware of, innocent and monstrous at once, by turns confident and hopeful, by turns confused and dejected— "pitiable, and laughable, and a wonder to behold" (*Rep.* 620a1–2).

NOTES

1. This is not to say that Megillos is uninterested in looking at "laws *or* regimes [*ê nomous ê politeias*] that preserve the beautiful and great things or, on the contrary, utterly corrupt them through and through" (686b8–c2; cf. 683b1–4. N.b. Megillos's almost redundant emphasis *diaphtheirousas to parapan* ["utterly corrupt them through and through"] evokes Thucydides 7.87.6: *panôlethriai . . . ouden ouk apôleto* ["none not destroyed with total destruction"]). But the fact that he does not want to *preclude* looking at them (which is all that he says—686b8, c2–3) does not mean that "one could not look elsewhere" than at them. Nor does Megillos conflate the "regimes" with the "laws" here (note the doubled *ê*—"or"): his statement does nothing to either overtly point to or to deny or diminish the regime of the soul. The establishment of what is noble—and beautiful and fine—and great (*kala kai megala pragmata*) by laws or regimes is clearly essential to the Stranger's purpose, though that purpose is not exhausted by such establishment (683b3–4). It is a foundation for something greater, but nevertheless the foundation without which the greater cannot exist. As we will see, this is in fact essential to the issue addressed in Book 3 in particular. Plato has given us ample reason prior to this to suspect that what is true of the Stranger here is also true of Megillos, and it may be noted that while Megillos brings the focus to what is "noble and great" here, whereas the Stranger spoke only of "what is preserved" and "what is destroyed" (683b3), he also brings the focus to the "laws *or* regimes,*" whereas the Stranger spoke only of "laws" (683b2). Cf., importantly, the Stranger's comment at 707d.

2. Strauss nonetheless brings the seeming contradiction to our attention here. A page earlier he had noted that "the Athenian proposes that they now begin a detailed examination of the Spartan arrangements without apologizing for the fact that some of these arrangements may prove to be defective. Megillos agrees with some enthusiasm. . . ." (Strauss 1975, 42). He is referring to 682e–683c. Note, though, that Strauss writes that "Megillos . . . *is* none too pleased . . . " (my emphasis), and not that, for example, "Megillos . . . *seems* none too

pleased. . . ." Strauss is very careful with the distinction between these two words. It is of course true that the Stranger also does not *alert* Megillos to "the fact that some of those arrangements may prove to be defective" *here*. But they have already discussed several ways in which they are, in Book 1 (632e–638e), and there too as a "new beginning" (632d8, 682e8–9, 683b5–6). Megillos would have to be blind indeed to anticipate no criticism of Sparta on this occasion. We might anticipate such blindness from Kleinias, but not Megillos.

3. We should not be too hasty to dismiss the naïveté of Kleinias's belief in the myths of Daedelus, Orpheus, and the like, as primitive. One may think of the easy belief that many North American adults have today that Copernicus "discovered" that the earth was not the center of the universe, or that the earth was "discovered" to be spherical only after the "Dark" ages (or perhaps even after the "Middle" ages), in Europe.

4. What the exact Cretan belief was about Minos, Zeus, and the provenance of Cretan laws, or whether it is in fact accurate to assume only one such belief rather than several, is impossible to determine today, if it was ever possible (determining the specifics of one predominating belief of any community may well be a dubious enterprise in principle, as the *Laws* in fact illustrates—what do "Canadians" believe about the origins of their own constitution and laws, for example?). As Morrow (1960) has argued and convincingly substantiated, however, it is almost certain that the interpretation advanced here by the Stranger (and by Socrates in the *Minos*), and which came to predominate written discourse on the subject (by later Athenians and others), does not precede Plato in any extant writing; later accounts in fact seem to follow the "Platonic" account (22–25). Indeed, before Plato, the character of Minos in Athenian tragedy and other poetry was that of a violent tyrant and Ur-enemy of Athens in general (ibid.; cf. 706a–c). The nearest extant reference—temporally, to Plato—to Minos as being celebrated for his virtue is a passing reference in an oration by Isocrates, in which Minos is listed as one of several ancient men "sung of" for their piety, justice, and wisdom (*Panathenaikos* 205). But Isocrates writes in the same oration that he is ninety-four years old at the time (ibid., 3), and he is therefore writing many years after Plato wrote the *Laws*: Plato had been dead for over a decade. It would appear that Plato thus effects *with* the *Laws* (and the *Minos*) exactly what he illustrates *in* the *Laws*: he gives an account of a man and a god that is then trusted as "most true" simply because he said it.

5. I am in agreement with Pangle (1988) that the Stranger's phrase in which he questions Kleinias about Epimenides is "hardly intelligible" in the MSS (521n3), and I agree with him in following Post's emendation (see Post 1930, *ad loc.*), though not for Post's own dramatic reasons. Burnet's minor emendation (*ar' ist'* to *arist'*—thus: "well done, Kleinas, for leaving out your friend . . . "; accepted by Des Places and England) seems unsound to me—not because, as Post says, it is not complimentary to Epimenides the Cretan and therefore not complimentary to Kleinias the Cretan (Post, ibid), but because Kleinias's *Môn phrazeis Epimenidên;* ["*Surely* you don't mean Epimenides?"] as a response makes little semantic sense with it. The Stranger *is* being complimentary to Kleinias here, using the fantastic legend of Epimenides to slip an easy wedge between Kleinias as a person and Kleinias as a Cretan patriot.

6. In Aeschylus's *Prometheus Bound*, it is Prometheus himself who relates that this was Zeus's desire, a desire prevented by Prometheus (lines 233–243). Just a few lines before this claim, Prometheus had twice stressed that what separates him from all the other Titans is that he knows that "wily contrivance" (208) and "cunning" (215), not brute force, are "foretold to prevail" (213–215, cf. 944; *Protagoras* 317a4–b6). It goes without saying that neither of the elements of this account is confirmed by Zeus, since he is not present in the play; but neither does Hephaestus at the beginning, nor Hermes at the end of the play mention that Prometheus has done anything other than bestow "honors" on mortals with fire and the arts (30, 946). Prometheus acknowledges that his own current situation bound to the rock was "seen and resolved upon long ago" (998)—Zeus's own desire and decision, if it is indeed what Prometheus says it is, need not be that the destruction of mortals occur immediately (cf. Genesis 2:17 with 3:19). In addition to fire, Prometheus says that he replaced mortals' foreknowledge of their fate with blind hope (250–252), and gave them the technological arts. Blind hope and technology are not necessarily separate gifts—whether as one, or as separate, they replace

foreknowledge of mortal fate. There is no "fourth wall" in Athenian tragedy, or in a Platonic dialogue.

7. The end of the "Minoan" civilization of Crete (c. 1400 BC) is believed to have been precipitated by a massive volcanic eruption, which provoked a massive tsunami. Needless to say, the mountain peaks of Crete may not have provided much refuge from the ensuing flood.

8. Consider as well 683e10–684a1, especially *peri kenon* ("about an empty nothing") at 683e11.

9. Meyer's discussion is good inasmuch as she provides several important references to other dialogues in which the phrase *archein hautôn* ("rule themselves") appears, usually in a "political" sense of a city ruling itself, rather than the "psychological" sense that the Stranger deploys with Kleinias at this point. I will not quibble here with the fact that Meyer pays no attention at all to the dramatic importance of Meno, Callicles, and Kleinias as the hearers of this phrase in the Platonic dialogues (aside from its *fortissimo* appearance in the *Republic*). What is important for our purposes is that Meyer (2015) is nevertheless correct that "the ambiguity might well be deliberate on Plato's part, as it allows the Athenian to appeal to the paradigm of virtue that resonates with his interlocutors (the 'victory' model), but without endorsing it himself" (171). I would add to Meyer's conclusions that this "psychological" interpretation of "ruling oneself" is Plato's own discovery, and that he is controlling the drama within which that discovery is misunderstood, rejected, discussed, reviled, and introduced (in that order).

10. It may be wondered whether *saying* that one is returning to a beginning impacts that "return" in a specific way. When the Stranger returns, at the outset of Book 4, to the beginning of Kleinias's discourse from the outset of the *Laws* concerning the "nature" of the Cretan landscape and its implications for habits and practices, he does not *say* that he is returning to that beginning. Needless to say, his own interpretation thereof differs on every significant point with Kleinias's.

11. *Sumpiptein* is the same verb used by Socrates in the *Republic* to describe the practically impossible coincidence of philosophy and political power (*Rep.* 473d3). It denotes an event uncontrolled by human beings, when things simply "fall together."

12. For some reason, most English translators use different nomenclatures for these two terms, implying a like difference in the Greek that is not in fact there. Both terms, in Greek, contain the identical suffix, *–idês*, which means "son of." Bury translates "sons of Heracles" as against the "Pelopidae"; Saunders translates "sons of Hercules" as against "grandsons of Pelops"; Pangle exaggerates the difference still more, translating "sons of Heracles" as against "descendants of Pelops." By translating the first term, but transliterating the second, Bury's translation (and note) implies that "Pelopidae" refers specifically to Agamemnon and Menelaus, and Saunders's translation implies the same. Pangle's translation implies that "sons of Heracles" is a kind of honorific title, whereas "descendants of Pelops" is a kind of "factual" description. In Greek, both are identically honorific. Jowett preserves this best, simply transliterating both—"Heraclidae" and "Pelopidae."

13. Cf. Xenophon, *Memorabilia* 4.6.15

14. And as such, the possibility of the desire for true wisdom enters the city (689d4–6).

Chapter Four

Responsibility, Indignation, and the "Instinct of the Secondary Role"

Indignation [is] a mean position between poisonous envy and enjoying others' misfortune, with respect to pain and pleasure about those in our proximity.

—Aristotle, *Nicomachean Ethics* 1108b1–2

It is remarkable, and of the utmost importance to understanding the *Laws*, that despite his rigorous and even relentless examination of human failures (personal and political), the Stranger is never once indignant about them. As we saw in chapter 3, he is quite clearly aware of Kleinias's major character flaws, and the serious limitations that Kleinias as a *type* will entail for any political community (cf. *Rep.* 520c–d).[1] Yet, far from being moved to indignation by this misfortune, the Stranger's treatment of those flaws instead resolutely attempts to spiritualize them into their highest possibility (which, it should be noted, is not a very high possibility). He treats them not as vicious facts to denounce and eliminate, but as opportunities, and indeed the only opportunities, with which to work.

In a later era of "social justice," in which indignation is explicitly prized and cultivated, this may strike many readers as odd. Indeed, modern proponents of social justice are likely to find the following commendatory "conviction," from a recent article in *Peace Review: A Journal of Social Justice*, to be virtually axiomatic: "Love of wisdom, the search for wanting to know more, the radical continuous thinking that Socrates speaks of and that is at the core of philosophy are attitudes that encourage the capacity for indignation" (París Albert 2013, 336; "conviction" is París Albert's word).[2] But Plato himself could not disagree more. For whatever its real or imagined

potential to contribute to "social change," indignation is the polar opposite of
genuine responsibility.

This is not to deny the important political place and usefulness of indignation, nor to suggest that Plato denied this importance. As several insightful
commentators and thinkers have illustrated, and as we will have cause to
further consider shortly, political indignation is as necessary as political courage (T. Pangle 1988, 452–58; L. Pangle 2009). What it is to deny is that
such indignation has anything to do with "the radical continuous thinking
that Socrates speaks of," and it is indicative of the essential sophism of her
statement to the contrary that while París Albert marshals the image of Socrates for rhetorical support, she provides no example of an indignant Socrates
from any writing of Plato or Xenophon in which he figures. Nor could she,
for Socrates is never presented as indignant.[3] For while indignation is as
important as—and is closely related to—political courage, its relationship to
continuous philosophical questioning and thinking is as remote as political
courage is from philosophical courage (it is a circumstance or disposition in
which, as Aristotle puts it, "spiritedness [*thumos*] seems to listen to reason
somewhat, but mis-hears" [*Nic. Ethics* 1149a]). And this distinction is in
every way related to the difference between the responsibility that indignation demands that others take, and the responsibility that the lawgiver
takes—a responsibility that is illustrated in the *Laws* as only possible in the
absence of indignation. Indignation, pointed in a specific direction, is praised
by the Stranger, as I will discuss in a moment. But this is coupled with a
subtle critique of praise itself, and the need for it—a critique that has deeper
implications than might initially seem.

Considerable difficulties of interpretation therefore beset us. In terms of
strict logic, the arguments of the *Laws* are to a very high degree subordinate
to the action (this too I will discuss at more length shortly), and do not follow
in any immediately clear way on their own. In terms of the dramatic action,
however, we can, for example, expect a real lack of condemnation on the
Stranger's part, and Megillos's, where they are most dissimilar to Kleinias,
and indeed, their very responsibility will require them to rhetorically mini-
mize the significant differences that exist between them. The action on its
own is no clearer than the arguments on their own. The Platonic dialogues
therefore mirror life in an uncanny way, and the "second sailing" that turns to
"the speeches" always entails turning to the speakers, and listeners.

With this as our watchword, we are in a position to consider the following: if in order to have any concrete effect with their words to Kleinias, the
Stranger and Megillos must speak in terms that he will not only understand,
but recognize himself in, then they will have to speak in terms that *he* does,
even and especially when they are attempting to shift the meanings of those
terms for him. The language of indignation—of condemnation and blame—
will be deployed by *kinountoi* (bear with me!—I will discuss this below) who

do not in fact experience it, in order to guide those who do, within (and in very rare cases, out of) the terms of justice as the latter imagine it. To use the ancient metaphor of the Midrash, the Stranger, and Megillos, will speak in the language of the sons of Adam—the language of human beings as they are (see also Maimonides, *Guide of the Perplexed* 1.26; cf. Cicero, *De legibus* 1.19, *De officiis* 2.35, *De finibus* 4.74). Discerning what they are *doing* in what they are *saying* will require exceptional care.

To add to the difficulty, we will see that part of the Stranger's effort involves using and provoking indignation as *testing* Kleinias and Megillos. Treantafelles has done excellent work on the ubiquity of "testing" in the Platonic dialogues, and points to just such testing in the *Protagoras*, there by Socrates, and of Hippocrates (*Prot.* 311b). As he rightly notes, "in administering a test the tester does not necessarily believe the arguments employed in the test itself (*Theaetetus* 157c)" (Treantafelles 2013, 163–64; also citing *Prot.* 341d). We may add that this can well apply not only to the arguments used for the purposes of testing another, but also to the comportment assumed by the tester in doing so. Of interest here is that what Socrates tests in Hippocrates is exactly what the Stranger tests in Kleinias: his "resolve," or the *strength* of his convictions (nor does the Stranger *tell* Kleinias that he is testing him, any more than Socrates tells Hippocrates). But whereas Socrates intends an at least moderate self-transformation of Hippocrates in the *Protagoras*, in the *Laws* the Stranger can hope for very little in this regard, with Kleinias.

In chapters 5 and 6, we will consider one particular issue, with very broad implications, that seems to be treated by the Stranger with condemnation and blame: extramarital sexual activity, and in particular, male homosexuality. We will see that things are very different than they initially appear there, provided one considers what is said with exceptional care. His purpose is to discover in Kleinias the dispositional truth of his erotic appetites—for both money and sex. And to do this, he must provoke him in the "language" that *Kleinias* understands and responds to: the language of indignation, and shame.

At this point, though, what is important is to emphasize that exceptional care is warranted, and pointed to by Plato as desirable. The seamless presentation of Book 3 of the *Laws* as at once bizarre *and* following a very strict logic does just that. Within that presentation, the equanimity with which the Stranger treats both the case of the Cyclops, and more broadly the case of Kleinias, also points to just that desirability.

The Stanger's reference to the Cyclopes stands out, and is intended to stand out, in the reader's understanding, or imagination. The Cyclopes are, for the Homeric Greek imagination, virtually the paradigmatic examples of monstrous wickedness that illustrate the divide between human beings and beasts: extremely aggressive cannibals with no respect for gods or human beings. As several commentators on Book 3 have pointed out, when the Stranger suggests that these postdiluvian survivors were "glad to see each other, given how few of them there were at the time" (678c5–6; cf. 678e9–679a4), that they were glad to see *dinner* is very much an unspoken possibility (Al-Farabi, *Summary* 3.2; Pangle 1988, 427–28; Whitaker 2004, 46). As we will see in chapter 6, the Stranger additionally goes to some length to subtly point to the necessarily incestuous nature of their erotic activity. However tempted we are, though, to interpret the Stranger's praise of these Cyclopean human beings as false or faint, it is surely remarkable— and it is intended to be remarkable—that he nevertheless speaks of them only with praise. The explicit blame and condemnation that we would expect (and that Greek readers would expect) to at least qualify if not replace that praise is never forthcoming. So we would be remiss to assume too easily that we understand the depths and complexities of Socratic or Platonic irony, and simply dismiss the Stranger's comments as "ironic" in the sense of deliberately untrue. This would be to assume that we can miraculously access depths without first seriously engaging and penetrating what lies in the surface. And as Leo Strauss (1978) so rightly put it:

> There is no surer protection against the understanding of anything than taking for granted or otherwise despising the obvious and the surface. The problem inherent in the surface of things, and only in the surface of things, is the heart of things. (13)

Provided that we are provoked not to dismiss, but to wonder at, the Stranger's resolute avoidance of assigning blame to the Cyclopes (and to Kleinias) in Book 3, later instances in which he does indeed appear to very heavily blame behaviors and characteristics of human beings will strike us as somewhat odd on principle. How is it that, on the one hand, he can be so indignant about the human love of money that Kleinias will see him as "full of hate" (832b5–6), and, on the other, completely lack indignation about the cannibalism of the Cyclopes?[4] How can he so vehemently seemingly condemn all extramarital sex, and homosexuality in particular, as "against nature" in Book 8 (835b6–842a3), and yet pass over the incestuousness of the Cyclopean regime—a regime that he seems to suggest is "the most just of all the monarchies"—in silence in Book 3?

Very provisionally, I suggest that the seeming contradictions here are manifestations of the fundamental tension of political philosophy—of political science—between nature and convention, between what is right by nature and what is right in law. As the contours of responsibility, in the Platonic understanding, emerge in our consideration of specific examples thereof, so too will this fundamental tension and the consequences it has for understanding or imagining what is. This is fitting, given the specific nature of responsibility, and the resolute engagement with the actual and real that it entails, and is. It is for this reason that we examined, in broad terms, such an engagement in chapter 3.

That being said, we must at this point remark again, and consider anew, that the first words of the *Laws* are: "[A] god or some human being, Strangers, has *taken* (*eilêphe*) the responsibility (*aitia*) for setting down your laws?" (624a1–2). There is an ambiguity here that intentionally mimics the tension between genuine responsibility and political responsibility, inasmuch as it speaks of one or the other depending on its listener's predilections and assumptions. The Platonic teaching on responsibility is in a sense entirely foreshadowed in the Stranger's opening question, and its reception.

Existing English translations uniformly translate this sentence as asking to whom the responsibility (or credit) is *given*. Des Places likewise translates as ". . . *celui à qui vous faites remonter l'agencement de vos lois?*" (*ad loc*); and Schöpsdau translates ". . . *dem ihr den Ursprung eurer Gesetzgebung zuschreibt?*" (Plato 1994–2011, vol. 1, *ad loc*).[5] These translations are not wrong, as it is necessary to choose between the active and passive senses of *eilêphe* in translation. *Eilêphe* is the perfect of *lambanein*, and *lambanein* is a curious Greek verb: its grammatically active voice can have senses ranging from fully active to almost completely passive, and this range is in full play in the Stranger's opening question. So while not wrong, these translations capture only the more passive sense that *Kleinias* hears, not the completely active sense that the Stranger also intends. And since "taking responsibility" turns out to be *the* act in which active human agency is realized—and only in which it can be realized—these translations miss quite a lot. We must therefore turn to the commentaries.

There is no significant dispute in the MSS as to the wording of the opening lines considered here, and none at all with respect to the key words (see also Schöpsdau 1994–2011, vol. 1, 153–54 for comprehensive consideration of the Greek text). England provides "has the credit" in his commentary (England 1921, *ad loc*), but this skips to the result without attention to the process, and it is the process that is questioned by the Stranger in his opening question. Strauss's (1975) "is responsible" is revealing in its neutrality (3). Benardete is the only commentator that I am aware of who explicitly considers the literal significance of *eilêphe* (and rightly calls attention to Kleinias's use of the same word in response at 625a2), suggesting that while "[w]e would have been inclined to take it neutrally," Kleinias suspiciously—and partly correctly—recognizes therein a subterfuge on the part of the Stranger (Benardete 2000, 5). According to Benardete, then, Kleinias hears "taken" in the *eilêphe* of 624a2, and responds with a similar sense of the word in his rejoinder at 625a3.

But is this a tenable interpretation? We should note that the Stranger's "*eilêphe tên aitian*" is an either/or with respect to whether it is active or passive. If active, it would be heard as "has taken the responsibility," if passive, as "has received / been given the credit."[6] Kleinias's rejoinder at 625a3, that Minos's brother Rhadamanthys "*ton epainon . . . eilêphenai*" ("received / was given praise"), though, is as far toward the passive as it can be. The direct object in Kleinias's use of the verb here is *epainon*—"praise"—one of a few words that, as the direct object of this particular verb, supplies that verb with the derivative sense of "has been given" (another is *kleos*—"fame"): if this particular thing is "received" (i.e., "taken" in what the *LSJ* calls the "more passive" sense), it must necessarily also be *given* by others. The *LSJ* supplies the definition "won," in this sense (see *LSJ* sub *lambanô* II.1)—that is, "won fame/praise"—but this is to translate as active in English what is a passive sense in Greek, and the colloquial English usage therefore obscures the semantics of the Greek grammar. If Kleinias is using the passive in response to the Stranger, he likely heard only the passive in the Stranger's question.

This interpretation is further supported by the motive that prompts Kleinias to respond to the Stranger in the first place. As Benardete (2005, 5) and Pangle (1988, 380) draw our attention to, Kleinias is plainly trying to deflect the Athenian's attention away from Minos and toward his brother Rhadamanthys, with his rejoinder praising the latter as having "become most just" (625a1), according to "we Cretans": "The Minos who demanded human sacrifices from the Athenians is not the Minos Clinias [Kleinias] wishes to defend" (Benardete, 2005, 5).[7] If this is the case, it would be reasonable to believe that Kleinias, in saying that Rhadamanthys also "received praise" (*ton epainon . . . eilêphenai*) for his part in ordering Cretan legalities, is suggesting an equivalency between this "praise" and the "credit" for establishing the laws that he has just admitted Minos shares with Zeus. "Praise" given by others and "credit" given by others are essentially the same thing. Neither has any necessary relation to the active sense of "taking responsibility," a sense that Kleinias seems not to have heard.

What is more, the actions of Rhadamanthys and of Minos, with respect to Cretan laws, are themselves suggested by the very way in which Kleinias compares them to have at least some equivalence here. Minos, according to Kleinias, had a role in establishing the laws. Rhadamanthys, according to Kleinias, is said to have "become most just" because "*tou tote dianemein ta peri tas dikas orthôs*" (625a2). Pangle translates: "because he regulated judicial affairs correctly in those times," which, while somewhat doubtful, is a possibility. It is more likely, however, that what Kleinias means is more specific: as Parens notes, he could well mean that Rhadamanthys "distributed judicial penalties correctly" in those times (Parens 1995, 155n16). In support of the latter meaning, we may add that *dianemein*—literally, to apportion or distribute—would be awkward with *dikê* in the sense of "judicial matters" broadly conceived (and indeed is a highly unusual combination, period),[8] and *dikê* as penalty is quickly picked up by both the Stranger and Megillos, before any other sense of the word is used in the *Laws* (632b8, 637b1—cf. chapters 1 and 3 on how the two first follow Kleinias's lead before shifting—and in order to shift—meanings of terms). What is more, as Pangle himself translates (correctly) at 728b2 in Book 5, the Stranger later returns to address this sense of the word, speaking somewhat pejoratively of "so-called 'judicial penalties' for wrongdoing" (*legomenên dikên tês kakourgias*); and he uses the word unmistakably in the same sense at 941d2 in Book 12 (Pangle there succumbs to the temptation of translating it as "judicial punishment"; cf. also 728c2 and especially 869b2). As Parens (1995) further notes, whereas Pangle's translation of 625a in Book 1 "may or may not mean that he [Rhadamanthys] participated in the act of legislating," if Kleinias is referring to penalties rather than judicial matters broadly speaking, this "makes it sound as if Rhadamanthus did *not* participate in legislating" (Parens, ibid, citing *Minos* 318d–20d; my emphasis). Distributing judicial penalties correctly seems to be advanced as having some equivalence with founding the laws in which that adjudication occurs, per Kleinias. Particularly given his deafness to the suggestion that the latter requires taking responsibility for the laws and the regime as a whole, whatever equivalence there actually is between the two[9] is unlikely to be the equivalence that Kleinias so easily assumes. Socrates, in the *Minos*, separates Rhadamanthys from Minos on this exact point, for his companion who makes essentially the same assumption that Kleinias does in the *Laws* (*Minos* 318d9–11, 320b8–c8). According to Socrates there, Rhadamanthys was "educated by Minos, and educated not in the whole of the kingly art but, as a servant (*hupêresia*) to the kingly, enough to have charge of the law-courts," and was thus not Minos's equal, but rather Minos's servant and "law-guardian" (*Minos* 320b8–c2; cf. *hupêresia* at *Laws* 729d7 and its verbal form at e1).

Kleinias's response, then, comes fairly close to a parody. If the incomprehension that masks itself as easy comprehension were mutual, it would be a comedy of errors. But it is not mutual, and Kleinias may be right, in a way, but for the wrong reasons. The responsibility of the lawgiver does indeed include—both immediately and in the much longer term—the education of auxiliary magistrates, for example, who are capable of distributing judicial penalties "correctly." And Kleinias is not wrong if he imagines, as he likely does, that he is just the sort of person for the job, for the responsibility that the lawgiver takes, and must take, is "to fit the gown he makes to cloth he has" (Dante, *Paradiso* 32.141; my translation). But for that very reason, that responsibility entails as well the education of the "safeguard" Megillos, and the regime they found must nurture his ilk throughout its lifetime. For what Kleinias is wrong about is *why* he is suitable for the political authority that would be impossible to establish without him, and impossible to preclude him from possessing. His preoccupation with penalty and praise bespeak a man who is susceptible to both, and it is no accident that when the Stranger later describes who "the great man in the city" will be, it is he who is to be praised for assisting the city's magistrates inflict punishments (730d5–7): the man of righteous indignation. This man is, in the same breath, in quiet but clear terms, separated completely from the qualities of moderation and prudence, and "all such good things possessed that allow one not only to have them oneself, but also give a share to others" (730e1–3).[10] Such "good things," the Stranger says, need be given the same "praise" (*epainon*) as that bestowed on the great man in the city, who is to be "publically proclaimed complete (*teleios*) and the victory-bearer in virtue" (730d7–e2).

As Strauss (1975) points out, however, the person who does indeed give a share to others of these particular good things is nevertheless "not praised as 'the great man in the city and perfect'" (68). It is these good things, or possessions (731a1), that need be praised, along with the great man in the city, as "perfect and the victory-bearer in virtue" (a1–2). The person who possesses them and shares them does not need praise for possessing or sharing them (nor could there be a properly directed penalty for not possessing or sharing them—cf. Montesquieu, *Spirit of the Laws* V, 7–9 with 13). It is not for such a person to "receive the victorious reputation for serving (*hupêresia*) their [city's] laws" (729d7). The person who possesses these good things and shares them may not even be recognized as possessing or sharing them, or want to be, by others or many others (see chapters 1 and 3). Such a person does not require praise for him- or herself in order to be "complete" (cf. 727a3–b3; and Strauss 1975, 71, on the shift of focus from the pleasure of good reputation to pleasures independent of reputation in the conclusion of the *Laws*' "prelude," a conclusion in which the "healthy" life quietly takes the place of the "just" life [732e–734e]).[11]

The "completeness" of this person is responsibility—responsibility *taken*. How this taking of responsibility is to be described is very difficult. No less a commentator than Marsilio Ficino, who rightly speaks in this context of *reverentia* (reverence) of one's own soul,[12] writes that "how truly important *reverentia* is for observance of the laws, I am unable to clearly explain" (*Argument de legibus libri V*, Ficino 1588, 538, my translation). He then goes on to attempt to do so, explaining that "whoever reveres, in his thought, the constant presence of his own soul as if it were a divinity, has a judge within himself—by whose law he directs himself in utmost completeness (*perfectissime*) even where there is no written law" (ibid.). The Stranger in this context speaks of "honoring one's own soul second after the gods" (726a6–a2, b3–4), and it is not hard to see why it is so difficult to speak of such honoring or reverence. Indeed, no sooner has the Stranger broached the topic than he must, responsibly, expect his statement to be largely misunderstood as praising self-love as it is commonly imagined (cf. 818a7–b5): indulging whatever pleasures occur to us, fleeing whatever might seem to harm us, valuing self-preservation and moneyed comfort above all else, and striving to provide the same opportunities (and example) for our children (727c–729c). To speak other than allusively and briefly about the rare kind of responsibility that he and Megillos embody (and ensoul) would be to valorize a kind of behavior that is completely contrary to that responsibility—one need only imagine how a tyrannical human being would be disposed to interpret a teaching on revering oneself as divine, or as a close second thereafter. The teaching on responsibility emerges largely in the behavior and action of the Stranger and Megillos, [13] and their interactions with Kleinias, for as the Stranger explicitly says, "education that makes a difference, both for the young *and ourselves*, is not a giving of counsels, but displaying the counsels that one might say to another in one's activity throughout life" (729c2–5). [14] Such a statement of counsel would for obvious reasons be self-undermining if its counsel were not also displayed in the Stranger's own activity. Attention to the actions of the characters in the *Laws* is therefore explicitly shown to be important by the most evidently philosophical character *in* the *Laws*: the demand for such attention is Plato's own (nor is this demand in any way restricted only to the *Laws*—see, as one example of many, *Laches* 188c4–189b7). [15] We must expect that those actions will shed important light on the counsels that are given, depending upon whether or not, and how, those actions display those counsels.

The attention we have thus far given to this aspect of the interplay between the *Laws'* characters already points toward a reflection on responsibility properly so called that is not immediately evident from the Stranger's first overt discussion of what human responsibility *is* in Book 5 (a discussion that, for the reasons noted above, quickly becomes one of what responsibility is *not*). We have already seen how "gently" the Stranger and Megillos have tested each other and Kleinias, how carefully and well they have understood each other's dispositions, and how completely the Stranger and Megillos accept and even affirm Kleinias's limited potential in order to lead him to fulfill it. Certainly their actions seem in this respect to be in diametric opposition to the Stranger's "counsel" on the city's praise for the "great man in the city," for example.

To this may be added that even within the realm of the political, in which it is proper to praise indignation of a certain type and directionality, the Stranger in the *Laws* draws an implicit contrast between the knowledge about injustice that "being gentle" requires (731d3), and indignation which is, as Benardete notes, "not naturally allied with any *knowledge* of injustice" (Benardete 2000, 157; citing 731c2–d4; my emphasis). [16] To direct indignation is to direct a certain kind of ignorance. And just as he has made a distinction between the politically just man (the great man in the city) and the person who possesses other "good things," so he recognizes a possible distinction between the unjust person and the person who possesses other "bad things"

(731d1). A just or a good person may "possess" a reputation for being unjust, for example, as well as the consequences that attend that reputation (see *Apology of Socrates*—both Plato's and Xenophon's—as a whole). And a good and just legislator by necessity must have many "bad things" with which he or she must work—a people that was simply just and good, and would remain so, would not need laws (875c–d)—and regardless if an imaginary "purification" of these things might be initially tempting as "best," reflection demonstrates such a purification to be impossible (735b–737b, especially 735d1–736b5). Indeed, even if one were to imagine such an initial purification as having limited aspects that are possible and desirable (and such a possibility, and desirability, does indeed seem to be assumed time and time again), they could in no way be assumed thereafter to be permanent.

The specific case that the Stranger and Megillos confront in the *Laws* illustrates the necessities involved here in spades. Having dismissed harsher purifications as impossible, the Stranger suggests they "assume"—"in speech but not in deed" (736b6)—that a limited "purification" has been accomplished for the as yet unnamed city they propose to legislate in speech:

> Having thoroughly tested, with every persuasion and with sufficient time, in order to discern those who are bad among the people trying to become citizens of the present city, we will prevent them from coming into it, whereas those who are good we will bring with us in as gracious and propitious a way possible. (736b8–c4)

But as we have seen, the Stranger and Megillos have been "thoroughly testing" Kleinias (and each other) over the course of their entire conversation thus far, and Kleinias has given ample indication that he himself meets several of the criteria that the Stranger has given before and is about to give again for being "bad"—most importantly, for the Stranger, his love of money (737a4–6). This is, particularly in a *founder*, a very bad thing indeed to the Stranger's mind, and despite his statement that they have escaped the extreme danger it would present to the city (737a2), he is well aware that this is not the case—he immediately appends: "All the same, it's at any rate more correct to discuss how, had we not escaped, we would prepare a refuge from it" (a2–4). As we will explore at length in chapter 5, the Stranger demonstrates ample awareness of Kleinias's failing in this respect throughout the *Laws*, and with ample reason. He knows very well that this failing in Kleinias (and in the majority of the new city's citizens) entails that the lawgiver must fall back on "prayer, and small, cautious shifts that over a long period of time slightly change [this disposition's] direction"—"shifts" that require a continual series of "reformers" (*kinountoi*)[17] to understand and attempt them (736d2–e3). This will be the permanent condition of the city (i.e., the permanent condition of any political community). The Stranger's statement that they had escaped this is part of, to borrow Nietzsche's phrase, his "genius for finery" (*BGE* 145).

Yet to prevent Kleinias from coming into the city because of this would be to abandon the founding of the city altogether: he is the man with the political power necessary to its establishment to begin with. As we will see in chapters 5 and 6, the testing of Kleinias will continue—and as we have already seen, and will see again, it is quite precisely "with persuasion" that he is tested—so we might perhaps be inclined to think that what is lacking at this point in Book 5 is merely the "sufficient time" necessary to truly discern his character. But the further testing of Kleinias will turn out to rely upon what the Stranger and Megillos have already discerned about his "bad" character through the previous testing. The further testing is concerned not with whether Kleinias has a "good" or "bad" disposition of character, but whether his failings can be turned to good purpose.

Thus, far from indignantly castigating and trying to purge the "bad," the Stranger and Megillos *take responsibility* for it. From their perspective it makes no difference—it may not even be true—that the "bad" thing in Kleinias's disposition for which they take responsibility is not "their own," or is something inflicted upon them by Kleinias. It makes no difference, because it is not true, that it is another person's "fault." Considered in conjunction with the characters' *actions* demonstrated here, the Stranger's description of responsibility at the outset of Book 5—which for the reasons stated above, he is compelled to phrase in the negative, that is, as a description of what is not responsibility—takes on a surprisingly all-encompassing scope. Rephrasing his statement in the positive, he had said there that properly honoring one's soul involves "holding oneself responsible every time for [one's] errors and greatest evils [*kakôn*—'bad things']¹⁸ (in both quantity and magnitude)" and not "considering others responsible for them and always relieving oneself of being responsible" (727b4–7).

Aside from the fact that one's errors and "evils" (or "bad things") cannot, on the Stranger's terms, be one's own "fault" or indeed anyone's fault (no one being willingly unjust), the "evils" that one has and must take responsibility for in order to properly honor one's soul do not seem to be limited—in the Stranger's actions, and Megillos's—to those things that in the commonplace use of the phrase would be gestured at by "our evils." They seem rather to include all the "evils" that one experiences, *tout court* (in the greatest quantity, and including the most grievous ones)—including those that in commonplace terms one would say simply happen to us, or are inflicted upon us. By taking responsibility (*aitia*) for these, one affirms that what one has experienced—all of it—is a part of one's soul: one locates the "cause" (*aitia*) of one's experience in one's soul completely, and self-identifies as the whole of that experience—not because "I *did* that," but because I *am* that:

I am a part of all that I have met;
Yet all experience is an arch wherethro'
Gleams that untravell'd world, whose margin fades
For ever and forever when I move.

(Tennyson, *Ulysses*)

This is taking responsibility, and is the only responsibility that can truly be taken, "with intrepid Oedipus eyes and sealed Odysseus ears" (Nietzsche *BGE* 230).[19] It is the responsibility of the lawgiver, the very nature of whose task demands no less. It is the action and disposition in which a human being usurps his or her natural condition in order to will, and it is easy to see how it might be seen as a usurpation of the divine (consider 716c1–d4, 829a1–5, *Theaetetus* 176a5–b2 [Benardete does not Christianize this, nor does Sachs; other English translations do], *Timaeus* 90d1–7). The Stranger's opening question in the *Laws*—"a god or some human being . . . has taken responsibility for the laws?"—is not a facile one. The difficult question of why the Stranger is at all interested in the project he undertakes in the *Laws* to begin with, or why Socrates or "the divine Plato" taught at all, could be considered with this in mind.

It is then in a way paradigmatic of true responsibility that it is not only free of indignation, but in particular is not indignant *about* indignation as a necessary political fact ("the truth of the matter is this: the good *must* be Pharisees—they have no choice!," learns Zarathustra [*TSZ* 3.12.26]).[20] Where indignation separates actions drastically into good and evil, responsibility just is a human comportment that is beyond that distinction. One may say that it was this insight that led Nietzsche to not even attempt to varnish the economy of value that obtains "beyond good and evil" with any kind of *different* mythological binary distinction. That economy of value is instead, for Nietzsche, *amor fati*, his own term for what Plato called "taking responsibility" (*lambanein aitian*—624a1–2), or "holding oneself responsible" (*hêgeasthai heauton aition*—727b5).

Accepting indignation as a human fact and quandary that is at once a problem and an opportunity is paradigmatic of true responsibility in a very helpful way. By that I mean, thinking through what it entails can let us glimpse a rare human possibility that would be impossible to describe *within* the indignant dynamics of valuing according to "good" and "evil."

It is important that what Plato means by responsibility is not an abdication of valuing, though. Very far from it. Distinguishing between higher and lower human possibilities, and choosing—or more accurately, being *unable not* to choose—the highest for oneself is a fundamental part of responsibility. Judging one's own tasks undertaken is likewise fundamental, with a crucial proviso: no mitigating circumstances are in any way permitted to soften one's self-judgment in these matters, for taking responsibility means taking responsibility for *all* of the circumstances and accidents that attend one's task.[21] There can be no special pleading. It is for this reason that the Stranger forthrightly judges the penal laws discussed in Book 9 to be "in a certain way shameful" (twice: 853b4, c3). That they are predictably and *unavoidably* necessary given the contingencies of being human is entirely beside the point with respect to the Stranger's self-judgment. That their necessity appears to arise from aspects of *others'* character that the Stranger himself seems not to share in at all is likewise entirely beside the point with respect to his self-judgment. *He* has taken responsibility for the laws, and therefore for educating the lawgiver, which laws (conventions) are by their very *nature* concerned with, and necessary because of, human contingency and accident. He therefore does not, and cannot, blame anyone or anything for his own failure: the penal laws are "in a certain way shameful" *for himself.* Where Kleinias would indignantly blame each criminal—and thereby absolve himself of blame—for destroying the laws and the entire city as far as it lies in him or her (857b4–8; *Crito* 50b1–2; cf. Crito's charge against Socrates at 45d2–3), the Stranger takes responsibility for—and therefore does not blame—even the severe moral failing that Kleinias demonstrates in doing so.

Yet at the same time, there is a single instance in the *Laws*, in Book 8, in which the Stranger does indeed seem to be indignant, and even extremely so. The occasion, as we will examine in great detail in chapter 5, is his discussion of the deleterious effects of the love of moneyed wealth, and so extreme does his indignation seem to Kleinias that not only does Kleinias cut him short, but he claims the Stranger seems to both him and Megillos to be "full of hatred" against this disposition (832b5–6). Is the Stranger, for all his understanding and forbearance, indignant about human baseness after all?

It is my contention that he is not, but that what is illustrated here is the inevitability of at least some use of the manners of indignation, wherever moral understanding is imagined in such terms—that is, in practice, everywhere and at all times. What is more—and not unrelated to the previous point—a person given to righteous indignation is likely to hear indignation in any judgment, regardless if it is there or not.

Let us note immediately that in the instance we are considering, Kleinias once again speaks for both himself and Megillos (*dokeis hêmin*—"you seem to *us* . . . "), without having any independent indication from the latter that he agrees. Here we must once again underscore the importance of the essential differences of character that emerged in our examinations in chapters 1 and 2, for those differences urge us to be cautious, as readers, about trusting that Kleinias is correct about the opinion or thought of his Spartan companion. This is to say nothing of the caution we might wish to exercise concerning Kleinias's judgment of the Stranger. As we shall see, it is quite important that this is *Kleinias*'s interpretation of the Stranger's comportment. That he could not interpret that comportment otherwise will entail grave consequences for the best possible regime to be established under the name of Magnesia. That the majority of us, as readers and as citizens and private people, can only with difficulty escape such an interpretation ourselves suggests that we also live with such consequences. For the education of Megillos in the *Laws* is only possible because he has at the outset already overcome his indignation that might be termed political, and that education is specifically focused and dependent on cultivating his own overcoming of the indignation that remains in him. Yet at the same time, just because indignation is in almost every case ineradicable, it is a significant lesson within such an education that political indignation—the righteousness and self-righteousness of the citizen—needs be directed in such ways that it supports rather than destroys the foundation of the laws and the regime.

It is in this latter sense that Lorraine Pangle (2009) rightly notes that indignation is necessary to any society, for "[a]s human beings live in ignorance of their own good and commit injustices upon one another, not only punishment but even the anger that fuels it is socially necessary," if that society is to have the stomach for the necessary punishment of law-breakers. "This fact," Pangle rightly notes, "casts a long shadow over the dignity of political life" (469–70). If Plato is correct in his estimations, however, this description itself, though correct, is already a kind of noble gloss on the deeper political quandary of indignation. For as we saw in chapter 2, Plato also illustrates that punishment is necessary for law-breakers precisely in order to *satisfy* the indignation of others (cf. especially 873e1–a3). This fact casts a longer shadow still, and brings into question any purpose or program that sees in indignation an avenue toward a higher or more inclusive justice, or even what Saunders (1994) rather blithely refers to as "some didactic and social function" (243)—beyond, of course, the "social function" of satisfying social indignation. For while indignation sees itself as clearly discerning and condemning what is transparently wicked and unjust, what in fact transpires, as Benardete (1991) puts it so well (commenting on *Gorgias* 461b3–481b5), is that "[t]he actual opacity of wickedness is replaced by moral certainty of the experience of injustice, which can work backward from its affect to what kind of wickedness initiated its experience" (58; cf. *Hipparchus* 225b10–c2; and the flip side of this comportment in Kephalos in the *Republic* 330d4–331b7).[22] Working backward from the affect of moral certainty in this respect is, of course, blindness convinced that it is clear-sighted, and indeed convinced that it alone is clear-sighted. Punishment and indignation are, on this understanding, both ineradicable facts of political life, bound together in a vicious circle.

As might be expected, this relationship comes to the fore most obviously in the proposals for criminal law and penalty in Book 9, and there Plato does indeed seem, as Saunders (1991) puts it, to allow, "as Athenian law allowed, the seriousness of the act itself to guide by inference a reconstruction of the state of the agent's soul" (251). To Saunders's credit, he is, rightly, not comfortable that this statement is entirely satisfactory. For as he modifies almost immediately, Plato's "discussion of murder in anger shows he is aware of the dangers of arguing directly from the act and the manner of its commission to the psychic state" (251). Why, then, does "Plato" seem to allow such a working backward from an act in the first place?

It may be worth considering what prompts this learned commentator himself to assume a "didactic and social function" in "Plato's" comments on indignation. This quote, from Saunders's magnum opus on the *Laws*, takes place in the context of his extremely brief discussion of the crucial passage from Book 9 in which the Stranger prescribes trials and penalties for both beasts of burden and inanimate objects that "murder" someone (873e1–874a3). That Saunders is sure that even here there must be a "didactic" lesson for citizens is indicative of how reluctant he is to acknowledge Plato's elision of indignation at crime in general with what he has Socrates elsewhere explicitly illustrate as a bestial anger that militates against the very basis and possibility of rational thought (*Rep.* 469d4–e2; Pliny relates that the image Socrates evokes here—"a stone bitten by a dog"—was in fact proverbial in Greek, *Naturalis historia* 29.102; cf. Erasmus, *Adagia* 4.2.22, "*canis saeviens in lapidem,*" in contrast with 4.2.18, "*omnibus vestigiis inquirere*").

For all of Saunders's detailed concern with the aspects of anger and spiritedness (*thumos*) that Plato takes into consideration with respect to the commission of crimes, there is nevertheless an almost complete absence in *Plato's Penal Code* (Saunders 1991) of attention to the aspect of *eagerness* to punish crime that is so important a consideration for Plato. For example, the crucial passage 730c1–731b2—on "the great man in the city"—is not mentioned by Saunders at any point in his book. Yet it is in this passage in Book 5 that the political necessity for indignation for punishment comes most prominently to light as a necessity that relies for its fulfillment upon a highly suspect and base disposition of character, and one moreover that is always dangerously close to poisonous envy or the delight in the pain of others (731a2–b3). Thus while Saunders (1991) is highly attentive to the *miasma* ("pollution," "defilement") entailed by, in particular, homicide—and rightly so—he persistently suggests that appeasement of primarily the *dead person*'s fury is what is attempted with the punishments and purifications of the crime, that is, that it is the dead victim who feels "vindictive and vengeful" (251–57). And while Saunders is certainly correct that appeasing the dead victim is much discussed by the Stranger in the *Laws*, it seems unwise to neglect that categorizing such appeasement as being of the dead can be a very effective way of symbolically diffusing the indignant demands of the living. At the same time, Saunders is quite correct that the principle of punishment as "cure" is constant throughout the *Laws*, but incorrect that the attempt to be as curative as possible is limited to only the criminal. Thus Allen too is incorrect, and for the same reason, when she proposes that Plato "did not use the trope of disease to argue that either the punisher or the community was made ill by and needed to be cured because of an act of wrongdoing. In Plato's usage, it is only the wrongdoer who is sick, and only the wrongdoer who needs a cure" (Allen 2001, 247; cf. 200–201). *Pace* Allen, and Saunders, that is quite precisely what Plato uses the trope of disease (and *miasma*) to do.

Let us return to our story. The Stranger's seeming indignation, in the examples we will shortly consider from Book 8, looks like real indignation, and is *intended* to look like real indignation if considerable, nonindignant reflection is not devoted to it—Plato tests his readers too. If law, as opposed to philosophical reflection on law, *requires* the mannerisms of indignant blame, how does Plato expect genuine responsibility to be discernible from the genuinely indignant blame of the Kleinias type? For certainly it is of the very essence of this type that such a person claims to take responsibility as well, by ruling others and wanting to rule others, and in fact actually believes that he or she does take responsibility thereby.

The first thing we must say is that *institutionally*, the differences here cannot be adjudicated. There is no possible institutional mechanism for differentiating the deployment of feigned indignation from the claims of real indignation—any more than there is a possible institutional mechanism for differentiating a philosopher-ruler from a usurper to that title. This is a major reason why Plato is in no way interested in granting institutional title or authority to either genuine responsibility or a philosopher-ruler—just the opposite, in fact. A person like Kleinias could never recognize a genuine lack of indignation in another.

But if we consider the Stranger's moment of purported indignation carefully, we will see that that is exactly what Plato is trying to illustrate with it. The interpretation that the Stranger is indignant is *Kleinias*'s interpretation. It is *Kleinias* who accuses the Stranger of being "full of hate" for the money-loving disposition (832b5–6), not the Stranger who avows it. In fact, the Stranger is quite clear that he does not *blame* anyone who suffers from this disposition, for according to him, that disposition arises out of a "lack of nature" (*aphueis*) for nobility and human excellence, or "bad luck" (832a2–3 and context). Nor do such people constitute agents who *could* reasonably be blamed, according to the Stranger, for they are themselves "utterly unlucky" just because they are "*compelled* (*ananke*) to go through their lives with their own souls always hungry" (832a5–7). The love of money is certainly a grievous misfortune for the city, according to the Stranger, but it is first and foremost a total misfortune for each person who is compelled by it. Thus where Kleinias sees hate and blame in the Stranger's words, the Stranger himself is comporting himself according to the principle that "no one is willingly unjust." If we resist being seduced by Kleinias's own indignation, we will see that Plato gives us ample reason to believe that the Stranger is not indignant at all here, though the Stranger is deliberately letting Kleinias experience his judgment as such (837b7). Kleinias hears of the extreme harm to the city that results from this disposition, and assumes as a matter of course that it—that *he*—is being blamed—and further, that if something is blamable in this way, that it ought to be punished (cf. his response to the Stranger at 857c7–e2). But that extreme harm does not in any way change the Stranger's own judgment that blaming people for this disposition would be absurd, nor does he merely voice this lack of blameworthiness and then lose sight of it (as many of us do when reality confronts what we assume to be our "principles") when he attends to the highly deleterious effects of that disposition: he voices that lack of blameworthiness *after* he attends to those effects.

It seems then that one way to discern between real and seeming indignation is to put aside other people's reactions—and especially indignant people's reactions—and both listen to what someone is saying (and doing) and seriously consider the principle, if principle there be, that the saying and the doing derives from. This is obviously easier said than done, and Plato knows it. It may well in fact be his point to illustrate how difficult it is to *do* this in general, even though it is perfectly obvious what one would need to do in order to accomplish it (cf. 839b7–c2). Even on the page, the reader is beguiled by Kleinias's interpretation of the Stranger's evaluation.

One may also note, not least importantly, the massive difference in dispositional response, between the Stranger and Kleinias, with respect to judging another human being to be without continence and thus compelled by forces, desires, and opinions for which he or she is not responsible. The Stranger's response, as is already clear and as will become even more abundantly so in Book 9, is identical to the response of Christ expressed several centuries later: "remit their penalty (*aphes autois*), for they know not what they do" (Luke 22:34). (This is *not* to say that the Stranger was a Christian *avant la lettre*, nor do I assert affinities beyond the specifics mentioned here.) Kleinias's assumption about what the Stranger's response must be, while completely erroneous with respect to the Stranger, reveals Kleinias's own response: hatred. Nor is this merely a function of feeling a secret aspect of himself to have been judged by the Stranger, and found wanting. Rather, his contempt for those he characterizes from the outset as "weaker than themselves" is a mirror of, and for, the contempt he is sure a superior person to himself would feel for him. He voices his rebuke of the Stranger as for hatred *tout court*, but it is the sting of hatred he is sure the Stranger must feel *for him* that provokes his anger. And it is his own contempt for the incontinence of others that, in his shame, he experiences as directed toward himself. He reads his own disposition into the Stranger's judgment.

There is a glimpse offered here into the unavoidable divergence from and perversion of even the soundest and highest principles that might somehow be established within the founding of a regime or constitution, and in its laws.

We might also note that when Kleinias finally cuts the Stranger off, accusing him of excessive hatred, the immediate statement to which he is responding is in fact the Stranger's assertion that the money-loving person is simply—and completely—unfortunate. As just noted, because Kleinias feels personal shame when he hears this from the Stranger, he also hears, and can only hear, hatred in the Stranger's statement about the unworthiness of such a person.

Yet Kleinias had not felt such great shame, and therefore anger, when the Stranger had, at the outset of Book 8, described the necessity and love of war in much the same way as he has just described the love of money (Strauss 1975, 118, citing 828d2[-3] and 829a7–8[6–7]).[23] And as if to evoke the affinity between the two poetically, the Stranger invokes the name of Pluto (the god of death and the underworld) as a god whom a warlike people ought not be disturbed by (828d1–3). As we will discuss at more length in chapter 5, the linguistic similarity of Pluto (*Ploutôn*), the god of death, to Plutos (*Ploutos*), wealth or the god of wealth, is such that one immediately conjures the other. We are reminded by this evocative affinity of the inclination toward love of wealth that Kleinias revealed in Book 1 to lie at the heart of what he is disposed to believe is his own love of victory (626b).

But if Kleinias did not immediately react with shame and anger to the Stranger's discourse on the necessity of war, he was nonetheless slow to respond, and hesitant to completely affirm what the Stranger says and implies there (note Kleinias's *schedon* ["almost" or "probably"] at 830c5, and *tach' an* ["probably" or "maybe"] at 831b9). To the Stranger's assertion that "if a city becomes good, it has a life of peace, but a life of war both without and within should it be wicked" (829a6–7, and consider context), Kleinias said not a word. He was already beginning to suspect that the Stranger was reevaluating the grounds on which stand, for Kleinias and likely for most Cretans, the superior man and the good life, and though he was unable to refute that reevaluation, he did not like what he was hearing. For implied in the Stranger's evaluation is that the victor in war is no less controlled by (i.e., a slave to) forces and desires that compel him, than is the defeated party. Nor is it any longer clear that any cardinal difference exists between the compulsion or necessity exerted by "external" forces of political enemies, and the compulsion or necessity of the "internal" forces of desire—of *eros*—over which one has no real control. Kleinias, who considers himself to be an exemplar of martial virtue, is no longer getting any credit for that virtue. And as if that weren't bad enough, if he had imagined the credit he *believed* he earned from that virtue to counterbalance or outweigh the indulgence of a "minor" vice or two—as so many people do—then he can be expected to be all the more ashamed by the harsh light in which those "minor" vices are cast in the sequel, provided that he in fact holds, in principle, that they are in fact vices. We will return to the quandaries involved here in chapter 6.

Just as with Book 3 of the *Laws*, which at first sight seems so strange and so bizarrely juxtaposed, the initial image we get of Book 8 as a hodge-podge of disparate elements or "digressions" (thus Gonzalez 2013, 154) slowly gives way to a strict logic. For its elements are deliberately planned, and its plan precise. And as with Book 3, the overwhelming *prima facie* impression of "sound and fury" is a mirror of the subject matter: here, though, of erotic compulsion in general—of the forces that lay claim to us, within and without, with what we experience as certainty of agency and purpose in each separate moment, but which reflection leaves us unable to account for as a coherent whole of which we are the agents: the seemingly paramount importance of now one, now another pursuit demanding our full attention, only to give way to the next without having been either fulfilled or comprehended; each with enough strangeness and allure to capture our fixation momentarily, yet each with enough and more than enough familiarity to fall back into quotidian formlessness without undue struggle.

Nor is Book 8 without consequence. It seems likely that Kleinias's willingness in Book 9 to entertain the Stranger's argument that "no one is willingly unjust" (860c–864c—note that that argument is made entirely in terms of broad generalities rather than in terms of specific injuries or injustices) follows directly from his semicloseted self-realization in Book 8 that he himself is not exactly the paragon of virtue that he had previously held himself to be. Certainly the Stranger did not even attempt to make that argument or have such a conversation when he first made mention of this principle, in Book 5 (731c–d). Indeed, the Stranger seemed to deliberately avoid having a conversation about this with Kleinias at that time, making only an extremely short and more or less innocuous defense thereof (a defense that is *different* in striking ways from the later defense in Book 9), immediately after proclaiming the spirited man who "relentlessly punishes" (731b6–7) incurable injustices to be "the great man in the city" (cf. Pangle 1988, 452), and sandwiching even that limited and misleading defense within what is, by far, his longest uninterrupted speech in the *Laws* (twenty-five full Stephanus pages, 726a–751a), a speech "during which the actual lawgiver Kleinias is not given an opportunity to ask any questions" (Pangle 1988, 458, citing in particular 746b).[24] Following what seems to be very high praise of the spiritedness necessary to relentlessly punish "incurable" injustices (but which praise is, as we have seen, mitigated by the fact that it is devoted to praise itself), the Stranger said:

> On the other hand, of those things which such people do unjustly, but that are curable, it's in the first place necessary to understand that every unjust man is not willingly unjust; for no one would anywhere any (*oudeis oudamou ouden*) of the greatest bad things ever willingly take possession, least of all into his own most honorable things. But soul, as we said, is in truth the most honorable thing for everyone; therefore no one would ever willingly take the greatest bad thing into what is most honorable, and live the rest of his life possessing it. Thus the unjust man and the possessor of bad things is entirely pitiable, and it is permissible to pity him if what he possesses is curable. . . . (731c1–d2)[25]

It may be noted that it is precisely this innocuous defense in Book 5, with its repeated (and repetitive) appeal to ownership and honor,[26] that Nietzsche so cuttingly calls "Socratism" (*Sokratismus*—n.b. *not* "Socrates"), and places at the heart of virtually "every utilitarian morality": "This way of reasoning smells of the *mob*," Nietzsche writes, "which sees in bad behavior only its disagreeable consequences and actually judges 'it is *stupid* to act badly'; while it takes 'good' without further ado to be identical with 'useful and pleasant'" (*Beyond Good and Evil* §190, Nietzsche's emphases; trans. Hollingdale). And indeed, Nietzsche's analysis is very much to the point, so long as one recognizes that the Stranger's initial defense of his principle in Book 5 is *intentionally* unobjectionable *to Kleinias*, and is for that reason put in terms that *he* would not disagree with immediately (cf. also 728b2–c2, 733e–734b). It is Plato's deliberate presentation of how that principle might be introduced to someone like Kleinias (who would certainly take offense were he to be overtly considered part of "the mob") without causing initial offense. The deeper psychological elaboration of the same principle—with its discussion of "tyranny in the soul"—would certainly offend Kleinias at this early point, before he has fully confronted the fact of tyranny in his own soul, a failing for which he is not averse to some clemency.

In Book 9, moreover, it will be precisely in immediate relation to the actually *criminal* love of money that the Stranger expounds at most length, and most directly, upon his true principle. Indeed, he quite deliberately—and idiosyncratically—intrudes the crime of theft into the conversation there specifically in order to address his principle, which applies equally to all injustice, to that crime in particular, and with Kleinias in particular (on which more below).

This is by no means the only instance in the *Laws* in which the timing and circumstances of a statement of principle on the Stranger's part in itself gesture mightily toward the profound conflict—and mutual dependency—between the lawgiver's lack of indignation and the expected serious indignation of the citizens of Magnesia. We may illustrate a related instance with the "preamble" that shifts the focus from homicide to "woundings" (*traumata*) in Book 9 (874e8–875d6). As Saunders (1991) notes, "[t]his preamble has little specific relevance to wounding: it could be attached to any part of the code"

(258). Yet Saunders does not go on to ask *why* the Stranger did not speak of it previously, given that, as a principle, it evidently applies in principle to all of criminal law (at least): "The concluding reflection is that law and regulation cannot provide for every individual case, but must express general principles" (258). Why then did the Stranger not attach this "preamble" to the previous crimes discussed, and their respective punishments—temple robbery (always capital), fomenting civil war (always capital), treason (always capital), and homicide (often but not always capital, but with no real discretion left to the magistrates regarding penalty) (853e–857a, 864c–874d)? Is it not perhaps because it is likely that the expression of doubt and hesitancy about what the law is and is not capable of seeing would be anathema to the indignation provoked by the crimes that are experienced as most severe? Just as the Stranger's vehement defense of the true principle that no one is willingly unjust might find a hearing in the *outrageously* out of place discussion of penal law for theft, but could not possibly be reasonably expected to be entertained during discussion of the penal law for homicide (864c9–10, 865a1–3)?[27]

This, then, is the quandary that the Stranger faces: he must at one and the same time both foster and direct the moral indignation of Kleinias, as a citizen, according to the disposition or regime of Magnesia; and attempt to provide Megillos, as lawgiver, with the guidance he needs to overcome for himself the remnants of his own indignation. But this must be accomplished with exceptional care and subtlety for the following reason among others: the disposition of moral indignation is not inclined to view a lack of indignation about human injustice as a morally acceptable alternative to its own certainty about and condemnation of injustices and the causes from which they appear to derive, a conclusion that modern research on moral outrage and indignation both supports and amplifies (e.g., see Rothschild and Keefer 2017).[28] Indeed, were the indignant disposition sanguine about the option of non-indignation in others concerning the specific injustices it perceives, it would by that fact alone already be on its way to becoming less indignant itself. The complete lack of indignation of the lawgiver as such, if perceived in its entirety by the Kleinias-type, would entail one of two things, or perhaps both. Either it would mark his or her laws as somehow unworthy of the sacred attachment of indignation-disposed citizens, and thus lead to the neglect of those laws or their spirit, or it would mark the lawgiver as a deserving target of indignation. The Stranger's task is a fraught one.

The last two chapters will examine in considerable detail how he approaches this task, with respect to a specific aspect of the laws: the erotic regime at the heart of Magnesian familial and social interaction. In order to see how the Stranger accomplishes his purpose, we will need to look closely at the images he deploys in pursuing it—of animal sexual behavior and the incest prohibition in particular—and at the very different ways in which

Kleinias and Megillos respectively interact with those images and the opinions they depend upon, and at the thoughtfulness they might provoke.

NOTES

1. The extent to which the type of person who *wants* to rule others is a problem of very great proportions is captured succinctly by Thomas More (2003), with the simple and absolute rule of the Utopians given in the second Book of his *Utopia*: "Any man who campaigns for a public office is disqualified for all of them" (82; cf. More's discussion, in the prefatory pseudo-Letter, of the "devout man and a professor of theology" who has campaigned to be named bishop of Utopia [5]—that the would-be bishop's ambition is, according to himself, "holy" and deriving from "piety," rather than done for "glory or gain," would not avail him with the Utopians). Needless to say, in all non-Utopian scenarios (i.e., in all actual political life), the problem is not so neatly done away with, and indeed such people are necessary. Raphael's utter refusal of and contempt for holding office is subtly presented by More as "utopian" self-righteousness, a self-righteousness—and a utopianism—that More himself eschews (12–14, cf. with 3–4).

2. I have deleted "of which" after "that Socrates speaks of and that" in the sentence, which I assume to be a typographical error.

3. Even where one might be inclined to see Socrates indignant, close reading and consideration reveal that the texts simply do not support such an image. For example, when Socrates speaks to those who have condemned him to die (*Apology* 38c1–5), he of course notes that others will blame (*oneidizein*) them—but this is merely acknowledging what others are bound to do, and in no way means that Socrates himself blames those jurists. Socrates uses reproach (*oneidizein*) only as instructive—as exhortative to self-reflection (*Apology* 41e1–42a2; cf. *Laws* 730b). A person who does not and cannot blame others for their "errors" is by definition incapable of indignation.

4. I will address the supposed manuscript problems that some editors have suspected in 832a11–b3 and b5–6 when I examine these passages at length in chapter 5.

5. As an aside, I do not think that Schöpsdau's informal or familiar "*ihr*" is suitable for translating the Stranger's quite formal or unfamiliar way of addressing these "strangers" here (nor is *Gastfreunde* [guest-friends] for the Stranger's *xenoi* when *Fremder* [foreigner] is then immediately used to translate Kleinias's *xenos* in response). *Sie*, not *ihr*, is called for—*ihr* implies a level of familiarity that renders the Stranger's "strangers" completely ironic from the outset, without substantiation. The movement between the three characters from formal/unfamiliar to informal/familiar address (and sometimes back and forth again) is important to consider in the *Laws*.

6. Note that *aitia* itself can mean either credit *or* blame, depending on context.

7. Minos's most prominent action in Athenian myth was his demand for human sacrifices from Athens "every ninth year," for the Minotaur to devour in Daedalos's labyrinth.

8. Maffi (2007) questions whether this might actually be "a *hapax* [only existing example] in the judicial context" (214; my translation). I for one can find no other examples, and suspect that Maffi is correct. "Distributing" (or "apportioning" or "dividing") is a normal Greek way of referring to penalties, to fate, even to music—in the Greek imagination, one receives one's "portion" of all of these. But it makes little sense in terms of "judicial affairs" in general.

9. Cf. *Minos* 318d7–8, especially *hôn hoide eisin hoi nomoi*—"These laws are theirs." This is not negligible.

10. "*Sin perfecionar las leyes / Perfecionan el rigor,*" says Fierro's son in *La Vuelta de Martín Fierro*: "Without perfecting the laws, / they perfect the punishment" (Hernández 1974, II.12.4143–4; my translation). Cf. Aeschylus, *Eumenides* 986: " . . . and [may they] hate with a single heart."

11. It is worth hearing Strauss (1975) at length on this: "In the concluding section of the prelude, the Athenian is completely silent on the pleasant character of justice. But in the statement on the poets' speeches [660d1–663e2] he had proved the pleasant character of justice

only by referring to the fame and praise from men and gods which attend justice, while in the present statement he is concerned with pleasure in contradistinction to good repute; he is now concerned only with that pleasure which men derive from their virtues, even if others are wholly unaware of these virtues; he is concerned only with the pleasures which are, strictly speaking, natural" (71).

12. Ficino uses *animus* rather than *anima* for "soul," which more usually means "mind" or "spirit."

13. This is one of the principal reasons that, within the drama of the *Laws*, the Stranger dictates that the conversation that transpires in the *Laws* is to be preserved in writing as the city of Magnesia's "canonical school-text" (Picht 1990, 31–37, my translation; 811b–812a), and is thus to be read by all citizens, and by some people time and time again (891a, 957d). What is more, as Wieland (1982) elaborates, "the discussion carried on in the *Laws* is itself [also] a model for literature, which is to be used as a basis for teaching the youth" (93; my translation).

14. What Brann (2004) writes of the *Republic* is equally true of the *Laws* (and all Platonic dialogues): "As so often in the *Republic*, the conversation makes its own mode the object of reflection" (160).

15. This by way of dispensing with the characterization of all such attention as "Straussian," for example. I do not pretend to be without indignation myself, though I hope that I have profited at least somewhat from the self-scrutiny—which is at times excruciating and even humiliating—necessary for any intimate access to the Platonic dialogues (cf. *Laches* 187e6–188c3). Rome being neither built nor burnt in a day, however, I have certainly not purged myself of all or even most of the flaws in myself that I can recognize. And I am weary of—and occasionally also indignant about—hearing the unsupported assertions that are regurgitated about Leo Strauss—about his "method" and his supposed politics—and the *reductio ad Straussem* in general. *Mea culpa.*

16. One may consider here the presence of indignation (*nemesis*) as a virtue in Book 2 of Aristotle's *Nicomachean Ethics*, and its absence in Book 4. As Burger (2008) notes: "Whatever intention, if any, may lie behind the disappearance of *nemesis* from Book IV, the effect of its absence is powerful: had it not been eliminated, righteous indignation would have occupied the culminating position in the discussion of virtues of character and cast the shadow of its underlying assumptions on the set as a whole. Instead, the discussion ends with a reference to the equitable person, anticipating the account of equity at the end of Book V; and that account occupies the culminating position in the discussion of ethical virtue as a whole, on its way into being absorbed as *phronêsis*" (92).

17. I borrow the translation of Saunders and Pangle here, though there is no happy English translation for *kinountoi*, which literally means "movers." There is a strong negative connotation to the word in general, for Athenians, which is partly captured by this translation.

18. "Evil" is almost unavoidable as a translation of *kakon* here (and in many other instances), and is in a certain sense correct: Kleinias almost surely hears something like the connotations of what in modern English is indicated by "evil." But it must be kept in mind that it also simply means "bad," and it is this word that I have been translating as such above. It is implied in the Stranger's very comportment toward the "bad" that there is in fact no human "evil."

19. Dostoevsky wrote repeatedly in his journals, regarding his novel *Demons*, that "Stavrogin is *everything*." Substituting Oedipus for Stavrogin, we could say that "Oedipus is *everything*."

20. Nietzsche, who famously has much to say about "*bad* conscience"(in the *Genealogy of Morality* in particular), is certainly equally if not more interested in the danger and harm—but also the necessity—of the "prison" of *good* conscience as well. It should be noted that it is precisely at the point when Zarathustra's own indignation and condemnation of "the good and the righteous" reaches a fever pitch ("Disgust, disgust, disgust!" he screams), that he collapses "like a dead man and lay . . . like one dead" for seven days (*TSZ* 3.13). In the originally planned three books of *Thus Spoke Zarathustra*, this is deliberately evocative of Matthew's account of Christ in the desert: "the great loathing for the human being"—Zarathustra's own condemnation of the all-too-small condemners, which is like a snake or monster that "crawled into [his] throat and choked [him]"—is the "last temptation" of Zarathustra. Had he been unable to

overcome it, he would have been no more than that which he condemned, and no more capable of transcending himself than Jesus would have been had he accepted the mere kingdom of the world (Matthew 4:8–11; in Luke 4:5–8, this is the second temptation of Christ, not the last).

21. It may be helpful or necessary here to think in terms of what has come to be called "aesthetic" judgment. Judging what is beautiful or not beautiful is an experience that virtually everyone has of judging without blame.

22. There is a typographical error of considerable consequence in Bloom's translation of the *Republic*, at 329d2–3. As it stands, Bloom's translation has Kephalos's statement there as "But of these things and of those that concern relatives, there is one *just* cause. . . ." (Plato 1991, 4; my emphasis). The Greek in fact does not have the word *dikaiôs* ("just") here: Kephalos speaks not of "*one just* cause," but of "*just one* cause" (*mia tis aitia*) at 329d2–3. The difference is quite crucial: it is of the utmost importance that Kephalos does not *ever* discuss, in his own name, what he thinks about justice in any other terms than *in*justice, and indeed in any other terms than particular unjust *deeds* (330d8, e5, e6, 331a1; and cf. 331b1–4). The *single* time that he uses the word "just" is to describe what *Pindar* said, and in doing so he does not notice at all the discrepancy between Pindar describing a "*just* and pious *life*" (331a4), and his own exclusive obsession with perhaps having committed some *un*just (or impious) *deed*. What Kephalos does not notice, however, Plato's reader must definitely notice. Kephalos's imagination of justice is informed exclusively by his experiential reaction (real or anticipatory) to what he is morally certain are unjust deeds, an exclusivity that wholly eliminates the possibility, for him, of even imagining a standard outside of that experience of certainty by which the truth of that certainty could be evaluated (he could never ask himself, "What is justice?"). Because he is unaware of this as a problem, though, he is not prevented by it from holding himself to be very certain about what justice is (cf. *Alcibiades Major* 110a–c). This is exactly the comportment of moral indignation, which in Kephalos's case is presented as turned upon himself.

23. Numbers in square brackets convert the line numbers of the edition used by Strauss (I am not sure whether this is Burnet's or Bury's) to those of the Diès and Des Places edition.

24. The problem here is not that Kleinias lacks a Nathan to tell him, "*You* are that man." He has one (he may even have two). The problem is that Kleinias is not a David who can hear it or bear it.

25. I have translated both *echô* and the perfect of *ktaomai* as "possess" here. With apologies for its impact on readability, my translation here is hyperliteral, in the interest of drawing out, on the one hand, the Stranger's emphatic appeal to possession and honor, and, on the other, his striking emphasis on the absolute applicability of his principle in each and every case—thus his "*oudeis oudamou ouden . . . pote*," for example: "no one, nowhere, nothing . . . ever" (Greek frequently uses the double—or triple—negative in a way that compounds rather than negates the negative, which limits the extent to which the Stranger's emphasis can be conveyed in English translation). What is presented here under the rubric of curable injustices as against incurable injustices in fact, by virtue of that absolute applicability, obviously applies to "incurables" as well (as the Stranger makes quite clear when he embarks upon the subject again at 860d1–2). "Incurable" injustice may be incurable just because it invites "relentless punishing." Certainly it is the injustices, and *not* the unjust person, that are classified as "incurable" here (*pace* Pangle 1988, 456)—the Stranger uses exclusively the neuter plural indicating unjust *things*, rather than the masculine or feminine unjust *person*, and repeats that neuter indication seven times in four lines (731b4–7; cf. 854b1–5, and *Euthyphro* 6e11–7a1 with 7a7–10; and my comments above on the "good things" that need be praised along with the "great man in the city"). If we are given to understand this specific image, it is one of incurable *injustices* and curable unjust *people* (which is not at all to deny that the Stranger does indeed conceive of some people as incurable—e.g., 853c8–d4). One may consider here the unfortunately many and various grotesquely brutal atrocities of the twentieth century, and ask ourselves whether their horror as *events* does not have something that is independent in our imaginations from our horror at any particular participant whom we hold to be an "agent" thereof. An ambiguity in the Greek should be noted: the word that I have translated "honorable" (three times in this passage) is *timios*, which can mean either "honor*able*" or "honor*ed*." The importance of this ambiguity—and its impact on how Kleinias interprets the Stranger's comments—becomes clear when we consider that it is not uncommon for people to honor most what is not necessarily most

honorable (727d6–7), and conversely—or therefore—may not honor most or even at all what is most honorable (727e1–3). Moreover, it is almost certain that the Stranger and Kleinias do not agree about what is most honorable (cf. 728c6–8 and d4–6 and context), to say nothing of the fact that there is a great difference between holding something to be honorable in opinion or speech, and actually honoring it in deed (689a5–c3).

26. In the discussion of the principle in Book 9, the only thing referred to as a "possession" is spiritedness (863b4), which in the Stranger's comments in Book 5 is remarked upon (as necessary) only outside of the principle, and at least formally as preceding it. Honor is not mentioned *at all* in the later discussion. As a "possession," I am intrigued by Ritter's emendation that would have the Stranger classify the form of error due to spiritedness as *luttê* (madness, frenzy) rather than *lupê* (pain) at 864b3 (see Post 1939, 100, for discussion), but cf. *Philebus* 40d–e. It may well be Plato's point that there is an experiential "slippage" that can be gestured at in Greek here: especially to the eye (ΛΥΠΗ / ΛΥΤΤΗ), but also somewhat to the ear, the two words were close to each other in ancient Greek, and Plato elsewhere makes it quite clear that he orchestrates important plays on such words (e.g., *ê* or *ei* at *Apology of Socrates* 42a4?—the MSS are divided for good reason on this point). There is moreover sound reason to think of spiritedness that is inclined to injure someone as both resulting from "pain," and driven to "madness." This may be a singularly appropriate passage about which it is fitting to say that our quarrel is not about phrases or names, but about what is (864a8–b1; cf. 627d1–4, 644a6, 710a5–6). It seems likely that Plato, for good reason, was not particularly interested in any decisive categorical correspondence between the various *images* of *n*–partite souls he presents in his dialogues, and what soul *is*. Pangle (1988) highlights an aspect of this very well: "In the manifold mystery that is the soul, the 'parts' are not distinguished by sharp boundary lines, any more than are the four forms of virtue or the forms of the various regimes" (454, citing 878b with 681d and 714b).

27. The Stranger begins his "digression" on his true principle (that no one is willingly unjust) after embarking on legislating the penal law for *theft*. When he returns to "legislating" after that discussion, he does so by saying that they should go back to where they were before digressing (864c9–10). Instead of returning to theft, however, the Stranger returns to the first three always-capital crimes discussed, and provides a measure of *leniency*. He then turns to *homicide*, not theft, immediately (865a1–3). His turn to theft was only to allow a hearing for his principle.

28. I thank Travis Smith for drawing my attention to this excellent article on the mutual implication of moral outrage, moral guilt, and moral identity. According to the research of Rothschild and Keefer, moral indignation is to a great extent bound up in the suppression of one's own perceived moral guilt, and the desire to participate in and establish a common moral identity with one's community, *just by* perceiving one's own moral outrage as an "altruistic" demand for justice (whether as retribution or restoration). Plato would agree completely.

Chapter Five

Nature

For in truth custom is a violent and treacherous schoolmistress. She establishes in us, little by little, covertly, the base of her authority: but by this soft and humble beginning, having matured and implanted it with the help of time, she soon reveals to us a furious and tyrannical face, against which we no longer have the liberty to raise even our eyes. We see her force, in every instance, the rules of nature [*Nous luy voyons forcer, tous les coups, les reigles de nature*].

—Montaigne, *Essais* I.23
"De la coustume, et de ne changer aisément une loy receüe"

Regardless of its original provenance, the distinction between nature and convention (or law) has for many centuries been—whether accepted or rejected—a conventional one for almost any heir or partial heir to the Greek tradition,[1] and as such requires examination as a necessary preliminary to inquiry into what has come to be called natural right or natural rights or rights simply. The quandary might be put, perhaps over simply, as such: is the distinction between nature and convention a natural or a conventional distinction? As Plato knew and illustrated, careful inquiry into this question entails its own particular consequences, but we do not and cannot avoid all of the consequences of the assumptions that would be brought to light in such an inquiry, by avoiding that inquiry. Plato's *Laws* might accurately be termed the Ur-text for the moral and judicial authority of natural right (a claim to be substantiated by the analysis thereof, not assumed to begin with), and Book 8 of the *Laws* specifically and subtly brings the double-edged nature of that authority to the fore, even as it cements that authority, by doing so.

At the outset of the Book 8 of the *Laws*, the twelfth month of the year—Scirophorion, or Pluto's month (though obviously not "the silver Pluto, or the gold"; 801b6)[2]—is devoted by the Stranger to the "chthonic rites" for the chthonic gods, which rites are to be kept strictly separate from the rites for the gods whom "one must call (*eponomasteon*] heavenly" (828c6–d6; cf. 717a6–b2).[3] The twelfth month is therefore devoted to the rites and gods of the earth and under the earth, or to the ground from which things grow (*phuein*) and to which, in growing, they return. The conversation that comprises the *Laws*, which is to be preserved in writing as the city of Magnesia's "canonical school-text" (Picht 1990, 31–37, my trans.; 811b–812a)[4] and is thus to be read by all citizens, and by some people time and time again (891a, 957d), and in which this devotion of the twelfth month to the gods of nature, or natural gods, occurs, takes place itself at the end of the twelfth month of the year (683b7–c5; Benardete 2000, 232). The *Laws* is then, in a sense, self-consecrated to the divinity of nature (*phusis*), though the rites and festivals by which this consecration is accomplished are devoted symbolically only toward death and dissolution (828d2–5, 955e5–8). The surface of the practice conceals what engagement or depth in the practice is intended to reveal, just as the practice of excessively drinking wine in the "symposium in speech" in Books 1 and 2 was directed toward sobriety and moderation.

The arrangement or plan of Book 8 can be seen at first glance under the rubric of nature real and imagined.[5] The final subject, the unlimited desire for and pursuit of wealth, is one that appears "natural" to those in its possession. Yet at the same time it is *the* paradigmatic conventional desire—money is convention as such. Likewise one of the most puzzling intervening subjects (puzzling in the sense of why and how and when it is introduced), the prohibition against incest, appears "natural" to virtually everyone, regardless of their particular political situation, yet the Stranger's "archaeology" of the nonpolitical (i.e., post- and prepolitical) society in Book 3 illustrates not only the absence of the incest prohibition in such situations, but its impossibility. What is more, there is no parallel for this unwritten law in any other species on earth, yet images of animal "nature" seem to be *the* guiding examples of sexual desire and behavior by which the Stranger orients his overarching program for the erotic regime of the city: the greatest possible elimination of sexual activity that is not monogamous, heterosexual, and for the purpose of producing children, with a particular focus on the elimination of *paederasteia* and homosexuality in general, practices for which the men of Crete are famous.

The relationship of appearance and "image" to what is thus seems itself to be the theme of Book 8. Bound up in this theme is the question of what an image is, and how and why images are necessary and useful. It may be worthwhile to first consider this generally, before turning to the specific images of nature advanced by the Stranger, and their contexts.

Images

In Book 4 of the *Republic*, Socrates pulls up the conversation he is having with Glaukon to remind him that the image of "one man, one job" is inaccurate, but that is precisely *why* it is helpful (*di' ho kai ôphelei*) (*Rep.* 443c4). It is not the "outer" (*exô*) but the "inner" (*entos*) practices that are the truth of this image—not a cobbler working on nothing but shoes, and a carpenter on nothing but houses, but each human being working on his or her own soul (*Rep.* 443c–e). And indeed, the very image of the soul as tripartite is also such an inaccurate and therefore helpful one (*Rep.* 443d7–8, 435c9–d4; cf. the myth of the four-part soul in the *Phaedrus* 246a–249d: winged chariot [this part is crucial, though almost always ignored], charioteer, dark horse, and light horse). *All* rituals and practices, particularly those designed for children (Al-Farabi, *Summary* 2.1), enact such helpful (or unhelpful) images, and produce dispositional images within both those who observe and those who enact them.[6] As Al-Farabi puts it:

> [A] human being either forms a concept of the principles of the beings, their rankings, happiness, and the rulership of the virtuous cities and intellects them, or imagines them. To form a concept of them is to have their essences sketched in the human soul as they exist in truth. To imagine them is to have their images, their likenesses, and the objects representing them sketched in the human soul. That is similar to what is possible with objects that are seen—for example, a human being. Either we see him himself, we see a statue of him, we see an image of him in water, or we see an image of his statue in water or in other mirrors.[7] (*Political Regime* §89; 2011, 45)

In this regard, we may recall that it was Megillos who brought in the importance of educative practices in the Spartan laws (633b–c). As we saw, Kleinias assumed a single, accessible, and final lesson as the immediate and continual teaching of the laws: because their images are observable to him largely as static, their character *as images* is not something that he is likely to notice, much less adequately reflect upon. It is improbable that he can be brought to see law in general as being differently disposed than this, regardless if he can be brought to see that the lessons themselves must be different than he originally imagined. Where Megillos looks to the manifold unfolding of practices over time, Kleinias interprets the immediate as the eternal, or as what ought to be. He does not perceive the subtle transformations that practices in general have on people's characters as they grow or develop, because he is largely blind to the transformations he has undergone himself.[8] The validity of an image must seem immediately apparent to him as complete in itself, its evocation corresponding fully and at once to what it signifies. The short and near road is "entirely long enough" for Kleinias (625b1–2), and not for him is the long road, or the far (*Laws* 683b–c; *Republic* 435c–d, 504b–d,

532e–533a; *Timaeus* 29b–d; *Sophist* 253d–254b). It is for Kleinias's sake that the Stranger does not say of his images, in the *Laws*, what Socrates says explicitly of his image of the tripartite soul in the *Republic*: "Know well, Glaukon, that in my opinion, with the modes (*methodôn*) we are using in the discussion now, we will never grasp the thing precisely; for the road that leads to it is a longer road, and hard" (*Rep.* 435c9–d3; cf. Dante, *Inferno* 34.95: "*la via è lunga e 'l cammino è malvagio*"). It is Megillos, not Kleinias, who is compelled toward the longer road (cf. 683c3–4), and one of the lessons of the longer and harder road seems to be discretion upon the shorter.

It is therefore for citizens and rulers such as Kleinias that the image of "one person, one job" must be seen and lived not with the understanding that it is merely a phantom image (*eidôlon*) of justice—as it is discussed by Socrates with Glaukon in the *Republic*—but with the belief that it *is* justice (846d–847b; cf. 918c–d, 919c6–d3). No native of Magnesia, nor any servant of any native-born man, is to practice any art other than "preserving and possessing the common order of the city" (846d5–6). Only strangers (foreigners and resident aliens) are permitted to be carpenters, smiths, and so forth, and if someone among them practices two such arts the City Regulators must "reprove him with fetters and fines and expulsions from the city, forcing him to be one only, instead of many" (847a7–b2). This image is therefore to bear fruit as a lived and living image in the "external" (*exô*) daily life of Magnesia, enacted by all of her inhabitants, and it is as such that it may turn some of them toward their own "internal" (*entos*) affairs (cf. *Rep.* 443c10–d1). The image in speech is an image of the image in deed.

It might of course be objected that the Stranger is not necessarily Socrates, and cannot be presumed to be aware of the latter's insight into the greater importance of the internal meaning of "doing one's own things" (thus Zuckert 2004, 379).[9] But the Stranger has, from the outset of the *Laws*, continually drawn the conversation from the "external" to the "internal," stressing above all the need for inner concord in soul and body (which he numbers among "the greatest of human things"—688c7–8) and the supreme dangers that the lack thereof pose to the city and man (688c–689e). But law cannot compel people to turn their attention and devotion to "their own" in the internal sense. It must use the external in ways that might lead them to do this themselves, sometimes unbeknownst to them, and law—all law—ultimately depends on at least minimal success in this regard (689d8–e1, 857e3–6, 870e3–871a1, 874d2–5, 880d8–e6, 957c3–958a3).[10]

What we should note here, then, is that the Stranger in the *Laws* is far more concerned to use images for *what* they do, than to discuss the subtleties of *how* they do it (as Socrates does throughout the *Republic*). But knowledge of the latter is obviously implied by his subtle use.[11] We must keep this in mind as we turn to the "erotic regime" and *its* images. And we should not expect every image to be identical in kind.

Nor, I think, should we assume from the outset that we know or fully know what any given image is intended to be an image *of*, and then devote ourselves only to discerning whether or not it is adequate for that purpose. Since it is the task of an image to gesture beyond itself to something that is, presumably, to the author's mind most adequately expressed or gestured at with an image for his purposes, there is good reason to at least provisionally assume that we do not know from the outset what exactly is being evoked with an image. Rather than restricting our reflection, then, to assessing an adequacy that we strictly speaking cannot assess at the outset, we ought also at every point ask ourselves what a particular image *is* adequate for. It is with this in mind that we turn to the Stranger's most pointed and perhaps peculiar images of nature in Book 8 of the *Laws*.

Images of Animal Behavior

An image of nature, unless it is super-natural (e.g., "the art of God"), is almost by necessity an image of a particular thing's place in nature as a part in the whole. The Stranger's rhetoric with respect to sexual desire and behavior, about what does and does not accord with nature, is based in the *Laws* on examples of behaviors of other species of animals (636b5, c3, c4, c5–6, 836c4, c5–6, 840d–e), from which he draws for his interlocutors basic natural principles for human behavior. As tendentious as those examples themselves are (which the Stranger is aware of—he clearly backtracks after suggesting that *all* animals by nature are monogamous, heterosexual, and have sexual intercourse [only?] for purposes of reproduction—cf. 836c4 and 838e6 with 840d4), the Stranger does not offer even a tendentious example in "the nature of beasts" for observance of an incest prohibition. [12] Since by the Stranger's own definition animals (or most animals, or at any rate many animals) select their partners according—aside from "natural" monogamous, heterosexual, and reproductive desires—only to what they find pleasing (*kata charin*—840d7), it would indeed be difficult to derive a "natural" incest prohibition for human beings from "the nature of beasts" (cf. 713d). And in fact, in his *Clouds*, Aristophanes had shown the very image of animal behavior that the Stranger deploys to be a highly permissive, rather than a restrictive one, justifying (according to his character Pheidippides) a son beating his parents, and with the strong implication that it would therefore justify incest (*Clouds* 1427–1432; cf. Strauss 1966, 42–43). What is going on here? [13]

We should note from the outset—and precisely because we are given to considering what a particular image *is* adequate for, in addition to considering its analogical and anagogical adequacy for what it appears to be of at the outset—that the examples of animal behavior entail the following difficulty: as the Stranger's own statements on what is indicated by those examples show, they are open to very broad interpretations, and can lend themselves to many ends. If the reproductive patterns of birds or bees, for example, are to be imitated by human beings as "according to nature" (636b5), why not also their hierarchies and "government" (cf. Calvin, *Institutes* 4.6.8)? The Stranger's own opening statement on the subject seems considerably broader than he knows the facts permit: whatever the implications might be for "natural" human behavior, it is not true—and the Stranger knows it is not true—that it is universal "animal nature" to be monogamous, heterosexual, and have sexual intercourse [only?] for purposes of reproduction (cf. 636b–d, 836c4 and 838e6 with 840d4). Indeed, the very hyperbole with which he celebrates the nature of "*many* [not *all*] birds and other animals" shows how given to excess his procedure is: the Stranger praises the "pure and chaste" lives of these animal "bachelors" during the time before the time comes to breed children, their heterosexual pairings—"according to pleasure"—at the appropriate time, and the "pious and just" life they monogamously lead together all of the rest of their lives, "cleaving securely to their first agreements of friendship": purity, chastity, and friendship precede piety and justice (840d4–e2). Which "many birds and other animals" could the Stranger possibly have in mind? And why does what the "many" do have such significance for human nobility, which is typically the provenance of the few? For in the final analysis, imitation of these animal examples is not explicitly advocated, but instead the Stranger appeals to the human respect for honor—a quality that he does not suggest any other animal species shares in[14] —in saying that the citizens of Magnesia must not be "worse" (*cheirous*) than these many other species (840d3–4), and indeed that they "need be better (*ameinous*) than the animals, at any rate" (840e2; the explicit theme is not restricted to Book 8: 814b, 824b, 875a, 963e).

It should remarked as well that within an earlier discussion of imitation and image-making, in Book 2, the Stranger had called attention to precisely the problem involved in simply conflating human and animal "rhythms." Favorably casting the Muses against human poets, the Stranger noted:

> . . . nor would they [the Muses] ever elide the sounds of animals and humans and instruments and every kind of noise, as if imitating some one thing. But human poets, by vehemently interweaving and confusing such things, absurdly, would provide a laugh for those human beings who, as Orpheus says, "are allotted the season of delight." For they see that these are entirely confused. . . . (669c8–d6)

This is obviously not the Stranger's, or Plato's, last word on the subject (cf., for example, 765e–766a, 808d–e, and 759a3–4 with 713d), nor is it free of ambiguity itself (is such elision only laughable to certain people, presumably adolescents?), but it is nevertheless important that the Stranger calls attention to the problem of easily and vehemently eliding animal and human "sounds"—the sounds that in music signify behaviors. And he does so well in advance of what seems to be his own easy and vehement elision of animal and human behavior.

What the Stranger in fact shows is that in correcting the standard of the gods as arbitrary with the standard of gods bound by nature, the standard of nature becomes as susceptible to justificatory myth-making as the standard of arbitrary gods (*Phaedrus* 229b–d). Or is it available as a standard just because it can be put in the service of justification? We should recall here the Stranger's accusation, concerning precisely the topic in question here, *paiderasteia*, that the Cretans had invented the myth of Ganymede in order to indulge it (636c–d; cf. Megillos on the Dionysia, 637b1–2): it is intentionally mirrored here.

It would not be controversial to say that the standard of nature is a standard of what is in principle observable. That something is in principle observable does not mean that all people will observe it, or be inclined to try. Observation—of nature, of artifacts, and even of old and new books—is as much a matter of character or "music of the soul" as it is of the senses, intellect, reason, and passions. It is telling that Kleinias, though he resists all change to the erotic regime with which he is familiar, raises no objection to the Stranger's hyperbolically anthropomorphic description of "nature"; whereas Megillos, with his characteristic subtlety, makes his own resistance to the Stranger's hyperbole clear to the latter when they engage each other on the subject of friendship, eros, and incest. As Locke noted, "reason, which is [the law of nature], teaches all mankind *who will but consult it*" (*Second Treatise* §6, my emphasis; Locke 2005, 19).[15] As we have seen in chapter 2, careful observation and consideration reveals that Kleinias is not a student of nature in Locke's sense.

In this respect, it should be noted that, with Kleinias in the position of immediate political power, the sexual laws do not in fact change (an important fact that we will need to return to). Like the common messes that received such critical attention in Books 1 and 2, and then are left more or less as they already were (842b), the erotic regime remains essentially as is. The proposal of the Stranger is strikingly similar to contemporary Athenian practices, and Kleinias anyway defers his decision about this indefinitely (842a). It could seem, then, that the entire point of the almost comical images of nature the Stranger uses in order to attempt to curb homosexual practices is to illustrate more the nature of an image than an image of nature. And by illustrating this even as much as he does, the image fails in its purpose, a failure that is one of the deeper lessons that the discussion is designed to teach Megillos—or, better, one of the deeper lessons that Megillos may learn. That homosexual practices could be selected as an area in which failure could not only be risked, but anticipated with deliberation, indicates of what little importance homosexuality is, *per se*, for the Stranger.

Nussbaum (1994, 1543 *inter alia*) is therefore correct that not homosexuality, but immoderation, is the target of the Stranger's efforts here (see especially 836a7–b3), in the same way that love of money is a target (835e5–836a2), though the latter is clearly a *much* bigger problem in the *Laws*. It may be remembered that for the guardians or auxiliaries of Beauticity (*Kallipolis*), among whom moderation is wished and prayed for as a whole way of character and of life, homosexuality and heterosexuality are not even separate issues (other than the breeding of children, of course), and can be equally indulged—even used as an incentive for valor in battle—provided, for *both*, that it is with *sôphrosunê* (*Rep.* 402e–403c, 468b–c).

But we can go further. While it is obviously true that the Stranger and Megillos hold moderation in sexual desires and practices to be civically necessary in general, and the Cretan regime no perfect instantiation thereof, the immoderation of Cretan *paiderasteia* is already sufficiently moderate to be civically acceptable. Kleinias defers his decision on whether or not to accept the Stranger's law(s) governing sexual practices for the colony, and never does get back to it (842a7–9). Given the reticence Kleinias has already shown to accepting any change in this regard (cf. 837e5–6), it seems reasonable to assume that he never will, and that the laws that *he* will write—with the nine other Cretan statesmen—will contain none of the Stranger's recommendations on this issue. But regardless if this supposition is true or not, what we can observe without supposing is that neither the Stranger nor Megillos will later return to Kleinias for his answer. *They* are satisfied to leave the erotic regime of the Cretans[16] essentially intact, just as they are satisfied to leave the common messes intact that were accused of giving rise to immoderate *paiderasteia* in the first place (842b, especially *kai gar nun emmelôs echein kateskeuasmena*—"for they're rightly ordered now" [b8–9]; cf. 636b).[17]

And indeed we can go still further. The Stranger in fact turns to the subject of erotics to begin with because the laws of Magnesia, as examined and imagined thus far, have in the Stranger's own estimation surely *lessened* the normal "excessive and servile labors that most stifle wantonness" (835d8–e1; cf. 779a, 806d–807d). And just *after* Kleinias's refusal to assent to the proposed erotic regime, the Stranger goes on to decrease such labors *even more*, suggesting that all of the colony's citizens be forbidden to practice any of the craftsmen's arts at all (smithing, carpentry, etc.—846d1–6).[18] Citizens who nevertheless take up a craft are to be punished with "reproaches and dishonors" (847a6), just as—in the "unwritten law" that Kleinias did not accept, which is perhaps "one or two laws," and which indicated "second-best (*deuteron*) nobility and shame, and second-best (*deuteron*) correctness" in the laws—it was to be considered shameful to engage in the things of Aphrodite without awe (*aidos*) and be caught (841a–842a). The Stranger certainly does not say even once of citizens who, in this already avowedly second-best (*deuteron*—739a4, 807b6–7) city, take up craftsmen's arts, what he says once and perhaps twice of those who indulge without awe in the things of Aphrodite without being caught—that "custom, through habit and unwritten law, should let their actions be noble" (841b2–4 and e1–2; cf. 847d8–e1 with 920a3–4).[19]

The Stranger's concern with the threat that Cretan homosexual desires and practices posed to the city's legislation cannot have been as great as he seemed to indicate, if after he saw that Kleinias was unwilling to budge on them, he not only continued with his legislative proposals that he knew weakened their restraint, but compounded them with proposals that weakened that restraint still further. One reason for this is to be found in the Stranger's earlier discussion with Megillos, in which the ending of homosexual practices and desires—along with all nonprocreative sex—were imagined to clear the way for deep bonds of friendship between husband and wife (838e–839b). We may recall again here the picture of "many birds and other animals" in the image of nature that "opposes" homosexuality—along with all nonprocreative sex—in which monogamous heterosexual parents live the entirety of their sexually mature lives "cleaving securely to their first agreements of friendship" (840d4–e2). The Stranger would seem in this respect to be in agreement with many modern "conservative" complaints about the effects of such practices and desires, though he does not think those practices and desires threaten *existing* bonds of marriage. Rather they prevent marriage from *becoming* an institution of genuine friendship in the first place (consider the surprise with which Herodotus relates that Candaules "fell in love with his own wife," and the unhappy ending for Candaules—1.8.1; such love was *not* the norm in any ancient Greek society).

But his actions demonstrate a stark disagreement with those modern voices (e.g., Finnis 1994, 1997) as to the political desirability of supremely strengthened family bonds (consider, again, the myth of the original lawgiver in Book 3, who must unite many families into one political order, with 708c3–d7).[20] Like Socrates in the *Republic*, the Stranger knows that rigidly cohesive family devotion can seriously undermine the cohesion of the city. As Kochin (2002, 100–11) insightfully illustrates, rather than attempting to eradicate homosexual practices and desires, the Stranger's laws depend on them to check (and balance, as it were) the citizens' potentially immoderate love for their families. We must go beyond Kochin, however, and stress that those laws depend on them even in their present fairly moderate immoderation (780d5–8).[21] For while Kochin assumes that the common meals for women as well would actually be established (107; citing 780b and 806d–807a), thereby meeting the threat posed by private families with respect to women as well, we must note that this does not in fact happen. For in the last passage cited by Kochin (806d–807a), the establishment (*kateskeuasmena*) of common meals for both men and women, segregated and with children accompanying according to gender, is strictly hypothetical. The passage is a single sentence and is almost Thucydidean in its complexity and length, but it is entirely in the optative: that is, it is suppositional. And when the Stranger returns to the topic in Book 8, at the point where, he says, they are "now *almost* (*schedon*) there where the common messes have been ordered (*tôi kateskeuasthai*)" (842b1–2),[22] he recommends ordering them as they are now in Crete, or in Lacedaimon, or perhaps "in some third way better than either," but supposes that it is neither difficult to decide which, nor of any great moment to do so, "for they're rightly ordered (*kateskeuasmena*) now" (842b2–9). Just prior to this, the Stranger had specifically said to the Spartan and the Cretan that as far as common messes for women go, "it still doesn't seem natural to your cities" (839d2–4).

We are of course reminded by the mention of a possible "third way" of the Stranger's earlier proposal for women's common messes as well. Diès interprets the phrase as referring to the manners in which the common messes were actually financed in Crete and Sparta—by the city in the former, by each citizen in the latter (n2, *ad loc.*). But while this is doubtless evoked here, this cannot be what is meant.[23] In his next sentence, the Stranger explicitly takes up how the "arrangement (*kataskeuê*) of the way of life" in the city will provide for the common messes (842c1–2), which provides the ostensible reason for the shift to the discussion of agricultural laws—as if the sole purpose of the entire agricultural economy of the city were to support the *syssitia* (though cf. 955d5–e4, in which, incidentally, the Stranger says—as if referring to a well-known fact that requires no explanation—that the common meals will be funded by taxed contributions from each of the 5,040 households, designated specifically for that purpose. No conversations prior to or after this one-line reference elaborate).

I have been highlighting the word *kateskeuasmena* in the contexts quoted here, as this word (and its cognates) is the word the Stranger uses throughout to refer to both the "establishment" of the common messes and their "ordering" or arrangement (twice, for example, in the passage 806e–807b). Thus to a much greater degree than my translations convey, the Stranger's last statement on the subject—that the messes are "rightly ordered now"—responds to the whole establishment and order of the common messes.

The Stranger had also specifically avoided, from the outset, saying that he would address *how* or *if* common messes for women might actually be established (781d3–6). As Strauss (1975) notes, "[h]e is silent on the question of whether what he proposes is possible as distinguished from desirable: just as Socrates, while taking up the question whether the corresponding proposal is possible as distinguished from desirable, drops it immediately (*Republic* 466d6ff.)" (98). The Stranger had preceded this pointed silence on discussing *how* or *if* this were possible by stressing exactly how difficult or impossible it might be: "for nothing would be more difficult for the race of women to tolerate…it will pull back in every way from being pulled into the light by force, and greatly overpower (*kratêsei*) the lawgiver" (781c5–8). At best, he had said, given that the messes were already in place for men in Crete, and thus are not an entirely new innovation there, the Cretan women would *perhaps* (*isôs*) tolerate the "correct" argument even to be spoken "without [them] just screaming" (781d1–2, but see 707e–708d). This is, to say the least, not a high expectation of success on the Stranger's part. If we approach the question of that success with the responsibility necessary to the task at hand, we have to assume, in the absence of not just some, but of very serious indication that what is desirable is immediately likely or plausible, that it is not in fact immediately likely or possible, and that the Stranger does not expect it to be. As it stands, there is no real indication that it is immediately possible at all, and given the extreme and "overpowering" resistance he anticipates to this innovation, we should not be surprised that the Stranger takes a piece of his own earlier advice in letting it go. For while he had insisted that the city in which men and women do not practice the same things is only "around half" of what it could be (805a7), and that carefully overseeing the men while leaving the women to a life of luxury and license condemns the city to only "about half of a completely happy life" (806c6), in Book 3 he had himself reflected on how a desire for the unachievable whole can hubristically undermine the attainment of the achievable and moderate half (noting that such a desire *had* done so in the case of the mythical league of Sparta, Argos, and Messene). Quoting Hesiod—indeed, "what Hesiod most correctly said"—he had there approvingly put it that "'the half is often more than the whole' [*Works and Days* 40]. For whenever to take the whole brings ruin, but the half is measured, he held what is measured to be more than the whole, the better one than the worse" (690e1–5).[24]

If we are judging according to whether the topics discussed are to be implemented as legislation or not, then the discussion concerning the attempt to institute common messes for women is as much a failure as that concerning the attempt to legislate homosexuality and extramarital sex. Nor does the Stranger ever give any indication that he expects, with the former, to immediately succeed in this respect, nor does immediate and full institution of the activity seem to be the point—as we will return to later. The discussion concerning homosexuality and extramarital sex must be considered with this in mind. The unconvincing images of nature that the Stranger deploys, then, seem merely to be a part of a strategy that *depends* on them being unconvincing for their immediate purpose, since he is likewise—just because of the "failure" of the women's *syssitia*—depending more, not less, on the homosexual and extramarital desires and practices that those images are ostensibly intended to dissuade.[25] Such is our image of that strategy as we have explored it thus far, though we will return later to the genuine effort that the

Stranger nevertheless makes, and needs to make, to convince Kleinias that homosexuality is or ought to be shameful.

To return now, though, to a crux of the matter, we recall that the Stranger's proposal for the erotic regime is *the* "law" in the *Laws* that is clearly not approved by Kleinias. Noting this, Gonzalez (2013) insists that this means "the problem of *erôs* . . . has not only defeated a particular law, but has undermined the very foundation of the project of legislation carried out in the *Laws*" (164). Leaving aside the question of whether the *Laws* actually presents a "project of legislation," I submit that the case is precisely to the contrary: this is a very great part of the foundation of the laws. The laws would be "derailed" (to borrow another of Gonzalez's descriptions [162]), only if Kleinias were to *accept* the Stranger's "proposition," for this would indicate a lack of attachment to his paederastic proclivities and lead—were the "law" to succeed not only in being laid down, but in being effective—to broadly pervasive close and closed family attachments that undermine broader political community. The Stranger is not trying to persuade Kleinias here. He is testing him to be sure that he can *count on* him being unsusceptible to persuasion in this respect.

This of course does not mean that the Stranger is blind to the many and varied absolutely necessary foundations and benefits that—in the *certain* (and thankfully certain) absence of the arrangement of the Kallipolis (739c–e)—only the family provide for children and for the city (e.g., 773e5–774c2). But nor does his recognition of the city's need for cohesive families blind him to the danger that such cohesion thereby poses to the city (e.g., 772e6–773e4)[26]—and families need the city as much as the city needs families. Awareness that this sword and others are double-edged is one of the principal requirements of those who are to "save" the laws (770b4–771a4), and this two-sidedness (at least) of all beneficial things[27] is why such "saviors" (*sôtêres*) are necessary from the outset (769b7–770a9, 772a6–d4). We are pointed to this conclusion still further by the apparent dissonance between the images of nature the Stranger uses with Kleinias to approach the topic of homosexuality, and the images of incest and its consequences that he discusses with Megillos.

Proposals for the Erotic Regime

To begin with, we should attend to the part of what Gonzalez calls "the digression" in the *Laws* Book 8 that Gonzalez himself does not adequately attend to: the Stranger's awareness, repeatedly stressed by him from the outset, that his "law" for the erotic regime stands almost *no* chance of being even remotely acceptable to—and therefore accepted by—Kleinias and the Cretans. Gonzalez (2013) does indeed note that the Stranger advertises several very problematic difficulties here (154–56). He rightly notes that "persuasion in these matters is indeed so difficult (*peithein chalepon*, 835c1[–2]), we are told that the task properly belongs to a god" (155—square bracketed numbers modify Bury's [?] edition to that of Diès). Gonzalez proposes that on the basis of 835c4–8[9], the "man acting alone and by reason alone is evidently, if not a god in fact, as god-like as possible" (155). He then asks, "What kind of law, then, is needed here and what kind of case can be made for it by our god-like legislator?" (156).

We may agree or disagree with Gonzalez that "a man acting alone and by reason alone" is godlike (the Stranger certainly does not himself apply this term to such a daring man—and consider 713e8 with 697b1; cf. *Soph.* 176b), but regardless of our agreement or disagreement on this issue, the Stranger does not say this task can be accomplished by a godlike man. Nor does he merely say that "properly speaking" it belongs to a god. He says that it "*above all* (*malista*) belongs to a god" (835c2; cf. *Phaedrus* 246a). Gonzalez goes on to say, "Absent a god, then, we require a bold man . . ." (156), and we are inclined to agree. But we would stress the phrase "absent a god," and remember the phrase that Gonzalez himself quoted to the effect that a god was above all needed for this project. The Stranger certainly does not say that a "bold man" would necessarily or even likely be adequate to this task—to the contrary. What he says is that the bold or daring man would be speaking to "utterly corrupted souls" (*psuchais diephtharmentais*), in "opposition to the *greatest* (*megistaisin*) desires, with no human ally"; and that not only will he be trying to "enslave a certain desire that, *more than any other* (*diapherontôs*), *enslaves* (*doulomenon*) human beings," but the customs of Crete as a whole, as well as Sparta, are "with respect to erotic things, *completely* (*pantapasin*) opposed" to what he proposes (835c6, c7–8, 836b8–c1, 838d4–5; cf. 636b–d, 782d–783a, and then 783c6–7: "*Let's guard the things that have just been said in our memory; for perhaps we'll have need of them all some time*").[28] Gonzalez is assuming that the Stranger *must* think himself to be in possession of some human remedy—must think therefore that there *is* a human remedy—for the malady that he is addressing, and thus Gonzalez makes his own enthymeme into a purported syllogism. In fact, though, the Stranger is frankly acknowledging from the outset that his proposals are beyond human power to enact.

In other words, when we look at what the Stranger actually says before his proposals for the erotic regime of Magnesia, his *clear* understanding, *before he makes his proposals*, that those proposals will *not* succeed with Kleinias becomes fairly clear itself. In addition, he makes comments throughout the brief discussion on the erotic regime that incline us to believe that he does not think that his unpersuasive argument is in fact persuading Kleinias. His "art" for establishing this law, he tells Megillos, "is in one sense easy for the present purpose, but in another *the most difficult in every single way* (*tropon pantapasin hôs hoion te chalepôtatên*)" (837e9–838a2).

The "easy" part, the Stranger says, is knowing *that* it takes everyone in the city being in agreement and holding the law sacred for the law to be "most secure" (838d3–e1), that "if it is made sufficiently sacred, the custom will enslave every soul and make it, using fear, obedient in every single way to the laws" (839c4–6). And knowing this is indeed quite easy! The hard part— the part that is "most difficult in every single way"—is getting them to *do* this (cf. 711c6–d4).

This part, the Stranger says, requires "beguiling" the citizens, from the time they are children, with the "most beautiful" (*kallistên*) image of the "much nobler (*kallionos*) victory" over pleasures, "using enchanting myths and phrases and music" (840b8–c2). Now quite aside from the fact that the Stranger's "model" here for Kleinias is not the beautiful image he gave of Socratic eros but the unwritten law against incest, and that he certainly did not describe the sanctification of *that* law as achieving "nobler" victories using "beautiful" images (see 838b10–c8), his very explanation of what it would take to "beguile" human beings into desiring differently, and to hold "most securely" to those different desires, itself shows precisely why he *cannot* and *does not* expect to convince *Kleinias* to accept his proposal to so enchant the city's children to begin with: Kleinias has been brought up on precisely the opposite myths, phrases, and songs, as the Stranger himself pointed out in Book 1 (636b–d, especially c7–d4), and shows no sign of having questioned these in himself. The Stranger is in fact illustrating *why* he cannot remove in a short time what Kleinias has acquired over a long time, any more than Socrates can do so with the "men of Athens" at his trial (*Apology of Socrates* 18c–19a). In order to convince Kleinias to approve of beguiling the city's children with a new myth and speech and song of Eros, the Stranger would have needed to beguile Kleinias himself with them since *his* childhood (797e–798b). His "solution" to the difficulty demonstrates instead the permanent problem that attends bringing in "new orders and modes" (cf. 752b–d).[29]

What is more, and more important, the Stranger explicitly acknowledges that he has already guessed—more or less from the outset—that Megillos *is* in harmony with him in making his proposals for the erotic regime. This is not surprising, given that, as we saw in chapter 1, Megillos had subtly and deliberately provoked the Stranger to raise this exact issue in Book 1, when he mentioned the license he had seen among Spartan colonists at Tarentum. This was just one action among many that led us to suspect that Megillos is a far more reflective man than he is usually taken (and that Kleinias takes him) to be.

We are led by the fruits of our earlier analysis, together with the present circumstances and indications, to grant a provisional hearing to the terms in which the Stranger here explicitly sets up his attempt or test of legislating Eros: we provisionally expect the Stranger to expect that all Cretans and

Spartans present, with the exception of Megillos, will disagree with the Stranger's proposals.

And they do.

This does not mean, however, that the Stranger does not make the strongest possible argument, in terms that would be *most* persuasive to Kleinias, against homosexuality and extramarital sex. It simply means that he does so without hoping to persuade him. What he actually needs to see is if Kleinias might be persuaded to budge, and if so, how far. Because if Kleinias—that exemplar of Cretans—can be so persuaded, if his commitment to the "natural" Cretan order of sexuality is susceptible to doubt or to shame, then the Stranger's regime will be in serious trouble. The Stranger needs to *know* that Kleinias's commitment to a society structured, for men, around extramarital homosexual relationships, is "most secure." And to know this, he needs to test Kleinias's commitment with the strongest possible argument. He cannot "trick" Kleinias in a merely verbal way, on this fundamental issue (as he had earlier with the discussion about being superior or inferior to oneself in Book 1, for example) because the regime *in deed* depends not on the tallied results of verbal jousting, but on the habituated state of character—the *hexis*—of noble Cretans, and in this circumstance, noble Cretan men (cf. 769d1–e2, 777b4–7). Nor can the Stranger depend on a mere verbal indication from Kleinias that his commitment is firm, given his experience with Kleinias's "willingness" to say one thing but hold another in his heart, and this concerning the gravest things (cf. 966b4–d3, especially c4–6). For example, as Kleinias has just revealed (and as we examined in chapter 2), while he had earlier voiced agreement with the Stranger in condemning love of wealth as destructive of noble dispositions (705b7–8), when the Stranger insists on dwelling on just how ignoble and destructive this love is—using, we should notice, and will need to return to, an analogy of man and animal and nature (831d8–e3)—Kleinias becomes ashamed and angry, going so far as to rebuke the Stranger for his excessive "hatred" of this disposition (832a7–b9; cf. *Gorgias* 494e).[30] The "*nature*[] and disposition[ ] of soul" (650b7) of Kleinias is not in all things in accordance with what Kleinias says he believes, and may even believe that he believes—and this most especially with respect to the most important political things, such as love of money ("Isn't it clear that the kings of that time were first to be seized by this, the desire for more than the laws set down [allowed], and that what they commended in speech and with oaths, they were not themselves in harmony with?"—691a3–5; cf. 918c–d). It is the nature and disposition of Kleinias's soul, not just his speech, that the Stranger must test. The question is not whether Kleinias will accept the Stranger's erotic law or not—for he certainly will not. The question is whether he himself harbors any secret doubts about the nobility of Cretan homosexual practices—whether, that is, he to any extent agrees or can be brought to agree with the Stranger's virtual equation of those practices with unnatural vice. If so, it is a safe bet that he will be pushed to shame and voluble anger when the Stranger basically declares them to be subhuman, just as he was when the Stranger asserted the same about love of wealth.

Nor is it merely incidental that the Stranger pushes Kleinias on his commitment to homosexual relations very soon after he pushes Kleinias on love of wealth and finds him wanting—only their brief return to the warrior festivals and contests intervenes (832e–835b). (This is not the only time the Stranger "casually" inserts a reflection on war and warriors—a much-favored topic for Kleinias—just before proceeding to a subject that he knows Kleinias will find deeply objectionable. Cf. 921d–922a with what follows thereafter, during which, it should be added, the Stranger addresses Kleinias by name three times in rapid succession.) For it now appears that the severe limits they have agreed to place on wealth in Magnesia, which are themselves not nearly as complete as those imposed on the guardians or auxiliaries in the *Republic*, are unlikely to obtain in practice—Kleinias certainly is not possessed of that "divine erotic desire for moderation and justice" that the Stranger had indicated was, as it were, to be prayed for in a ruler with whom a lawgiver might ally (711d6–e3; cf. Al-Farabi, *Summary* 8.7—Al-Farabi here assumes, without explaining why, that the prohibition against the arts and trades for citizens will not obtain. This is why). And the conjunction of opportunity for great wealth and close-knit families is the polar opposite of the coinciding of philosophy with rule: it guarantees a life of civil partisanship and war within the city, preserving and compounding that *stasis* through generations, and by them (cf. 715a7–b6, 716a4–b5, 832c2–9). It guarantees, that is, what the Stranger had paired with love of money, just after his heated exchange with Kleinias, as one of the "two main causes of almost everything, and certainly of [the prevention of the choral and warrior education designing thus far]" (832c7–9): the "unregime" (*oupoliteia*)[31] that is "faction-'i'-city" (*stasiôteia*)—"willing rulers ruling unwilling subjects, always with some kind of violence" (832b10–c5). The "two" causes are not really two, but one, and the question now is not whether this cause can be avoided, but whether and to what extent it can be mitigated. As Müller insightfully notes, "*all* empirical forms of government are *stasiôteiai* because someone is always oppressed. This assumption is already bound up in the ideal of the mixed regime" (Müller 1951, 168n1; my translation and emphasis). Faction is unavoidable even in the second-best, or the best practical, regime (cf. the Stranger's seemingly firm statement on having avoided the "two" causes at 832c9–d1—"the present regime, which we're giving laws for, has escaped both"—with his immediate qualification of that statement at d2–4: "it is least likely that they will become lovers of money, I think"). As we have seen, the attempt to establish common public meals for women has by no means immediately succeeded. Private homes must therefore still be presumed to be a dominant custom in Magnesia. All the more is a "device" necessary for avoiding the fatal conjunction of love of money and singular devotion to family, and Cretan homosexuality as encouraged by the common public meals for men is therefore much *more* to be desired.[32] Its "naturalness" among Cretan men is an *opportunity*.

It is of course true that when the Stranger and Megillos discussed gymnastics and the common meals and their attendant homosexual practices, in Book 1, the Stranger had warned that "while they help cities in many other ways, in time of factions (civil war—*staseis*) they are difficult (*chalepa*)" (636b1–3). It should be noted, though, that he did *not* say that they play any particular part in *bringing* faction or civil war—they are "difficult"[33] *in a time* of civil war (*pros tas staseis*): extramarital homosexual relations can potentially pose the same problem for the city that heterosexual marital and familial relations can—this is why the Stranger is interested in balancing the two in a kind of erotic competition, not eliminating one or the other. And the only thing *not* difficult in a time of civil war is the man of perfect virtue, or of perfect justice (630a–c). It is, moreover, important to note that this warning is part of a larger quandary that the Stranger is addressing, in one unbroken speech addressed to Megillos, which he begins:

> It is highly likely that it is difficult for regimes to achieve the same lack of contention in deed as in speech; just as it is with bodies, for it's next to impossible to assign one practice for *some one* body that would not appear to contain both harmful *and* helpful things for *our* bodies. (636a4–b1; cf. *Rep.* 588c–d)

The Stranger then discusses gymnastics and common meals as the same in this respect for the city—with benefits and difficulties according to time, place, and amount, including what seems to be (*dokei*) the Cretan corruption of the ancient law "laid down even according to nature," for human beings and beasts, against homosexuality. Then he returns to the main theme:

> Concerning human beings who are thoroughly examining (*diaskopoumenôn*) laws, almost their whole examination is concerned with the pleasures and the pains, both in *cities* and in *private dispositions*. These two sources flow freely *by nature* (*metheintai phusei rhein*),[34] and the one who draws from them as needful (*dei*) in place, time and amount is happy—this is the same *for city, private men, and every living thing* (*zôion*)—and at the same time the one who [draws from them] not having knowledge, and missing the critical moments, that one has a life (*zôê*) that is opposite. (636d5–e2)

Rather than an initial wholesale condemnation then, the Stranger has, from the very beginning, discussed precisely homosexuality and the common meals under *this* rubric of specific relativity. And by the time of the action and arguments of Book 8, he has seen that for *this* city, homosexuality offers

natural benefits that would be foolish to refuse. But he must be sure that this
custom is deeply ingrained and "most secure" in the natures and dispositions
of Cretan souls.

If the Stranger makes a half-hearted attempt at persuading Kleinias in this
respect, he cannot possibly know more than half of Kleinias's heart in return.
He must argue in earnest, translating the highest experience of philosophical
eros between human beings into terms and images that are Kleinias's own,
and that he will understand. The regime does indeed stand or fall by Kleinias's "decision" with respect to the erotic things, for the regime is to be an
enactment of love of the whole that is the city, which is a living image of
love of the whole that is the good. And this means that atomized and close-
knit individual families are, far from the desiderata they seem to be presented
as, anathema if there is no counterbalancing challenge to their exclusivity.

As the Stranger proceeds with his test, he must take his bearings by
Kleinias's agreements, disagreements, questions, confusions, and silences.
Kleinias's agreements are few and far between, are either hedged (840c9) or
on subsidiary or general points that do not nearly extend to agreement on the
Stranger's proposals as such (837b1, 839e4, 840b3–5), and are outweighed
by his questions and confusions (835d1–2, 837a5, 840c3, 841a1–2, a5, c3).
His disagreement in speech emerges only at the end of the conversation on
the topic, and then only in his refusal to give his assent in response to
Megillos's explicit assent, and Megillos then noting that Kleinias must speak
for himself on this (842a4–9).

But Kleinias's lack of any specific agreement on the regulations of practices proposed by the Stranger is telling in this test of nature and disposition
and deed. For when Kleinias has approved of the Stranger's suggestions
throughout the conversation, he has *said so*, as in fact he did just prior to the
turn to the erotic regime: in the matter of warrior contests, training, and
festivals, Kleinias interjected his own approval several times in rapid succession (832d7, e7, 833a3, a6, c4; cf. 781d7–8, 801a3–4). Kleinias's lack of
explicit agreement speaks volumes in the discussion of the erotic regime, and
the Stranger can easily see that he is therefore *not* in agreement as he proceeds with his effort to persuade him. In response, the Stranger steadily
decreases his "demands" on erotic restraint, testing whether Kleinias will
give a yard where he won't give a mile, an inch where he won't give a yard.
Because if he will, as we noted above, they are in real trouble. Fortunately,
Kleinias will not budge.

It is in light of these assessments that we must consider the Stranger's
argument for the elimination of homosexuality and extramarital sex, and in
particular the images of nature he deploys within it. And we must remember
at every point that the Stranger's hope that his argument will *not* be persuasive is—for the very reason that he so hopes—coupled with an effort to be as
persuasive as possible, which means that his argument is tailored very

carefully to the habitual proclivities, capacities, and limits of Kleinias's imagination. But it is tailored as well to draw the attention of the far more philosophic Megillos to a crucial aspect of political things that he has not yet fully considered, and a consequence thereof he wants to resist (or vice versa): an illness that must be hidden from the patient, but not the physician (804b5–6, *Republic* 476d7–e2).

With this in mind, we recall that in Book 1, the Stranger specifically avoided asking Megillos to challenge Kleinias on the one topic that Kleinias himself had identified as resulting from "suitability" (*summetros*)[35] to the "nature (*phusis*) of the *surroundings entire* (*chôra pasa*) of Crete" (625c10–d4), as opposed to the "nature" of political things (626a4–5): the weapons that the Cretans use. For although the Stranger began the inquiry into Cretan customs by asking why their laws ordered "the common messes and the gymnastics and their commitment to the weapons they use (*tên tôn hoplôn hexin*)" (625c7–9), when he turned to "testing" (632e3, 633a1, a3) his Dorian interlocutors on their practices with respect to courage and other virtues—specifically bringing Megillos in after the latter suggested testing Kleinias first, and with Megillos then volunteering his own test first—he dropped "weapons" altogether, asking only about "the common meals and gymnastics" (633a4–5). As we noted parenthetically in chapter 1, this change is more important than it initially seems. The Stranger did not *want* to challenge Kleinias's picture of nature seen broadly, nor his faith that the gods' (or at least Zeus's) laws were reasonable in light of nature so seen. He tested Megillos to gauge if he might understand this. Megillos met the test with aplomb, subtlety, and understanding, and they were therefore able to shake Kleinias's faith in the *political* "nature" that so transfixed his imagination, without shaking his faith in the basic relationship between laws and nature (and Zeus) more broadly seen. And in fact the relationship between "the virtue of the regime," "the nature of the *chôra*" (i.e., nature broadly understood), and "the arrangement of the laws" (707d1–2) is the *first* thing the Stranger emphasized, at great length and depth, once Kleinias revealed that he is in fact to be one of the founding fathers of a new Cretan colony (704a–707d). Plato did not *want* to shake this faith, and rightly did not want to, for its theme is in every way the theme of philosophy, and illustrates quite beautifully a genuine belief in natural right.

In order to be understood by Kleinias, and to make the strongest argument possible *for him* concerning the desirability of moderating desires and practices, the Stranger uses images that are more or less absolute—and images that are presented as reality rather than as images (and furthermore as reality that is practical and easily observable rather than abstract). This is in keeping with the practical consequences of the disposition of a man like Kleinias, whose reflective capacities are far from Socratic: to have any possibility of working minimally, the image must be seen and heard maximally. The problem that attends this procedure, though, is that Kleinias is by no means the least reflective citizen or ruler that Magnesia is likely to have, and images that seem absolute are also likely to create—and in some way depend on creating—zealots. This is so of any such image, and modern zealous atheists should not relish this statement as vindicating their impressions of modern zealous religionists. One need only consider two of Socrates's companions, for whom Socrates was a living image and idol, and whose zealotry *per se* eclipses that of any Miletus or Anytus: Apollodorus and Chaerophon.

The images of nature, however, cannot be simply for men like Kleinias. The sense in which they are more revelatory of human nature than influential of behavior is reflected in the thematic shifts of Book 8. To bring these images together into a more complete image, we could say that the surface analogy has only a very tenuous hold, and breaks down almost immediately upon reflection, whereas the ground beneath that analogy holds firmly. The themes of Book 8 are: festivals, then erotic engendering, then agricultural continuity. This is the natural movement of laws that the images of "many birds and other animals" also reveal: initial play, coming together to make children, and then remaining together the rest of their lives preserving the first agreements of friendship. First agreements of friendship thus become habitual dispositions from which these birds and other animals cannot depart. The continuous agricultural language of Book 8 (cf. Benardete 2000, 244–45 and 249, discussing 838e8–839a3 and b4, 844a1–3 and d5, for example) enacts an apparently parallel image of nature, inasmuch as the fertility of the earth and climate must first be assessed, appropriate perennial seeds and tree-nuts selected and planted, the earth tended, and the harvest brought in. The fundamental process of nature—of growing—is the same whether in the untouched forests or the carefully tended vineyard. This analogy too holds firm with human communities, and by the same nutritive, metabolic process that it holds firm with birds and all other animals—what appeared to be parallel analogies are the same analogy or process (cf. 736c–737a).[36] And the play and playfulness of images, and images of images, with and in which Plato enacts his (and our) turn toward nature as a political standard, is bound by the very process he describes, and vindicates it. Plato's general purpose is not exhausted by the Stranger's relatively insignificant particular purpose as we have elaborated it here.

Nevertheless, our only access to the general is through the particular, and we must therefore return to it. The way of nature that is at once variously and uniformly analogized in the *Laws* shows us why the women's common mess-es cannot be taken for granted as existent once they have been decided upon in the discussion. They are still seeds just planted. We have noted that the women's meals are not in fact established in the *Laws*, but we should also note that the training maneuvers and war games that *are* instituted, with women included, would "naturally" require common messes for the women who were participating whenever they took place. Each is to occur "not less than once per month" (829b–c, 830d–e), and clearly does not include all of the women in the city.[37] Nevertheless, these activities are like a seed planted in fertile ground. *This*, and not the immediate establishment of common messes for all women at all meals, is the point of the Stranger's efforts.

On the other hand, the incest law that is invoked in Book 8 reminds us, among other things, that the solidity of the mature and ancient oak that grows from such plantings, and that is fundamental to reseedings inasmuch as the specific fertility and stability of the earth is deeply affected by and in some cases dependent upon the older and ancient growths whose roots inhabit it in symbiotic nourishment (and thus become the ground themselves), is not the solidity of the tentative and still-fragile seedling.[38] The tests that the Stranger runs on the ground and on his seeds are therefore related but not equivalent. The failure of Kleinias to take heed of more moderation with respect to his "infertile" erotic desires and practices is itself a particular demonstration of the fertility of deep tradition, habituation to it, and resistance to hasty change. The "failure" of the women's common messes to take root is not a failure, and our assumption that it is proves to be as overly hasty as the assumptions of success that we criticized. We cannot judge, in the *Laws*, whether it is a successful planting or not—nor can the Stranger or Megillos or Kleinias. They, and we, can only witness, or neglect, how the seed is planted (cf. 960b–c).

We have so far largely neglected, however, the role of Megillos in this discussion, which we will consider in some detail in chapter 6. By way of forecasting that consideration, the digression with Megillos—specifically Megillos—into the incest prohibition in Book 8, will be a lesson in moderation for Megillos. Recall again that it was Megillos who, in Book 1, deliberately provoked the Stranger's attack on paederasteia (see chapter 1), and that the Stranger *knows* that he already has Megillos's agreement when he brings him into the discussion in Book 8 (837e2–3, especially *hoper kai etopazon*— "as I had guessed"). Megillos is very much on board with the Stranger when it comes to the necessity for moderation, and erotic moderation in particular. But he does not, before this conversation, see the extent to which political moderation depends on balancing immoderation, excess, and transgression, while seeming to advocate moderation *simpliciter*. The Stranger and Megillos will briefly evoke and discuss examples of tragic characters who engage in incest, and the punishments entailed, which allows the Stranger and Megillos to seriously consider balanced immoderation, and at the same time not disturb moderation *simpliciter* for Kleinias. The "exceptions" to the dire self-punishment for incest ("with one's sister") that the Stranger will suppress in the tragedies he mentions do not, as popular examples in *drama*, threaten the rule. What the Stranger does, essentially, is pull Megillos aside to show him this, and also the essentially involuntary nature of erotic direction. Political direction of eros does not and cannot depend on voluntary askesis: individual reflection in the true sense is almost entirely ruled out by such political direction (or: political direction in this sense would be, at least, simply redundant if genuine individual reflection and self-reflection were the norm). That Kleinias does not have any idea that this has happened is part and parcel of that lesson, not only (though it is that too) a condition of its efficacy.

The lesson is in many ways the lesson that Plato would have modern and thoughtful conservatives learn, for the sake of political community and thereby themselves. Obviously reflection on and moderation of sexual desire is a desideratum for any individual or private human being, and the more such truly reflective and moderate citizens that there *can* be in the city is a desideratum for the city. But the capacity for self-reflection and moderation is severely limited by nature, and given this, the moderation of the city as a whole (one obviously ought not to speak of the self-reflection of the city as a whole) *depends* on the natural immoderations of its citizens being balanced against each other in an artful way. This is especially so during times where the basest of human desires—for moneyed wealth—has assumed the mantle of "virtue" (*Rep.* 550d–551a; Thucydides 3.82.4–8), and it may be remarked here that while the Stranger clearly indicates that his comments on restricting homosexuality may be somewhat in jest, the desire for wealth is *never* treated with anything that could be confused with mirth anywhere in the *Laws*. (It is not Plato's position that immoderate private "interests" *automatically* lead to public benefit, obviously—very far from it.)

At the same time, this is a lesson for modern and thoughtful liberals, for the sake of themselves and thereby political community. Plato certainly agrees with the liberal position that homosexuality—and indeed sexuality of any form or direction in general—is neither "aberrant" nor "perverse" by nature: they are all quite natural. But *for that very reason*, the satisfaction and gratification of sexual desire of any kind is *not* an enactment of "autonomy" or "agency." It is not voluntary, but only an image or phantom of voluntary.

NOTES

1. My focus on the Greek tradition does not mean that there are no other traditions to which this might apply. One may think here, for example, of the teachings of the Chinese philosopher Laozi (or Lao-tze) on the *tao* (the way of motion) and *t'ien-tao* (the way of heaven or nature), and their influence. This and many other traditions are outside the scope of my own competence, rather than the scope of my inquiry.

2. *Ploutôn* is the god of the underworld, and an alternative name for Hades. *Ploutos* is the god of wealth. As the Stranger's remark at 801b6 indicates, the two were sometimes conflated.

3. Cf. Strauss (1975): "the greatest god (821c2) does not wish and does wish to be named Zeus" (116; citing Heraclitus fr. 32). The Heraclitus fragment that Strauss cites, using *Zênos* (cf. *zaô*, "to live") for "Zeus," is: ἓν τὸ σοφὸν μοῦνον λέγεσθαι οὐκ ἐθέλει καὶ ἐθέλει Ζηνὸς ὄνομα—"One only, what is wise, not wanting and wanting to be called the name Zeus." It is possible that the *Laws* reference Strauss cites (821c2) is a typo and should in fact be 821a2: *Ton*

megiston theon kai holon ton kosmon, "the greatest god and the cosmos as a whole," rather than c2 (cf. *Epinomis* 977b2–3). Of this "greatest god," the Stranger says (or rather, "we say") that investigating and trying to discover its causes is not and is pious (821a2–b2; cf. 966c–968b). Impious and pious is not identical with not permitted and permitted. Compared to the Stranger's reference to *ton megiston theon* at 821a2, his reference to the sun and moon as *megaloi theoi* ("*great* gods") at 821b6 clearly reflects a lesser dignity. The god mentioned by Kleinias at 821c2 is *Heôsphoros*, the "Morning-bearer," or morning star, which he swears "By Zeus!" (c1) he has often seen in motion, as also the evening star (c3). Strauss's reference to 821c2 may not be inaccurate.

4. What is more, as Wieland (1982) elaborates, "the discussion carried on in the *Laws* is itself a model for literature, which is to be used as a basis for teaching the young" (93; my translation).

5. Lewis (1845, 17–18) suggested, influentially, that the division of the *Republic* and the *Laws* into books was not Plato's own. I cannot deny this possibility, but it is worth noting that Lewis's argument rests on two and only two points that Lewis believed he had discerned: (1) that Aristotle does not refer to either the *Republic* or the *Laws* by book number, though he "gives a detailed criticism" of both in the *Politics*, book 2 (ibid., 18); and (2) that "[t]here is no internal mark of the division of books" in either the *Republic* or the *Laws* (ibid.). As to the first point, it can hardly be dispositive that Aristotle does not refer to specific books in his criticism. Machiavelli, for example, does not refer to specific books of Livy within either the *Prince* or the *Discourses*, and he certainly knew that Livy's work *was* divided into books (the title of the book commonly referred to in English as the *Discourses on Livy* is in fact *Discorsi sopra la prima deca di Tito Livio*, for example). Ficino cites specific books of the *Republic* and the *Laws* in his commentaries devoted specifically to those works, but never when he refers to them in his commentaries on other Platonic works, nor does he cite specific books of the *Republic* when he refers to the *Republic* in his commentary on the *Laws*, and vice versa. Vico never cites the book numbers or chapters of any author he refers to in the *Scienza nuova*, even with respect to what he considers "golden sentences." And Aristotle's criticism in book 2 of the *Politics*, to put a period on what would be an endless list, cannot by any stretch of the imagination accurately be termed "detailed." As to the second point, since Lewis does not say—in the single paragraph that he devotes to this subject with respect to Plato (Aristotle's work, by contrast, receives five pages of detailed attention: 18–23)—what would constitute an "internal mark of division," one can only guess what he meant, if anything, beyond an explicit citation within the dialogues to a book number. As I am attempting to illustrate here, there might well be thematic internal divisions that are not necessarily as readily apparent as explicit citations, but would nevertheless be part of a Platonic structure that accords with the division of the *Laws* into twelve books. That being said, I am illustrating an order here that accords with this structure, not relying from the outset on there being one.

6. Some recent and commendable groundwork in the "political culture" and discursive institutional approaches to comparative politics has begun, with narrower focuses than Plato, to illustrate the ubiquity of such images in political life. See in particular Ross (2004, 2009) on rituals as "psychocultural dramas"; and Wedeen (1999, 2002) on symbolic context and "semiotic practices." Schmidt (2008) provides a useful discussion on how this groundwork retrieves a deeply contextualized focus on "discourse" and "practices" from the arbitrary decontextualization of postmodernism. What is interesting for our purposes is not so much any particular focus of these analyses (e.g., the complexities of group identity, conflict, and reconciliation in Ross 2004; the dynamics of political compliance in Syria during the regime of Hafiz al-Asad, in Wedeen 1999), but their logic. That logic points to the necessity of such images and praxes for political animals—that is, to their necessity not, or not only, in the vulgar sense of "necessary for maintaining political power," but in the rigid sense of inevitability, for good and for "evil," and, as it were, beyond. For very good discussions of specific modern images and their praxes, see also Manning (2005) on Marxist "maternalism" during the Great Leap Forward in China; Belge (2011) on Kurdish "nationalism" in Kemal's Turkey; and Schneider (2014) on "development" in postcolonial Tanzania.

7. This passage may itself be an "image . . . in water": Al-Farabi had discussed, just prior to it, the need for cognition of "the principles of the *ultimate* beings, their rankings, happiness, the

first rulership that belongs to the virtuous city, and the *rankings* of its rulership" (*Political Regime* §88; 2011, 45, my emphases). Among other things, Al-Farabi is illustrating with this image the elisions and losses that attend images and mirror images, and yet how those images nevertheless point—*per speculum in enigmate* (1 Cor. 13:12)—at something that is contained but not achieved in themselves. Al-Farabi's image of cognition does not single out or explicitly rank the ultimate beings as prior in time and in dignity to "the beings" in general, nor the first rulership as prior in time or in dignity to rulership in general (cf. *Epinomis* 974d–975a). But these are entailed, unbeknownst to the beginner, in the fruition of the task and therefore, to some degree, in its progress. Cf. Averroës (2011), "Decisive Treatise," 11–15, especially the quoted directive of ʿAlī ibn Abī Ṭālib (15, toward the end; 2011, 128); Maimonides, *Guide of the Perplexed* 1.34 and then 35, with 3.20–21 and then 22–25; John of Salisbury, *Metalogicon* 1.24.854c–856c, 2.19.876d–877a, 3.5.902a–c, 3.10.910a–c (1991, 67–70, 117–18, 170–71, 189–90); Locke (1996), *Some Thoughts Concerning Education* §128–9 and 147–156; Tocqueville, *Democracy in America* 2.2.9, 3.2.8.

8. It must of course be remembered (and first, realized) that everything presented by Plato on the topic of images (and other topics) is explicitly presented in images and images of images.

9. Zuckert's broader thesis, that the *Laws* is set, dramatically, before the Peloponnesian War and before "the emergence of Socratic political philosophy" (2004, 376; 2009, 53–4), is untenable. Megillos is the eldest of the three very old men (712c8), and his *ancestors* fought in the Persian Wars (699d5–6). And at the time of the conversation, there have already been *several* Persian kings after Xerxes (695e4–5). At the time of Plato's death (believed to be around 348/347 BCE) the fourth Persian king after Xerxes, Artaxerxes III, was still ruling. Plato set the *Laws* in the future, not the past. There is no reason, based on the dramatic dating of the *Laws*, to assume that Socrates's "discovery" was not yet discovered.

10. As Benardete (2000) notes with respect to the criminal law in Book 9, and its curious placement *before* the civil law in Book 11: "The criminal law keeps intact the innocence of the law-abiding, which they themselves are led to believe education supports all by itself. The Stranger therefore has preserved in the preposterous order of criminal law first and then civil law the true order of becoming. . . . What was presented to us as the experiential deviation from the law proves to be the precondition of the law. The ordinary citizen, however, takes in, and is expected to take in, with his law-abidingness a self-congratulatory vanity that assures him that the punitiveness of this part of the law had not in any way contributed to his behaviour" (253–54, citing 927c7–d3; cf. also Whitaker 2004, 151; Pangle 1988, 500).

11. The "images" that the Stranger employs extend far beyond mere *paradeigmata*, and include the dispositional harmonies of music. Indeed, as Valiquette (2013, especially chapter 5, 163–202) has illustrated, the mimetic regime of the *Laws* is fundamentally musical, as the leading of human beings toward civic and human excellence is by necessity a musical composition.

12. Cf. Maimonides, *Eight Chapters* 6.9 (especially the words and context of ben Gamaliel) with respect to *Mishneh Torah*, Melachim 9.1, 5, 6; and consider *Guide of the Perplexed* 3.41 on "precepts" with respect to "punishment."

13. There is, to be sure, a further glaring inconsistency—or at any rate an unacknowledged incompleteness—to using the argument about what "all animals do" as an evident guide for human behavior: "all animals" certainly do not think about what "all animals" do, and indeed, it seems highly likely that *no* animal other than a human being is capable of considering this. What is more, it cannot even be said that all human beings *do* consider what "all animals" do. And even those who do imagine an aspect of this do not necessarily imagine *everything* that "all animals" do (as we will have cause to return to in chapter 6, when considering the human incest prohibition).

14. Cf. Cicero, *De officiis* 1.96, 97, 107.

15. Cf. §123, especially "the greater part no strict observers of equity and justice" (Locke 2005, 72). As Locke puts it elsewhere: "It is not uncommon to see men rest their opinions upon foundations that have no more certainty and solidity than the propositions built on them and embraced for their sake" (*Of the Conduct of the Understanding* §6; 1996, 175). Cf. Hobbes, *Leviathan* 1.15.35, 4.45.30 (last sentence), 4.46.18 (last sentence, especially parenthetical re-

mark) [paragraph numbers from Curley's edition, Hobbes 1994]. We may note here, with Mathie (1986, 290–92, 298), that Hobbes's *analysis* of prudence and therefore observation that leads him to declare men to be equal in prudence (*Lev.* 1.13.1–2) is itself evidently a demonstration of uncommon or eminent (i.e., unequal) prudence and observation. On some ramifications of this deliberate "insincerity" for Hobbes's other declared "equalities," see Kang (2003, 378–79).

16. Indeed, as Benardete (2000) points out, even the "compromise" suggestion (that Kleinias also does not accept) "is nothing but the unwritten law as it now prevails almost everywhere (cf. *Philebus* 65e9–66a3)" (246). The passage from the *Philebus* that Benardete cites is Protarchus's matter of course description of what "we" (i.e., "we all") do: "Whenever we see anyone taking pleasure in pleasures, and even almost the greatest [pleasures]—when we see either the ridiculousness or the complete shamefulness that sets in, we become ashamed ourselves and, withdrawing from sight, we hide as much of it as we can, giving all such things over to the night that should not be seen in the light."

17. Thus it seems that the Stranger's earlier insistence that women too should participate in the common messes of the city (780d–781e), which the discussion for over sixty Stephanus pages was ostensibly to show was "good and fitting" (781d4–5 and d9–e3, 783b3–c4), is here dropped. [Text of 783b3–c4 is problematic, though the sense is clear. See note by Diès, *ad loc.*, and Pangle 1988, 529n36.]

18. That the desire for wealth is addressed within the general context of providing for food, and following inquiries into dispositions toward war and incest, seems to evoke Socrates's comments on the dreaming tyrant at the outset of book 9 of the *Republic*. This tyrant, Socrates says, dreams of fulfilling "paranomal" [sic] desires that "likely come to be in *everyone*" (571b4–5): "intercourse (*meignusthai*) as he understands it (*hôs oietai*) with his mother, or any other human being, god or animal whatsoever; and any polluted murder whatsoever; and not refraining from any food at all" (571d1–4; cf. *Timaeus* 45e–46a and Adam 1902, *ad loc.*, who notes that "not refraining from any food at all" refers to cannibalism, citing Aristotle, *Nic. Ethics* 1148b20–25. The evocation of the Cyclopes in Book 3 obviously comes to mind here—see Homer, *Od.* 9.287–298). "As he understands it" (*hôs oietai*) is key here. The dreaming tyrant, or the tyrant that desire becomes in the dreamer, "understands" its desire to "have intercourse" or "engage" with mother and any person, god or beast as a sexual desire. But the word *meignusthai* has a hostile sense as well, and conveys engaging another in battle. The connection between coupling and battling, Aphrodite and Ares, is one of the principal political problems attending intergenerational incest. We may note as well that in the passage from the *Ethics*, while Aristotle specifically writes that such desires are not for "natural pleasures" (*hêdea phusei*), they can certainly arise "through depraved natures" (*dia mochthêras phuseis*) and such desires therefore come into being "by nature" (*phusei*) or habit (ibid). In other words, there can be a natural desire for an unnatural pleasure, per Aristotle. Cf. 831c–832c.

19. The clause translated as "custom, through habit and unwritten law" presents difficulty for literal translation into English, and is an adnominative little jingle in Greek (no pun intended): "*nomimon ethei kai agraphôi nomisthen nomôi.*" Pangle translates: "custom *laid down* in habit and unwritten law" (1988, *ad loc.*), which is both better, inasmuch as it captures the aspect of laying down of "law" in *nomisthen*; and worse, inasmuch as it thereby subdues the aspect of "customary belief." What is important here is that the Stranger makes the clause say "custom—believing—law," in that order, and with three words sharing the same root, *nom-* ("law"), or to be more etymologically precise, *nem-* ("boundary stone"). En quam modice habitat philosophia.

20. Finnis focuses on what he calls the "common good" of marriage (1994, 30) and the "common good of the two spouses" (1997, 134)—based, so far as I can see, on the assumption that "common" means "common good," or else on the quasi-Hobbesian assumption that whatever one (or two) *makes* is one's (or two's) "good" (cf. *Euthydemus* 289a5–8)—and dismisses the "political common good" as "instrumental" as opposed to "basic, intrinsic, or constitutive" (1994, 33–34). Regardless of the validity or nonvalidity of this or any other claims that Finnis makes, such an approach cannot begin to make sense of either the *Republic* or the *Laws*, to name just two obvious examples among many, since it does away with the question of what is *one's own*. (We may mention in passing that such an approach would similarly fall flat with

anyone who, for example, married once only, had seven children with that one woman, and eloquently exhorted his fellow Christians to penitence, and yet also claimed to love his own fatherland more than his soul.) It is additionally worth asking whether the husband of Xanthippe, and the father of Lamprocles, Sophronicus, and Menexenus, had any commitment to family whatsoever beyond fulfilling his *instrumental* civic duty to procreate (cf. Xenophon, *Symposium* 2.10). As for Plato himself, there is no indication that even this duty was of significance in his own life. Cf. *Laws* 721b–d.

21. Consider especially *ta polla* ("*most* things") at d7–8 vs. *pan* ("everything") at d5.

22. "Almost" and "most" are words that the Stranger uses with care. Cf. 751a1–2 ("Almost [*schedon*] the next thing for you [Kleinias] to specify is the establishment of the ruling offices of the city") with 751b2 ("But let's hold on a little before choosing them . . . "); also 658e8–659a1 ("almost [*schedon*] the noblest Muse is she who delights the best men [*beltistous*—i.e., highest social class], and the sufficiently educated men; but especially so is she who delights the man who is always outstanding in virtue and education"); 679b8 ("almost [*schedon*] the noblest dispositions . . . "); 636d5 (*oligou pasa*); 834d9–e2 (*pantôs* versus *pleista*); *inter alia*. See also endnote 21.

23. Pangle (1988) reminds us of Aristotle's severe criticism of Sparta's method of thus financing (532n16, citing *Politics* 1271a27ff and 1272a13ff). Grote draws our attention to discrepancies between Aristotle's and other classical accounts of the *syssitia*, particularly with respect to Crete (Grote 1888, vol. 4, 360n274).

24. Note that neither Hesiod nor the Stranger says that the half is *always* more than the whole.

25. *Pace* Schöpsdau (2003), who suggests that "laws of sexual morality" are instituted because the women's messes are only realizable in deed through a process of education that creates their "necessary preconditions," and that these "still-to-be-created preconditions include the heightening of sexual morality, so that men and women first learn to control their drives" (255; my translation). Schöpsdau notes that the women's messes are acknowledged by the Stranger to be practically impossible in the short term, but does not address, with his speculation, that the laws of "sexual morality" are themselves said to be practically impossible. Okin (1977) rightly stresses that a very great deal of the "traditional" private—and essentially *owned*—role of women, which is bound up with ensuring lineage and thus perpetuating family fortunes through private households, follows directly from the acceptance of private property; but she too assumes that both the women's messes and the Stranger's proposal for the erotic regime are instituted as law and practice in Magnesia (365, 368). Okin is correct to see just how much Plato's hands are tied—both with respect to the political role of women, and otherwise— by the inevitabilities of private property (and, we may add, love of private property), but she neglects the Stranger's efforts to ensure that the relationships entailed by love of property remain undermined or challenged by sexual desire directed outside of those relationships.

26. As Strauss (1975) notes, the Stranger's proposals for "the way of life of men and women" in the *Laws* are "much less shocking than what Socrates said on this subject in the *Republic*. (But see 781b6–c2.)" (97) But less shocking proposals do not mean less awareness of the fundamental problem: see 690a–d, especially *kai hoti pephukota pros allele enantiôs*, and so forth. ("and are therefore by nature opposed to each other . . .") at d3–4; 714d–715d, especially *kai empodia hetera heteroisi* ("and they are obstacles to each other") at 714e6, and *mête autois mête enkgonois* ("with neither them nor their descendants") at 715a9–10; also 739c–e on why the regime of the *Republic* is not suitable to Magnesia; and 775e–776b, 780a–b, 790a–b, 804d, 807b, 810a, for example. And follow Strauss's advice, and "see 781b6–c2."

27. Cf. 751b5–c2, 819a3–6, 937d6–e1; *Republic* 497d, *Symposium* 180e, *Meno* 87e–89a, *Euthydemus* 281d, *Crito* 46b. Plato draws our attention to this in the *Symposium*, where he has his Pausanias suggest that nothing is, *in itself*, noble or base, but that everything depends on *how* something is done (180e; cf. *Laws* 716d–717a). The important irony there is that Pausanias is himself putting this very argument into the service of a *base* cause (cf. *Lovers* 133b–d). "The way up, the way down—one and the same" (Heraclitus DK fr. 69).

28. 836c7–8 should be noted here, but the manuscripts have clearly lost something small but essential from the passage. As the sentence stands in the MSS, the Stranger says that if someone argued for the proposals he is making based on "the nature of animals" and on

homosexuality thus being "not according to nature," "his argument would probably be declared persuasive (*pithanôi*), and (*kai*) not at all in consonance with your cities." This cannot be right. Diès (*ad loc.*) adopts Badham's emendation of *apithanôi* ("unpersuasive") for *pithanôi* ("persuasive"), which seems likely to me, and which Pangle follows in his translation (see Pangle's note in Plato 1988, 532n11); Hermann suggests *ei kai* ("even if") for *kai* ("and"). Gonzalez (2013) seems to want to accept the manuscript reading as is (166–7n4), but so far as I can tell, does not seem to recognize that the problem lies not in whether one or the other clause makes sense on its own (each clearly does), but whether they make sense together. Gonzalez writes: "The argument based on nature is certainly presented as a persuasive one elsewhere in the dialogue," but provides no textual support for this claim. And if by "the argument based on nature" Gonzalez here means the argument based on nature *against homosexuality*, as I presume he does since it would be necessary to his claim here, then I for one find no such textual support to be had. This is the only statement the Stranger directly makes on the persuasiveness of that argument, and it is that statement that is in dispute.

29. Munn (2013) thus both points to and misses the decisive point when he writes that, "*Erôs* among [the people who must come together to found a new city] is ungoverned, possibly ungovernable except through the dictates of an impassioned tyrant. But once a new civic order is in place, and its own generation and regeneration is underway, it is possible, by starting with the young and carefully schooling their passions, to direct them constructively toward the greater good. This is the fantasy Plato entertains in the *Laws*" (43). We can only agree that this would indeed be a fantasy. Cf. Machiavelli's remarks on *nuovi ordini e modi* in *Prince*, chapter 6; with *Discourses* 1.16–20.

30. As mentioned in chapter 2, Hermann, Apelt, and Wilamovitz wish to give this interjection to Megillos rather than Kleinias; and Hermann, Apelt and Burges wish to do likewise with 832a11–b3. Diès accepts both emendations, and Burnet rejects both. All MSS have Kleinias for both, and the reason given for emendation is a supposed dramatic inconsistency with the plural *xenoi epeplêxate* ("you have chastened me, strangers") at 832b7 (see Wilamowitz-Möllendorff 1920, 403–4, for a review). Wilamovitz adds that Megillos is "the more sensible (or: insightful—*einsichtigere*) of the two" Dorians, though Wilamovitz seems to want by this to damn with faint praise. He further notes that Megillos "judges quietly that what people strive for above all else is to make their living, and to acquire all the things they think they need for their *bios* [way of life]" (404, my translation), and therefore interjects. It is difficult to see how this banal sentiment—which, if it told the whole story here, would neatly do away with most of the political problems addressed in the *Laws*, and (because the *Laws* is that kind of book) most political problems in general—passes for an "insight." Surely the same could have been said of the ancestor of Gyges when he was just "a shepherd, serving the ruler of Lydia" (*Rep.* 359d2–3), but this is called seriously into question when this "everyman" finds a certain ring. A great deal is revealed—not changed—about the structure of his desire (and Glaukon's) when opportunity presents itself, which is otherwise concealed in quotidian concerns for livelihood and the accoutrements of lifestyle. As to the plural address at 832b7, this is a rhetorical strategy frequently employed by the Stranger. He almost always addresses *both* of the Dorians, even when Kleinias is the one with whom he has been speaking, when Kleinias responds to a particular point or conclusion with anger, shame, doubt, or concern (to give some of many examples from Books 7 and 9 alone—to choose the two surrounding Books, in the first of which Megillos speaks a total of three lines, and in the second, does not speak *at all*—see 789b1, 792c7–8, 797a1, 860e4–5, 862a2–3, 862b1, 863a7; the last is a prime case in point: the Stranger responds here to a concerned question from a dubious Kleinias by speaking as if *both* the Dorians had asked the question [*hôs keleuete*], though Megillos at this point has not spoken for over twenty pages [since 842a9]). This strategy is a response to Kleinias's habit of answering for both himself *and* Megillos, and especially to the clear indication that Kleinias had given, at the beginning of the conversation (see discussion in chapter 2), that when proud of a particular "insight" of his own, he puts himself forward as an "I" (625c9, e1, e5), but when those insights run into trouble, he withdraws into the shelter of the communal "we" (628e2–5, 629b6, 630d2). The Stranger knows that Kleinias, under fire, prefers "we" to "I," and he responds accordingly. In sum, there is no dramatic inconsistency in the Stranger addressing both Dorians after speaking only with Kleinias, and after having seriously upset him. To the

contrary, it would be dramatically inconsistent if the Stranger did *not* address them both here. The reading given by all of the MSS should stand.

31. I treat this as one word, as it obviously may have been intended, in play with the Andocidean neologism *stasiôteia*. I depart from the manuscripts in this, without further defense.

32. I therefore agree with Gaca (2003) that the Stranger's effort here is tied to "having to accommodate the family, clans and the marketplace in Magnesia" (55), but disagree that it results from a concern that "these customs give sexual desire a ready way to breed myriad vices," inasmuch as Gaca means sexual vices. Gaca does not explain the immediate connection she draws (and says Plato draws) between the very existence of the "marketplace" and myriad sexual vices, nor does there seem to be an adequate explanation at hand. I set aside her identification of the existence of *any* commerce in the city with a "free market" (55), which is quite obviously egregiously inaccurate, and which a modern American reader (for example) might easily associate with a broad range of other modern legal and moral permissiveness, bound up with a general conviction that the "pursuit of happiness" is unquestionably to be determined for each person solely by that person's whims, proclivities, and desire for self-preservation (cf. Hume, *A Treatise of Human Nature* 3.1.1–2; Lenzner 1999).

33. Compare *ôphelei . . . chalepa* in the sentence here, with *blapton . . . ôpheloun* in the previous sentence (636a7–9). The whole of what the Stranger says in this passage is a consideration of the fact that "it is highly likely that it is difficult (*chalepon*) for regimes to achieve the same lack of contention in deed as in speech" (636a4–5). *Chalepon* ("difficult") is not necessarily the same as *blapton* ("harmful").

34. N.b. "These two sources flow freely *by nature*" (*phusei*). This is not the same thing as "*seems to be . . . laid down even according* to nature" just prior (636b4–5; transposing *tas*, with Paris and Vatican MSS [best manuscripts], *pace* Diès). The metaphor of "flow" is essential to a Platonic understanding of nature (cf., e.g., *hotan euroia hêi tês geneseôs*—"when there is good flow of conception"—at 784b2–3), just as the metaphor of "drawing" (as in "drawing water") is essential to a Platonic understanding of law. In Book 6, the Stranger describes nature as not eternally stable, but as "eternally becoming/engendering" (*hê aeigenês phusis*—773e6–7) (cf. *Symposium* 206e, *Statesman* 309c). *Aeigenês* is a rare word for Plato, and in general. Plato uses it only three times, and in each instance it is clearly relying upon and drawing out the aspect of engendering (*gennêsis*) and becoming (*gignesthai*). In the *Symposium* it is specifically used as not identical to "immortal" (*athanatos*), and therefore must be interpreted as meaning more than just "everlasting" or "eternal" (the definitions supplied by Liddell and Scott). Pangle's "eternal coming-into-being of nature" (1988, *ad loc.*) also brings this out well.

35. Here I would propose a rare outright correction to Pangle's on the whole excellent translation. Pangle translates *summetros* as "harmonize," and "to harmonize" (*sunarmottein* at 628a9; otherwise *sumphônein*; nouns: *harmonia* and *sumphônia*) is without a doubt one of the most important themes in the *Laws*. Kleinias does not recognize "harmony" here, but rather proportion, or suitability. *Summetros* literally means "commensurate," in both the mathematical and the ethical sense of that term.

36. Of the need for, and difficulties attending, the "small effects of prayer and slow and careful changes over long periods of time" (736d2–4), and effected only by "continual innovators (*kinountôn*—literally, "movers")" of considerable real virtue, the Stranger says: "This, as we say, we are escaping. However, it is more correct to discuss in what way we would devise an escape from it, if we have not escaped it" (737a2–4). Cf. Aristotle, *Politics* 1268b22–1269a28, noting that the fundamental criticism there of "innovation" with respect to law, is of Hippodamus's innovation whereby "honors" (*timê*) would be given for such innovation. Aristotle is in agreement with Plato: such innovations are best implemented quietly, and certainly without hope for being honored for them.

37. There is also the possibility that women will participate in the duties of the Agronomoi ("Field Regulators," to borrow Pangle's translation), since as with the required number of such Agronomoi, there is ambiguity in the Stranger's allotment (760b7–c1—*dôdeka tôn pente ek tôn neôn* could well include young women). The Agronomoi serve for two years, and during that time they must live together—sleeping and taking common meals together (762b7–d1). As Pangle (1988) notes, the number of people required to serve these two-year terms of duty is

quite large compared to the number of households (5,040) in the city—204 on the low side, 780 on the high—with potentially almost all young men *and* women needed to serve them (528n12). It may not be tangential, for our purposes, to note that all of the possible permutations result in numbers of Field Officers, on the one hand, and Regulators, on the other, that evenly divide the number of households in the city: 5 officers from each tribe, or 60 in total; 12 or 60 regulators from each tribe, or 144 or 720 in total. Whereas if the officers and their subordinate regulators are added together—both ranks treated as numerically equal—none of the resulting numbers yields even division of the city's number: 17 or 65 from each tribe, or 204 or 780 in total. [Post (1939) suggests *ek tôn neôn* at 760c1 might be emended to *ek neôn* for clarity (94). But the Stranger seems to be keeping his numbers here deliberately obscure, and therefore permissive of multiple legal interpretations.]

38. The unwritten law against incest is unique inasmuch as it seems to obtain for "all human beings" regardless of place. This does not mean that there are no particular laws in particular places that are not met with "sacred awe" of similar magnitude in and for those places.

Chapter Six

Law

It matters not how strait the gate,
How charged with punishments the scroll . . .

—William Ernest Henley, "Invictus"

It is customary, most of the time, for the last substantive chapter of a book to bring the argument to its head, and attempt to clinch it. I am not sure if this custom is proper or properly understood, nor will I be able to fulfill the better part of the expectations derived from it. In this respect, the *Laws* themselves militate against their fulfillment, with their final requirement of a "divine assembly" (sullogos—969b2) sending us back, as it were, to the beginning (cf. Sanday 2013, 230–31). The laws, and the *Laws*, are by their very nature unfinished and unfinishable. It cannot be responsible to end a serious argument merely for the sake of winning it.

We have stressed that the Stranger must make the strongest possible argument in favor of his proposals for the erotic regime, for Kleinias. It may be objected, though, that the argument he makes is not in fact a strong one, and indeed we noted in chapter 5 that it is plagued with rather bizarre weaknesses. This does not refute our claim, however. Absent being able to call on a god (which will not avail the Stranger, for as far as Kleinias is concerned, homosexuality among Cretan men is sanctified by the highest god), or ancestral tradition (which, for obvious reasons, he cannot do), the only completely reasonable argument is to suggest that Socratic eros is the highest eros, because voluntary to the highest degree, and ought to be the standard of natural right by which others orient themselves in disciplining and cultivating whatever natural dispositions they have (which are almost surely not naturally equal to the Stranger's or to Socrates's or to Megillos's natural disposition). The Stranger does in fact make this argument, knowing that Megillos is in harmony with him on it, but that it stands no chance of persuading Kleinias (cf. 966b4–8).

Aside from these three possibilities, there in fact *is no* strong argument to make—that is, demonstrative and reasonable argument—and this is among the first things that Plato would have us realize.[1] The institution of heterosexual marriage is not disputed here, nor the necessity of producing children. The sole disputed thing is whether there ought not to be homosexual relations or extramarital sexual relations of any description.

It is not the case that eroticism as such between people of the same sex is condemned, nor is extramarital eroticism as such condemned. Were that the case, Socrates, for example, would no more agree to this for himself than Kleinias agrees to it. Socrates, who it is easy to see *making* this argument to Kleinias (and those who believe that the Stranger *is* Socrates do see him making it), would by no means accept such an argument for himself, and clearly *did not* accept it for himself. Nor would anyone whom the Stranger describes as disposed to soul-to-soul, rather than body-to-body, erotic relations. The higher eros and the lower, as it were, mirror each other.

This may seem like a bold claim, so it will be helpful to see how it stands up to objections.

The neo-Thomist John Finnis is among the most prominent and articulate modern proponents of an at least ostensibly non-revelation-based "philosophical and common-sense rejection of extra-marital sex" (Finnis 1994, 1066), and the basis of his arguments is worth considering carefully. For Finnis, the rational basis of this "rejection" is fundamentally the potential for producing a child that is only available, by nature, to a man and woman together. Frequently drawing on Thomas Aquinas, Aristotle, and Plato, Finnis (1994, ibid.) calls this potential or actual production of a child the "common good" of marriage (30) and the "common good of the two spouses" (Finnis 1997, 134).[2] But *pace* Finnis, this is not at all obvious as a common *good* necessarily or even often on Socratic terms: Socrates's own children, being apparently without any philosophical promise, were neglected by him in favor of the company of more promising youths. Socrates quite clearly does not confuse "his own" in this sense with the good or the best. And in the absence of the child being a common *good*, Socrates would not even acknowledge anything *common*—anything *his own* in or of the marriage and the children—as he demonstrated with his own wife and children in deed. As Strauss (1991) notices, it is remarkable that Xenophon simply includes Socrates among the unmarried men (196; citing Xenophon, *Symposium* 9.7).

To return, then, to the Stranger's proposition, we should further note that even in the case where a philosophic soul ended up—by choice or by the arrangement of others—in a marriage with another philosophic soul, and both enjoyed each other for the sake of excellence and magnificence alone, it would be plainly absurd to think that *either* of such people would choose in advance to forego similar relationships with other people of similar ilk, should they appear (i.e., in the admittedly rare circumstances in which multiple such people were to be found together), whatever their gender or age. Such a "spouse" would be choosing beforehand to repudiate "the best" for the sake of "their own" (731e3–732a1)—a beloved of Socrates, for example, could never be a lover of Aristotle (to speak, with Nietzsche, "in Greek, and not only in Greek").

The weakness of any possible argument, based on unassisted human reason, for any *specific* sexual regime for "lower" erotics (to speak somewhat playfully) for all human beings always and everywhere, is a mirror of the impossibility of any such argument, unassisted by force, being effective for higher erotics. Why then is a specific sexual regime necessary for a city? *Is* it necessary?

The Stranger believes that it is. I have dwelled at length on the fact that his proposal for a heterosexual and monogamous regime is not in fact something that he desires for Magnesia, but this does not mean that he does not desire a specific erotic regime—by which I mean, a generalized habituated custom of sexuality that pervades the whole city. In fact, as we have seen, he goes to some length to be sure that the Cretan (male) customs in this respect are very secure, and that he can depend on the city's citizens living those customs as the obvious, and only, "correct" way of sexual relations.

As to *why* this is necessary, the answer lies in the very images of animal nature that the Stranger used to ostensibly promote his radically new sexual regime of heterosexuality and monogamy.

Those images depend upon human imaginations that focus on the lack of any external law corresponding to human law on other animal "natures," and are drawn to that lack. Such imaginations are in a way blind to, or persistently forgetful of, the thousand-fold iron necessities to which animals—and Socratic lovers—are subject, both internally through "instinct" and externally through the circumstances of their environments (or, to use a less anachronistic word, their *chôra*). Indeed, it was this very blindness or forgetfulness that the Stranger depended upon when he tested Kleinias's desire for moneyed wealth. "Because of an insatiable desire for gold or silver," he said, "every man is willing (*ethelein*) to abide every art or device, both noble and more shameful, if it is likely to bring him to wealth; and to do anything— pious and impious and totally shameful—without feeling disgust; if only it brought him the power to completely allow himself, *just like a beast* (*kathaper thêriôi*), the complete satiety of every kind of eating and drinking and likewise of [every] sexual desire" (831d4–e3).[3]

This statement seems to present us with a contradiction. In *this* comparison, animal behavior appears to be completely licentious, not completely moderate as it is later said to be in Book 8. How can the Stranger move from such a characterization of animals to his "pure and chaste" bachelor animals just a little while later? Earlier, in Book 7, the Stranger had specifically highlighted the "natural erotic longing" for food and drink of "every animal"—and it is "frenzy" (782e). Whereas the natural erotic longing for sex, he says, affects only human beings with "madness" (783a). He had stressed to Kleinias that they must keep these three erotic longings in their memories (783c).

In fact, the Stranger has not attributed to the "beasts" here any of the *insatiable* longing and frenzy for food and drink and sex that he suggests is normal for every man (*panta andra*—he does not necessarily suggest this is normal for every woman). He gives that impression, on first hearing—and that is almost surely how Kleinias hears him—but what he actually mentions is only the *satiety* (*plesmonê*) that beasts experience of these things—and that is not at all contradictory to his previous or later statements. Beasts *do* experience satiety of all these things. But precisely because their longings in that regard are not insatiable ("every man," by contrast, wants to both continue to experience insatiable appetite *and* experience satiety of that appetite).

Recognizing the seeming contradiction here is important, but resolving it analytically is a relatively minor concern. What is more to the point is understanding the imagination—and the desires that inform and drive that imagination—that does *not* recognize the contradiction. This is what the Stranger is illustrating for Megillos, and Plato for his reader. *Kleinias* does not say to the Stranger: That makes no sense! He does not note or notice that beasts[4] actually do experience satiety with respect to eating and drinking (and water, not wine!), to say nothing of sex. Instead, he is wounded to the quick by the analogy precisely because his own desires lead him to imagine the "freedom" of beasts with a longing that blinds him to the reality of animal nature *and therefore* to the contradictions inherent in the images thereof: he imagines them as having the freedom to endlessly satisfy these desires, not as having satisfiable desires that have an end. Beasts' desires of course recur—no lion eats its fill and is then never hungry again—just as men and all humans will temporarily reach a point at which they are unable to indulge further in food and drink and sex. But no beast hoards without measure—they do not wish to eat their cake and have it. Why do men? Is the answer truly reducible to food and drink and sex?

It is Kleinias, not the Stranger, who anthropomorphizes animals in his imagination, giving them his own desires coupled with what he perceives (or longs for) as their "freedom" from law: a Kleinias in wolf's clothing (cf. 669c–d, 710a, 963e–964a; *Alc. 1.* 132c–135b).[5] It is Kleinias's *own* image of "animal nature" that the Stranger presents to Kleinias, but articulated in words. And Kleinias responds to the severely negative light in which the Stranger casts that image, not to the image's lack of connection to the reality of animal nature. He is ashamed, and accuses the Stranger of excessive hatred (832b).

But that very shame alerts us to something that also tends to accompany wealth, the desire for which can certainly be a part of the desire for wealth in general, and which the Stranger apparently neglected in his description thereof: honor. Given what we have come to know of Kleinias, we may be in a position to articulate the argument that he does not or cannot articulate himself, but that lies at the root of his vehement objection to the Stranger's statement (and given the vehemence of that objection which, we remember, has no analog in anything else Plato ever wrote, we may even be obliged to try to articulate this): not all men hoard in order to later indulge their appetites for the triad of desiderata emphasized by the Stranger. Great wealth also usually means or is coincident with great honor, and in Kleinias's estimation can facilitate (rather than, per the Stranger, summarily preclude [831d1–4]) a proper focus on what is noble and good. Kleinias sees the desire for wealth as a point of articulation between the baser appetites and desire for honor. The love of wealth is shared, agrees Kleinias, but for diametrically opposing reasons: desire of wealth for honor is different in kind, per Kleinias, from desire of wealth for appetite indulgence.

The Stranger does not agree. After being accused of hatred by Kleinias, he almost immediately turns to a lengthy discussion of the city's martial contests and prizes—that is, of contests for honor (832d–835b; with young women included—833c–d, 834a, 834d). Needless to say, this turn pleases (and placates) Kleinias, who is quickly back to his enthusiastic agreement with the Stranger as to the purpose and manner of the contests (832d7, e7, 883a3, a6, c4). But that enthusiasm is to be short-lived, for while Kleinias imagines the pursuit of honor as raising itself above the baser appetites, the Stranger's purpose is to suggest that this devotion to contests and honor— and the release from the "harsh and illiberal labors" that honor despises— will, unchecked, lead precisely to extremes of sexual appetite, to "hubris" (835d6–e2). *Pace* Kleinias, honor seems, in the Stranger's treatment, to be the default human "solution" to the desire to eat one's cake and have it, and the desire to preserve (and even augment) one's appetite in the very act of satisfying it. Unfettered, its propensity is to become infinite. As Shakespeare's Ulysses puts it:

> And appetite, an universal wolf,
> So doubly seconded with will and power,
> Must make perforce an universal prey,
> And last eat up himself.

(Troilus and Cressida I.iii.574–577)

For honor, unlike the desire for food, for example, can never have its plate cleared after having been satisfied: clearing honor's plate even temporarily instantly invokes not just the return, but the extremes, of appetite for honor.

And indeed, Kleinias himself illustrated this in spades in his reaction to the Stranger's insistence that love of wealth was only focused on fulfilling the basest desires. The dishonor Kleinias felt in hearing this is what provoked his inordinate castigation of what he could only see as the Stranger's excessive "hatred": the instant Kleinias's appetite for honor was not satisfied, that appetite compounded and asserted itself.

Kleinias experiences the honorable life as essentially stable and free, and superior to the life of satisfying base appetites (the life of those whom he calls "the mindless many"), because he has never recognized the things to which his own appetite for honor is tethered and by which it is directed, constrained, and made meaningful and fruitful. As we noticed in chapter 1, with respect to education, he does not see how a thing learned or experienced in childhood *unfolds* into a later disposition of character—a disposition experienced later (by Kleinias and by many) as having always been such, and as correct. He therefore imagines his own disposition as independent of baser appetites without realizing that it is still grounded in those appetites and the tyrannical ways in which certain appetites, and certain ways of indulging them, have become either honorable or dishonorable. He imagines, that is, that his own "natural" honorability is what has *discovered* what the truly honorable—and at the same time what the truly shameful—manners of restraining and indulging those appetites are. Kleinias finds the image of a human being as insatiably desiring repugnant and shameful, but he does so because his own insatiable desires have been directed in ways he cannot see. In Platonic terms he is possessed of "true opinion" in this respect: he is right, but cannot understand why, much less articulate it.

It is all well and good to rank the three "loves" in the Platonic image of the soul—love of gain, love of honor, and love of victory—and Plato himself seems to do this, most famously in the *Republic*, and in that order of ascension. But this is always provisional (and of the three corresponding "lovers," only the lover of honor would even care about such a ranking) for in practice, with the exception of those who are utterly shameless, they always contaminate each other. Not to mention that the three "loves" can hardly be said to exhaust the facets of the human soul, even without considering the genuinely philosophical soul (what of love of adventure, for example? And love of God or gods?). It may be remarked that none of the three appetites is discernible in the character of the Stranger or Megillos, or Socrates. They are general— very general—human appetites, but not universal (cf. 875c).

Of the appetites discussed by the Stranger, only those for food, drink, and sex have a satiety that is not necessarily relative to others' enjoyment thereof (as opposed to the *desire* for indulgence, of course, which is potentially unlimited, and potentially envious in a profoundly relative way). There are limits after which even the most hedonistic human being (barring a disease or disorder) will be temporarily sated. By contrast, honor and victory are, in principle and in practice, relative to the core. The only way to limit them—and therefore also truly profit from them—is to limit the appetites whose satiety is not necessarily relative, and to which they remain connected. To liberate those baser appetites is to potentiate the in-principle infinite appetites for honor and victory. The political necessity—which is also always the only political opportunity—is to turn the appetites for honor and victory in part on the baser appetites, and both celebrate their dominance when they are dominant and deplore their weakness when they are weak in this respect.

It is this that leads the Stranger to see that a disciplined sexual regime of a certain type is necessary for Magnesia, and for all cities. The highest end of such discipline is the potential for self-discipline in some human beings. The lowest or urgent end is the constraint of the random directions of drives that enslave their "subjects," into a basic common direction, to *appeal* to honor in doing so, and to thereby generally limit the potentially (and in principle) infinite scope and permutations of the honor-lover. This is the same for food and drink as it is for sex. And to do this means directing desire itself by habituating it to yearn for a noble common object and shun the ignoble. To the modern objection that this restrains freedom of desire, the Stranger would completely agree. It *does* restrain the freedom of desire. But to the modern assumption that "I" as an autonomous subject am infringed upon with respect to "my" desires, the Stranger would emphatically disagree: a desire comes when *it* wants to, not when "*I*" want it to (cf. Nietzsche, *BGE* 17, and above all 188). The modern objection is confused here as to which is the subject, and which the predicate.

Megillos is a different story. Megillos does not follow an analogy around as if "it had no bridle in its mouth." He "pulls it up, like a horse" instead (701c–d). This is not evidence of a slow intellect incapable of following an argument, or impatient to have done with it, but of a keen and thoughtful mind reflecting on what is said, what that means, and the understandings, perplexities, and objections that are part and parcel of such reflection. Megillos and Kleinias each raise a different and severe objection to the Stranger's discourse—Megillos in Book 7, and Kleinias in Book 8. We have examined Kleinias's objections, so we are prepared to examine those of Megillos.

"For the sake of brevity," as Marsilius of Padua likes to say, it may be helpful to consider Megillos's objections in Book 7 in schematic outline.

Book 7

Megillos's first objection: The Stranger says outright that "human things are not worthy of any great seriousness, though it is unfortunately necessary to take them seriously," that human beings are "mostly puppets, but share in small portions of truth," and that playing games as divinely directed is what their children should believe is correctly dictated, in order "to live throughout their lives according to the way of nature" (804a4–b4). Megillos responds with dismay: "You hold our human race in complete contempt, Stranger" (804b5–6).

Megillos's second objection: The sequel to Megillos's first objection—which is the Stranger's "response" to Megillos—includes the Stranger's own most pointed objection to Cretan and Spartan law, and the most insulting to their legislators. Not "the many," as Kleinias believes, but the Cretan and Spartan legislators, have been "most mindless of all," for they have enacted or allowed through neglect the almost complete separation of male and female practices (805a). Megillos had directly addressed the Stranger concerning the whole of "our human race," with his first objection. He now turns to Kleinias to ask *him* what they ought to do about the Stranger disparaging *Sparta* (as opposed to the whole of our human race) (806c). Also: the Stranger has deliberately phrased this as a specific criticism of the Laconic regime and lawgiver, but it applies in spades to the Cretan regime and lawgiver as well. We are reminded of the way in which Megillos rose to the defense of *Sparta* in Book 1, when it was *Crete* that the Stranger had criticized (636e–637a). Following this, one of Kleinias's most substantial changes of heart occurs (805b–c).

Consider: What Megillos first objects to is something that, if true, is extraordinarily difficult for most human beings to accept: human beings are for the most part puppets (*thaumata*) or playthings of the god or gods—however god or gods are to be understood—sharing only in small portions of the truth. Aside from those small portions, human life as a whole is contemptible for anyone who would take no satisfaction in merely being a plaything of the gods. What Megillos has not understood—has perhaps resisted understanding—is that satisfaction is in fact enjoyed in such an existence, though no one who found such satisfaction would be likely to attach to such an existence such a description of it. This is what the Stranger will guide him to reflect upon in their moment of "stepping aside" in Book 8 (which we will discuss shortly), and indeed was recognized by at least one pre-Platonic philosopher as at once the impetus to philosophy for some very few, and a complete obstacle (*skandalon*) thereto for others (Empedocles frag. B2.1–8). It is *not* the case that Plato presents Megillos here as completely and finally foreclosed to acknowledging this possibility about human existence. What must be seen is whether or not Megillos can come to entertain that possibility as a possibility, and it is perhaps not so damning a mark of his character that he does not leap too eagerly at this possibility as a conclusion to be satisfied with, or to relish. Nor is the turn toward the divine or the whole cosmos implied in the affirmation of such a conclusion as easy in deed as in word. One may indeed ask whether guidance along the edge of this potential abyss is not one of the principal purposes of any philosopher's teaching, and further whether this very purpose does not mark the essential difference between the few philosophers' teaching, and the teachings of the more abundant and prolific nonphilosophers. Megillos has, on his own, come to see the limitations of Sparta, of Crete, of Athens, and perhaps of Hellas in general. But he seems to have in the process placed his hope in the human species as a whole, in "*our* human race." Confronted with the essential limitations of our species as a whole, he is initially dismayed, and perplexed. He is wayless, and in need of a guide.

We may suggest here that those critics of Megillos who write him off as merely "political" for his objection to the Stranger's criticism of the human species, or who judge him based on this objection to be narrow of mind and spirit, have not for one instant demonstrated by those criticisms any awareness of the "abyss-deep" confrontation he is facing. Certainly, for my part, I am far more impressed by Megillos's objection, which indicates such an awareness; than by Glaukon's easy acceptance of Socrates's denigration of "human things," an acceptance that seems to derive from a complete *lack* of awareness of the consequences of that truth (the Stranger's statement on human things not being "worthy of any great seriousness" at 803b3–4 is almost word-for-word identical with what Socrates says to Glaukon in Book 10 of the *Republic* [604b10–c1]).[6] This is to say nothing of the easy criticisms of scholars who seem to categorize Megillos as somehow deficient in character, without themselves demonstrating any awareness that there is even a confrontation to face.

This does not of course mean that I accuse all scholars who give no explicit or easy evidence that they are aware of this confrontation and its gravity of having no awareness thereof. There are quite valid reasons for declining in ordinary circumstances to force this confrontation on one's readers and on those who surround us.

The other side of this scholarly or scholastic problem, however, is to include the awareness of human insignificance *within* what is insignificant. Thus Hobbs (2000), for example, too easily assumes that what Socrates means by his statement in the *Republic* (and presumably, what the Stranger means in the *Laws*) is that if "[m]an does not matter much," then "the perception that this is so does not matter much either" (217). She assumes, that is, that this "perception" is a predicate of the subject "man," which is precisely the grammatical relationship and ethic that the *experience* of this truth undermines (cf. 951b4–7). We would suggest that this suggests a lack of proper reflection on, among other things, the Book of Job; and above all a lack of experience of the confrontation that such a parable attempts to relate or perhaps provoke.[7]

In the *Laws*, the envelopment of this "subject" by this "predicate" is gestured at with what Dunshirn terms the "autoreferentiality" of the Stranger's comments on human beings as "playthings of god" (803c4–5), inasmuch as the Stranger is a "plaything" of Plato—Plato, the "demiurge of the dialogues that mediate, in the action (*Bewegung*) of figures similar to himself, a reflection of the infinite dialectical motion (*Bewegung*)" (Dunshirn 2010, 59; my translation). As Dunshirn then goes on to rightly say, "It is up to each reader of the Platonic dialogues to see to what extent *he* is spoken to by such self-referential passages in those dialogues" (my emphasis). We may note here that Hobbs's reference to "perception" is inaccurate, in Plato's terms, and perhaps commits her grammatically to her assumption (cf. Nietzsche, *BGE* Preface on the "seduction of grammar"). The "small portions of truth" to which human beings have potential access are not *perceived* in Plato's terms or the Stranger's, but *participated in* (*metechontes*—804b4). Plato's Stranger is not teaching a doctrine to be merely observed and analyzed here, but provoking in Megillos what Dunshirn—following Heidegger—calls an *event* (*Ereignis*) to be experienced.

One may seriously ask whether this moment is the parallel to Kleinias's moment of shame that reveals Kleinias to be in "the greatest ignorance" with respect to the value of moneyed wealth. Does Megillos in fact *know* the Stranger to be correct in his assessment of human things, while desiring this to be otherwise? Does his heart deny, at this point, what his head cannot?

We turn to Book 8.

Book 8

In Book 8, very briefly, the Stranger and Megillos "digress" to speak of the incest prohibition that obtains in all political communities (838a–d). That digression is carefully orchestrated by the Stranger, with the willing help of Megillos. We are tempted to search for—and to find—an obvious connection between the Stranger's proposals for dishonoring or prohibiting homosexuality, and the incest prohibition that he invokes after making those proposals (thus Schöpsdau 1996–2011, vol. 3, 189). But the connection between the two is far from clear. The conversation follows immediately on the Stranger's discussion of the types of friendship, and begins with the Stranger explicitly asking Megillos, in very warm terms, whether he agrees that they want, if possible, only that friendship in the city that is based on virtue, and that desires the young to become the best [they can?] (837d4–7): "What do we say [about this], Megillos *my friend* (*ô phile Megille*)?" (327d7–8; Megillos is "my friend" again almost immediately, at e2–3). It ends when the Stranger explicitly includes Kleinias in the discussion again, asking if "you both want (*boulesthe*) me to attempt to give you both (*humin*) a somewhat persuasive argument" that reforming the erotic regime of the Cretans is possible (839d8–10).

Here's the set-up:

As we noted earlier (chapter 1), when the Stranger, in Book 8, overstates the case that tragic characters always immediately commit suicide if they engage in incest, Megillos—very diplomatically, it should be noted—declines to agree with him (838c9–d2). The Stranger, speaking of a "little phrase that quenches all such hedonisms" (i.e., of incest), describes that phrase as:

> The one that declares that these things are in no way pious, but hated by the gods and the most shameful of shameful things. Isn't the cause in fact that no one ever says anything else, but from the moment of birth each of us hears people saying these things, always and everywhere? In jokes and in every serious tragedy isn't it frequently said—and when they bring on Thyestas [plural of Thyestes] or those Oedipuses, or those Macareuses who secretly have intercourse with their sisters, isn't it seen that they promptly inflict upon themselves the penalty of death for their transgression? (838b10–c9; Pangle's translation with minor modifications).

What Megillos responds is this: "You speak most correctly to this extent, that a kind of amazing power falls to an utterance, when not even a single person attempts at any time to *breathe*[8] against the law in some other way" (838c9–d2).

Just as with his response "*kalôs men oun*" (617d6) that we considered in chapter 1, Megillos's response to the Stranger at 838c9–d2 presents itself initially as agreement, but closer consideration reveals that agreement to be qualified in such a way as to express *dis*agreement in a key respect: his explicit agreement in one respect is so phrased as to be a *lack* of explicit agreement in another. He begins, "you speak most correctly" (*Orthotata legeis*), exactly as he had spoken shortly before in the conversation, when he responded to a much broader solicitation or statement of agreement between himself and the Stranger (837e8, cf. 838b6). There, however, he offered his statement without qualification, whereas here he continues: "*to this extent . . .*" (*to ge tosouton . . .*), and then describes the "amazing power" that falls to an utterance that is not even breathed against (cf. Strauss 1975, 120–21), while offering no agreement whatsoever about the Stranger's examples from Athenian tragedy. But it was about precisely those examples that the Stranger had inquired, and in asking whether Megillos concurred about his characterization of three tragic characters' immediate suicide following incest, the Stranger had spoken as if he expected Megillos to be familiar with these examples (something he never does with Kleinias).

Thus whereas Kleinias did not challenge the Stranger's universal images of animal nature, Megillos here gently refuses the Stranger's discourse on the universal fate of incestuous characters in tragedy. But nor does he loudly advertise this refusal, and our careful reading of Book 1 suggests that this is not surprising, and that we should not simply assume his subtlety to be a sign of ignorance. And as a matter of fact, the Stranger has almost completely mischaracterized the fates of his tragic examples, Thyestes, Oedipus, and

Macareus. In no extant version or fragment of the plays in which these characters feature do *any* of them "give themselves without hesitation the penalty of death for their error (*tês hamartias*)" of incest. Pangle (1988) implies that Macareus does, noting that he "killed himself after committing incest with his sister Conace" (532n13), but the fragments of Euripides (16, 18, 19, 27, and 28, Nauck) and Ovid's later *Heroides* (Ep. 11) tell another story: Macareus kills himself in grief after Conace carries out the order for her suicide by her father Aeolus—an order given, it should be added, not because she committed incest, but because that incest was adulterous (she was betrothed, after conceiving a child with Macareus, to a *different* brother). Thyestes—who, it may be remarked, was also the unwitting cannibal of his own sons—does not kill himself, and in fact succeeds in the purpose for which he raped his daughter to begin with. And if Oedipus does in fact kill himself (the fourth episode of Sophocles's *Oedipus at Colonus*, presents his death as an apotheosis announced by Zeus, at the end of Oedipus's very long life—and suicide does *not* seem to be suggested [*Oed. Col.* 1656–1664, 1678–1682]), it is certainly not "without hesitation" (he is a middle-aged man when he discovers he has committed incest, and a very old one when he dies), as the Stranger later makes perfectly clear that he knows (931b5–7). The only character involved in these incestuous relationships who does immediately commit suicide is Jocaste, the mother and then wife of Oedipus, and then only in Sophocles's version (she obviously has not done so at the outset of Euripides's *Phoenician Women*, and in that play kills herself in grief for the deaths of her sons).[9]

Megillos's refusal to agree with these flagrant mischaracterizations confirms, to the Stranger and to us, that he is familiar with Athenian tragedy, and that we might call the "problem of Oedipus" has the opportunity to come to light (recall that Megillos had made it explicitly clear, in Book 1, that he had attended at least two, if not more, tragic festivals [637b]). The subtlety of that refusal—his phrasing it in such a way that Kleinias, who is not at all familiar with Athenian tragedy, will not hear it—confirms his shared understanding with the Stranger that the light into which this problem comes must necessarily cast the shadow of its beholder—the shadow of Megillos—on that problem.

Before turning to that problem, though, we should remark that Megillos's subtlety here demonstrates as well his recognition that the tragic examples of Thyestes(es) and Oedipus and Macareus observe the law in the breach. They do not, in breaking this law, "attempt to breathe against the law in some other way," nor do their poets (Sophocles and Euripides) do so with their characters. Their notable breaches reinforce the strength of the unwritten law, rather than threaten it.

In fact, those breaches and variations, in the sacred stories we hear, are necessary for any law that is not simply determined once and for all by nature (such as "human beings must breathe to live"), and even more so for laws by which it comes to seem "natural" to believe and behave in a way that would not necessarily be expected outside of a political order (665c). As Winch (1959) puts it, in a slightly different context, a society without such breaches, but that would still somehow keep the law constant within, would be a society like Swift's Houyhnhnms, who cannot say what is not (246–47). And while Clark (2003) is correct to note that in this respect "[t]he words of the poets, repeated by the masses, are infinitely more effective in restraining sexual desires than the most strong-armed legislation could ever be" (137), he thereby misses the point that the poets are as much bound up in "breathing" the unwritten law against incest as "the masses" they speak to: the poets—unless they *happen* to be philosophers too—are part of the masses (670e5–671a1, 802b7–c2). The philosopher alone is capable of truly reflecting on the contingent character of such unwritten laws (*Rep.* 461b10–e3, 463b9–e3).

This is so because reflection requires a lack of indignation: one cannot begin to consider anything when one has already decided in advance both that it is bad or evil, and what its cause is, and both of these with the punitive sureness to which indignation commits us (compare 634c5–8, 638c2–4, 640d9–e6, 660c6–d1, especially 693a5–b2, 730b5–c1, and 934d1–935c7 [n.b. *thêrioumenos*—"becoming a beast"—at 935a5]; with 717d1–6, 730d2–7, 739d3–6, 798d1–5, and especially 822e4–823a2; also *Apol.* 35e1 and 38c1–5; Nietzsche, *BGE* 26; Parens 1995, 126–27).[10] Perhaps the most remarkable, and most important, thing we should therefore note is that Megillos demonstrates no indignation at all in response to an issue that provokes indignation in virtually everyone, and that the Stranger seemed to *try* to provoke specifically in him. The Stranger has seen that Megillos could be so provoked—the latter's response to the characterization of human beings as puppets who participate in only small portions of truth showed that very clearly. And the Stranger's description here of human enslavement to the unwritten law reiterates precisely that earlier charge: "Do you see?" he says to Megillos, "Puppets—nor is that necessarily a bad thing." With Megillos's earlier pronounced indignation on behalf of "our human race," Plato draws our attention to its absence in his response here. Something has changed for Megillos.

The Stranger in fact confronts Megillos with dueling indignation provocations. On the one hand, he is reiterating his earlier judgment of human beings as puppets. On the other, he is presenting exactly that legal opinion which, with *its* claims on the indignation of all citizens of all cities, illustrates why the Stranger made that earlier judgment. And he presents that issue in the strongest political terms: incest is "in no way pious," "hated by the gods" and "the most shameful of shameful things" (838b10–c1). In tragedies, incestuous characters immediately commit suicide, and rightly so (though of course, as we have seen, none of the characters the Stranger mentions actually do so—which might itself provoke indignation in a good citizen).

Megillos responds with no indignation at all, instead going to the heart of the issue. He can agree that the unwritten law against incest is most certainly just and necessary without feeling any indignation about this. He can also, as we will examine shortly, freely consider whether the unwritten prohibition against incest is by nature, or whether it is in fact a law properly speaking: that is, he can consider *human* nature because he is not a mere puppet of the cities' opinion, regardless of how just or true that opinion is. [11]

It is worthwhile noting a little word play the Stranger had used during the conversation in Book 7 that Megillos indignantly rebelled against. In calling human beings "puppets," he had picked up on his earlier image or myth (from Book 1), using the word *thauma* (804d3; cf. 644d7, 645b1). A *thauma* is indeed a puppet, but literally it is "something to wonder at"—the Stranger speaks the word of philosophy: "Here is something to wonder at," he says. Of course, philosophical wonder about, and therefore clear-eyed examination of, human beings and human things leads to his meager assessment of the seriousness they deserve, an assessment that Megillos indignantly objects to. In response to Megillos's objection, the Stranger switches immediately to the word of the city, of politics and law: *Mê thaumasêis*—"Don't be amazed!," as Pangle translates, but literally, "*Do not wonder*" (804b7; cf., importantly, *Crito* 50c7–9). Philosophy says, circumspectly: this provokes wonder. The city—or "the cause"—says: Keep moving, folks—nothing to see here. Megillos was sorely tempted. [12]

That being said, we return to the problem of Oedipus. The Stranger had obliquely drawn our attention to this problem mere moments before he takes Megillos aside for the conversation we are considering. He did so by evoking "the law as it was before Laius," Oedipus's father, in order to mythically locate the origins of legally acceptable practices of homosexuality in Laius's rule (836c1–2). According to a scholiast (at Euripides, *Phoenician Women* 1760; quoted in full by Sewell-Rutter 2007, 61–62), Laius was the "first to have this unlawful [*athemiton*] eros," raping Chrysippus and going unpunished for the offense by the Thebans, whom Hera therefore cursed with the Sphinx (and perhaps with a riddle more terrible by far than the Sphinx's riddle). This curse is what leads—by curious pathways, and by curses of successive generations of fathers on their own children (a tradition that Oedipus himself will continue and thereby end)—to the parricide of Laius and the incest between Oedipus and his mother: Oedipus knows neither that Laius is his father nor that Jocaste is his mother when he later meets them. He is neither a witting parricide, nor a witting participant in incest.

But if he is not a witting participant, it is hard to see how he can be a willing (*hekôn*) one, and here the problem of Oedipus arises. For Oedipus and Jocaste are condemned in our imagination (and, as it were, in their own) by the unwritten law against incest just as much as "willing" participants such as Thyestes or Macareus, or Conace (and whereas, for example, the parricide could potentially be "cleansed," the incest certainly could not). Indeed, the shame of this unwritten law extends even to those, such as Thyestes's daughter Pelopeia, who are raped incestuously.[13] A later synopsis of her story (no classical references to her story survive) relates that when Pelopeia discovers that her son is a child of incest, she kills herself (Hyg. *Fab.* 88). Such themes are, to say the least, the same in virtually every modern society as well. When the Stranger speaks of refraining from incest as something everyone does "not unwillingly (*akontes*), but willingly (*hekontes*) to the greatest degree" (838a a6–7), he speaks of this restraint in the same spirit that he did of the "power of money" over "every man"—as an "enslavement" (838d4) by a desire—*against* incest or *for* money—that one is "compelled" (832a6) to desire. He speaks of something the anathema of which seems to have nothing to do with "willingness" whatsoever. If by "natural" we mean "involuntary," and by convention or law we mean "voluntary," both the human desire for money and the human revulsion at incest seem to be natural.

The lesson that Megillos has learned, with the Stranger's subtle pointing, is that the nature of "voluntary" self-restraint with respect to the things of Aphrodite looks nothing, in general and in deed, like the reflective moderation exhorted by the Stranger in his testing of Kleinias's erotic drives. Rather than depending on a reflective desire (for honor) to be "better than the animals at least," effective restraint of erotic desire depends on "devices" that direct the same *lack* of reflection that makes animals "virtuous" in their sexual activity—the same lack of reflection, we recall, that was said to lead to such "virtue" in the postpolitical Cyclopean peoples.[14] These families do not appear to be so remote in time as the Stranger's myth seemed originally to suggest.

The Stranger had already understood that Megillos was in harmony with his advocacy of moderation when he turned to Megillos to ask whether they were in harmony. It was Megillos who had subtly introduced the practice and consequences of *paederasteia* at the outset, and thereby opened it for criticism (637b3–5); and it was Megillos who showed himself to have already understood that the Spartan institutions are somehow directed at developing moderation, and not just courage, as a specific goal, in Book 1 (633d4, 636a2–3)—he understands this because *he* experienced those institutions as such.[15] Megillos is both reflective and moderate in the highest sense of both of these dispositions (which means that his devotion to reflection is the only thing untouched by his moderation). What the Stranger must draw his attention to is the gulf that thereby separates him from a man like Kleinias, without at the same time drawing Kleinias's attention to this, and he can count on Megillos's reflective capacity to enable him to see the hint, and on his moderation not to reveal what he comes to understand with its aid. We must therefore completely disagree with Clark (2003), who interprets this as "a little trap" for Megillos (136). It is a compassionate and philanthropic lesson from a philosopher for a potential philosopher. The Stranger has brought the conversation with Megillos full circle, back to the discussion that drew from him such dismay: human beings as puppets. But there is a difference.

The immediate political purpose of that lesson is to show Megillos why he needs to move from focusing on bringing the erotic restraint suggested by the Stranger to fruition (838e), to letting the whole topic go. The test that the Stranger puts Kleinias through (as discussed in chapter 5) is also a demonstration *to* Megillos *of* that test. "You have something like this in mind for moderating sexual excess, I think," implies the Stranger to Megillos. "Your expectations of human beings are more excessive than the sexual license that you, not without reason, would like to change—pay attention while I show you something." But to show him this, a much deeper lesson is needed, and Megillos must be provoked again to look closely at the whole of "our human race," without flinching at what the examination yields. He had flinched in Book 7; he does not here.

And indeed, following his discussion with the Stranger on the unwritten law, Megillos does in fact completely let go of the topic—sexual license— that had earlier inspired him to concerned and hopeful intervention, cheerfully acknowledging that while he would accept the Stranger's law concerning the restraint of erotic behavior, Kleinias must decide for himself (842a). Kleinias defers his own decision until later—which turns out, as expected, to be never—and Megillos is willing to leave it at that. Megillos has understood the Stranger's effort to tutor him, and why that effort was made. It behooves us to situate the short but intense conversation that provoked that understanding and change of heart in the ways in which its theme has been building since much earlier in the *Laws*.

This brings us back to our earlier statement concerning the Stranger and Megillos, and their free consideration of whether or not the incest prohibition is "by nature." For while the sexual behavior advocated by the Stranger with respect to heterosexual, monogamous, child-producing relationships is explicitly said by him to be "laid down according to nature" (839a6–7),[16] since child-producing through intercourse is "according to nature" (838e6); the unwritten law against incest is said to obtain its force because "everyone, both slaves and free men, and children and women and the entire city" hold a "[prophetic] utterance *sacred* (*kathierôsas . . . tên phêmên*)," a "little utterance," the "utterance that [incest] is in no way pious, is hated by the gods, and is the most shameful of shameful things" (838b7, b10–11, d6–8). The very example (and exemplar) of a law that the Stranger says will demonstrate how his "natural" law might in fact be possible, is not, as Strauss notes, said in any way to be natural (Strauss 1975, 121).

Not only this, but the implications of the Stranger's mythical "archaeology" in Book 3 on clan life and the rule of the Cyclopes specifically, if subtly, develop a picture (which, to stress it again, is a mythical one and, for the Greeks, a terrible one at that) in which incest does appear to occur naturally if it is not constrained politically. He stresses that these regimes were of "single families and clans" (680d7–e4, 681a7–b7), and it does not seem to the Stranger that it was easy for the people of that time to "mix with each other," given that there were virtually no means of transportation left (678c6–9). The Stranger's quote from Homer on the Cyclopes is remarkable: it highlights only the aspect of the isolated family as comprising the whole of each regime (680b5–c1, quoting *Odyssey* 9.112–115), and Homer's account as a whole— that is, beyond the few lines quoted by the Stranger—seems exaggeratedly inappropriate for supporting almost any of the other claims that the Stranger is making about the "simple" or childlike people of the postdiluvian time in his myth. For example, the lack of hubris of these simple people (679b8–c1) is the opposite of what Homer's Odysseus says of the Cyclopes (*Odyssey* 6.5, 9.106); and the lack of the "arts of war" (679d5–6, 678e2–4) certainly does not mean that the Cyclopes were not aggressively warlike (*Od.* 6.4–6), though the Stranger claims that war (and civil war) was in fact "destroyed at that time" (678e6–7).[17] The first mention of the Cyclopes by Homer—in his own words, incidentally, not in the mouth of Odysseus—illustrates precisely their warlike ways (*Od.* 6. 4–6). And the Cyclopes are hardly a model of "delightedness and friendliness" (678e9–10; cf. c5) upon seeing strangers!

What they are a model of is the isolated political community that is a single family, and whose generative activity is *ipso facto* "incestuous."[18] As Ficino stresses, it is this community or regime that is based "on nature" (*Arg. de leg.* book 3; 2009, 87–88). We will resist the temptation to call this Plato's "state of nature" (though the influence of this section—and the *Laws* in general—on Hobbes in particular may be remarked), for it would more accurately be called his "city of pigs" (cf. 819d1–8 with *Rep.* 372c5–d6). What is more, as the Stranger obliquely indicates with his citation from Homer, each of these families must have its own language (681e5; Homer, *Il.* 20.217, especially *meropôn*; cf. Strabo, *Geog.* 13.1.25, especially *hê tôn onomatôn kat' oligon metalêpsis*—"the translation of the [many] names into few").[19] The "general *nomos*," to borrow Averroës's term, that unites these diverse families into a single community, must establish at the same time a common language and a basic common measure of esteem which it will be unwise in the future to directly alter (Averroës, *On Plato's* Republic, Rosenthal p. 47; cf. also 57 and especially 62–63 on "the general common nomos that not a single nation can help choosing"; 2005, 47–48, 64–65, 74–75).[20] It is not necessary, or in fact possible, to ascertain *exactly* how such a "general nomos" first came to be, nor is that the Stranger's point in elaborating his myth. What is important, for understanding, is that the existence of any particular human *political* community presupposes and is itself the evidence of such a nomos. Is that nomos natural?

It is also important that this nomos be both symbolically and demonstratively untouched and untouchable, that that cohesion be as demonstrably evident to the lawgiver as according to nature for all cities as it is unquestionably obvious that it is by nature for all human beings to all citizens. It is in this sense that the universality of the unwritten law against incest is an image of nature in the deepest sense, though it can only by suggestion be paralleled with those images of natural conduct that are observable in other animal species and seem worthy of imitation.

That being said, we must note that *precisely if* we understand the Stranger's analogical assertion of child-production as the only natural direction and compulsion of human sexual desire, then the unwritten law against incest *cannot* be natural in this way.[21] Likewise, if we accept as true that our revulsion at incest is natural, as we are certainly inclined to do, then sex-as-reproduction cannot be natural in the same way, or as the Stranger seems to assert it. The necessities of the city necessarily and naturally (and polemically) intrude on the necessities of nature. The *polis* is in that case naturally at war (*polemos*) against nature, and every city *will* lose, as Plato emphasizes in his myth of the *Laws* (cf. Thucydides 3.84.2).[22] We are thus brought to the inevitable conclusion—a conclusion that Plato does not dissemble—that winning this war was not Plato's point (cf. the theme of *oligon chronon* vs. *polun chronon* in *Apology of Socrates* 18c, 19a, 21b, 24a, 32a, 33b–c, 37a–b, 38c; with *husterôi chronôi* at 32b, *tosouton chronon* at 39e, *prosthen chronôi* at 40a, *ho pas chronos* at 40e, and *ton loipon chronon* at 41c).[23]

The introduction of nature as the standard of right is thus accomplished by appeal to a fairly pedestrian or common intuitive reliance on the easily observable, and analogy with the easily observable, but the establishment and use of that standard undermines that very common intuition completely. What is more, the unwritten law against incest brings into specific focus the massive ambiguities attending the experience of the voluntary and the involuntary, for "most human beings, howsoever lawless (*paranomous*) they are, precisely reject intercourse with beautiful people [from their families], not unwillingly (*akontes*), but willingly (*hekontes*) to the highest degree . . . [for] there is *no desire* at all among the many for such intercourse, neither by openly sleeping together nor hidden away, nor by any other embrace" (838a4–b5). But this is no more "willing" or "voluntary," on the Stranger's terms, than the Cyclopes' "naïve" relations alluded to in Book 3. In fact, this is clearly a pedestrian and common intuitive image of what "voluntary" is like, and the Stranger (like Socrates, and like Plato) very obviously holds a very uncommon and reflective view of what voluntary is. In the unreflective image, what is "conventional" differs from what is "natural" merely by historical accident: those who "voluntarily" desist from incest under the unwritten law are compelled in a direction opposite to that of the "voluntary" actors under the paternal law of the Cyclopes, but by the same process of the soul (cf. 835e6–836a1 and 838b4–5; Al-Farabi, *Summary* 8.7: "being mindful and controlling something not distinguishable from its contrary is very difficult"). And those Stavrogins and Verkhovensky's of the spirit who would perhaps "willingly" flout the convention are in fact compelled by the identical process, with an additional step, and become obscene parodies of "liberty" (cf. Benardete 2000, 243; citing *Rep.* 571b3–d4). They understand themselves no more at the end of their stories than does Raskolnikov at the outset of his: ideological commitments, convictions of one's own superiority to the mob, arguments for the spiritual ends of extraordinary means—all conceal from the pale criminal his akratic "longing for the bliss of the knife" (Nietzsche, *TSZ* I, "On the Pale Criminal"). The compulsion of the unwritten law here directs the erotic nature of longing—of "willingness"—in the transgression itself.

Does the unwritten law pertain to the kind of "friendship" that the Stranger and Megillos agree is the only truly desirable one for their city—the friendship based on virtue and desire that the young become excellent? Or does it really only pertain to the other kinds of "friendship" that are based on or at least include bodily desire—"hungering for the bloom of youth like it was ripe fruit" (837c1–2)[24]—the kinds that the Stranger and Megillos agree would, if possible (and it obviously is not), be forbidden in the city altogether (837d4–7)?[25] As we observed at the outset of this chapter, for those rare Socrates-types for whom the first kind of friendship is the only kind, the unwritten law against incest would seem to be as negligible as the unwritten law directing one to devote one's time and attention to raising and nurturing one's "own" children because they are "one's own" rather than, say, the best children because they are the best (*Crito* 48c; cf. 45c–d and 50d). If all citizens and inhabitants of Magnesia were of this sort, neither the "natural" law that promotes moderate sexual behavior, nor the unwritten and seemingly "unnatural" law against incest would be necessary. In this respect, we might consider which law "*this* law" [*houtos ho nomos*] refers to (837e9, 838l e5, e5, 839a3, b2, b5, c2, and c6 [*touto*]) with respect to the "tens of thousands of good things" the Stranger forecasts, if "this law becomes perpetual and prevails." Along with eliminating "erotic frenzy and mania and all adulteries," and making friends of husbands and wives, the Stranger claims that this law would also prevent "all drinking and eating without measure" (839a3–b3). Does the Stranger mean the law governing sexual behavior that he discussed with Kleinias (836c1–e3), or the law concerning friendship that he discussed with Megillos (837d2–8)? Which, or what, is "the *true* law in [his] mind" (*en tôi nôi nomon alêthê*—836e5)?[26] The "good things" that the

Stranger says would follow from "this law" would indeed seem to follow immediately if the soul-to-soul friendship that he and Megillos admire were the rule rather than the exception: the city would have no one but Strangers and Megillos's and Socrates's (cf. 627e–628a, 631a–632b)! And it is difficult to believe that the Stranger assumes that severe restriction of sexual behavior would decrease, rather than increase immoderate drinking and eating in the short term. The short term, however, is not his point here (*pace* Clark 2003, 137), for he explicitly speaks of the effects of "this law" *if* it "becomes *perpetual* [*diênekês*] and *prevails* [*kratêsas*]." Setting aside the extreme difficulties of the short-term *establishment* of the law discussed with Kleinias (which difficulties, as we noted in chapter 5, the Stranger does not in fact believe can be overcome here), the Stranger seems to suggest that the long-term constant prevalence of such a law—if it were to obtain (and one might fruitfully consider Jewish, Christian, and Islamic laws of sexual moderation in this regard)[27]—would direct the habituations and practices of its subjects *toward* (*pros*) soul-to-soul friendship as the highest human relationship (cf. Schöpsdau 2003). Is this kind of friendship, then, naturally right—"the true law in mind"?[28]

It would be difficult indeed to see how such friendship or *erôs* "accords with nature" in the sense that the Stranger says that monogamous heterosexual coupling for the sake of child-making does, for nothing indicates that monogamy or heterosexuality[29] are, or ought to be, even considerations for this second *erôs*; and this sort of lover "considers the sating of body by body to be wanton (*hubris*)" (837c6–7), and "wants rather to be always chaste (*hagneuein*) with a chaste beloved" (c8–d1): even where heterosexual, the increasing "vehemence" of this *erôs* would only make the possibility of human offspring more remote. Lovers of this sort would most especially have to be compelled to produce children (783d8–784b6). Such a lover, moreover, "stands in awe of and reveres what is moderate, courageous, magnificent, and what is sensible (*to phronimon*)" (837c7–8). Of his or her reverence or awe of justice and right the Stranger says not a word. Would a person who *is* just be someone who does not stand in awe of justice, and would need no reverence for it? Does the standard for right itself hold or need to hold that standard? To put it in more Platonic terms, does the form[30] of justice participate in itself in the same way that "the just things" participate in it? Or to use an analogy that is incomplete at best, if there were a book—and some would say that there is such a book or books—in which was reflected the complete understanding of law or justice, properly speaking a reader ought to be in awe of and revere that book and its author. But one would not expect the same reverence or awe from the book for itself, nor from the author for him- or herself, and the regard of the author for the book would not be characterized by the same reverence and awe as that of a novitiate to that book. Ion is like neither the Muse nor Homer just as Euthyphro is like neither Zeus nor

Hesiod. Conversely, a Socrates does not require any awe (*aidos*) or reverence for justice to live without harming anyone—as a way of life, this is self-evident to him: *er kann nicht anders*; whereas as a *principle* or *maxim* of justice, "do not harm anyone" (to say nothing of other maxims) can only be enjoined by persuasion or compulsion and sacred awe. This is the quandary that the Stranger addresses under the name of "the greatest ignorance"—to believe something is noble or true, but to lack the complete desire to act in accordance therewith, or to have desires to act otherwise.

The tensions between the two are in a way imaginatively resolved in the tragic experience of the incest prohibition, which in its absoluteness refuses to acknowledge the innocence of any participant—no matter how unwitting or unwilling—and is thereby a higher reflection of natural right than is normally imagined. Before this law, in Greek tragedy, there can be no special pleading, no acceptance of innocence whatsoever if a transgression has occurred, no pardon (this is not the case in circumstances of *non*-incestuous rape—Iole in Sophocles's *Women of Trachis* being a supreme example of this). The incest prohibition insists, regardless of any notion of fairness or equity, on the guilt of anyone involved in its transgression, and therefore dimly reflects the disposition of genuine responsibility, which must necessarily, voluntarily, gather the *whole* of one's experience without exception into one's agency—into autonomy in its only true sense.

Where the complete desire for the noble or true way exists together with knowledge concerning these ways, reverential awe for justice is superfluous. That awe (*aidos*), which is a kind of fear called "shame" (*aischunê*), is a political or conventional substitute for this desire, and is a fear of the opinion of others or the "noblest fear" of the gods (646e11–647a6, 671d1–3) on account of which the unwilling are made "willing" to be "enslaved to the laws" and thereby made friendly to each other (698b–c, 699c). But the conventional aims at the natural, at what is right by nature. This may, where it does indeed so aim, be called "rational laws" (*sic*), but with the ambiguity of that term as it is alluded to most particularly by Maimonides and Halevi (see especially Maimonides, *Guide* 3.29 [cf. beginning remarks on the doctrine of the Sabians with *Laws* 821a2–b6]; Halevi, *Kuzari* 2.47–8, 3.7–11; Strauss 1988a, 95–141; also Al-Farabi, *Summary* 7.12–13; Ficino, *Arg. de leg.* 12): truly rational is the guidance given by the wise to the wise—that is, to themselves and to young or old natural philosophers;[31] second in terms of "rational law" is its image, which is incomplete by nature and necessity, and is the law given by the wise to those who are in "the greatest ignorance" with respect to the noble or the true (cf. 711d7–712a3).

"Third in virtue," one may say, are the laws that make "friends" of the parties, and allow the legislator—through laws that extend far beyond his or her lifetime—to comprehend and welcome the broad diversity of human failings and opportunities that must necessarily exist for any community to establish itself and thrive. And that allow the legislator to "take aside *his* [*or her*] *own*, drawing the heatedly wild and chafing youngster away from those he grazes with (*sunnomôn*) and, currying and gentling him, bring in a private groom, giving him everything that properly belongs to the rearing of [that] child" (666e3–7). This is, properly speaking, the rational law, the law that neglects no part of the whole and which, for that very reason, accords with nature.

Having provisionally accepted the distinction between nature and nomos, we are now in a position to qualify it. Nature is, as we have seen, involuntary in the strictest sense. The nature of the philosopher's disposition toward truth—the complete accord of his or her desires with the investigations of unassisted human reason—is natural. It cannot be "willed" into being, though it can of course be cultivated or neglected or perverted. Nomoi, inasmuch as they are taken responsibility for, are voluntary (the Stranger comes very close to explicitly saying that a "worthless lawgiver" is simply a part of "nature"—747c6–d1).[32] But this does not mean that all or even most who are under such nomoi behave voluntarily. Nomoi work by producing natural responses and behaviors to themselves—for example, the unwritten nomos against incest. While the vast majority of people refrain from incest in deed and in desire—and therefore "with the greatest willingness"—their willingness in this respect is no different than a willingness to breathe, or than the willingness of "most birds and other animals" to couple and create children: we are "somehow compelled to sing willingly" (670c9–d1). We are not in "the greatest ignorance" about this law, for our desires accord with our opinion that incest is, to say the least, ignoble. Nevertheless, that opinion, however true it might be, is not knowledge, and in fact is an opinion that actively prevents the serious reflection it would require to become such. What "will" there is belongs to the opinion itself here, which we are not *responsible* for (an entry point, incidentally, for considering Nietzsche's "*Wille zur Macht*"; cf. Aristotle, *Metaphysics* 982b25–26; Al-Farabi, *Political Regime* 71–72; Locke, *Conduct* §24; Nietzsche, *Dawn* §202). It is virtuous, rather than vicious, but it is no more voluntary for that. It is only an "image of voluntary" (cf. 867a1–2 with b3–4) and will be as such *the* quandary and opportunity of criminal law—and fundamental to understanding how and why "no one is voluntarily unjust" is simply true (Book 9, in the *Laws*). In this respect, the liberal view of progressive gradualism (i.e., modern historicism), whereby there is no separation between nature and convention, and all human things are natural (or, which is the same thing, all human things are conventional), is quite correct, and could not be imagined otherwise.[33] It is not in principle impossible that societies were known to Plato and his followers in which the vast majority of citizens great and small may be said to exist, at one and the same time, both in a city of laws, and in a state of nature.

Leaving such difficult speculations aside, other animals are chaste and pure and pious and just without effort because those distinctions are meaningless to them. They do not negotiate license and liberty—their moderation is truly moderation and not self-restraint. It is involuntary moderation. But in the decisive sense, human beings who lack moderation and self-restraint act, and live, no more voluntarily than animals that act and live instinctively (consider the "power of money to produce tens of thousands of erotic desires for insatiable and limitless acquisition, because of nature and also the evil that is lack of education"—870a4–6).[34] They merely serve a different master. And the subjection to this master is insidious because it masquerades as "freedom," a belief made possible by precisely the same error that "conventionalists" make in order to believe that the cities' laws arise through art rather than nature (and indeed for the same reason—890a2–4): the arbitrary ignoring or forgetting that whatever art is being spoken of, itself arose through nature and chance and their attendant necessities (889a–890a; Al-Farabi, *Summary* 3.2; cf. Strauss 1975, 144 [citing *Minos* 316b6–c2 and Xenophon, *Memorabilia* 4.4.12–14]).[35]

The unwritten law against incest does not substantially differ from this animal involuntariness. That law of course cannot be found anywhere else in "nature"—that is, other animal species—but the behavioral patterns of other animal species are only an image of human nature for human beings. The incest law is precisely natural for human beings, in the same way that the distinction between nature and convention is also natural for human beings. Human beings cannot help but make the distinction of rank that the incest law requires, nor can we help but make the distinction between nature and convention any more than we can help but make the distinction between "the laws of god, the laws of man." This means all these distinctions, and all the terms within them, as well as the distinctions themselves between the terms, are natural. The true distinction is not between nature and convention, but between natural and voluntary, between the life and action that cannot help but be moved and the life and action that moves itself.[36]

We recall again that Kleinias had demonstrated, very early on, how "all or nothing" his beliefs about what he knows are. This is deliberately mirrored in the Stranger's exaggerations, both with his examples of animal behavior and the supposedly universal response to transgression of the unwritten law against incest. To be persuasive to Kleinias as the standard of right, the image of nature must be of nature as an efficient cause. Nature *produces*, as it were automatically, the achieved forms of justice and right in all or most animals, and those forms are visible for all to see. Nature provides constraint, not license. Nature is therefore not merely a material and formal cause, for example, nor merely a final cause in the sense of holding out higher or spiritualized human possibilities that are not necessities. The problematic relationship between necessity and possibility, with respect to right by nature, can be illustrated by the point that Averroës stressed, in opposition to Avicenna: what necessarily exists by virtue of something else (i.e., which has an external efficient cause) does not have the possibility of existing by virtue of itself (i.e., have an internal efficient cause), because it does not have the possibility of *not* existing (see Wolfson's [1950–1951] careful reconstruction of Averroës's lost work on the prime mover).[37] A command that one cannot help but obey is not a command that one *may* obey, and vice versa.

It is the internal instinct toward a specific pattern of sexual behavior that is highlighted by the examples of animal species—not the patterns themselves. *Is* it desirable to develop such instincts in human communities by way of laws, and if so, how? The postdiluvian human beings—simple, childlike— are not driven by desires that are incompatible with necessities of life as generative and regenerative. There is nothing recognizably distinct as human to them, and Megillos's judgment concerning the aptness of the Stranger's use of Homer and his Cyclopes to illustrate this, is itself apt: whereas Kleinias finds Homer's verses to be "very urbane" (Pangle's quite precise translation—*mal' asteia*, from *astu*: "town" or "city"; 680c3), Megillos focuses on how Homer accounts for the "ancient" or original ways of the Cyclopes: "savagery" (*agriotêta*—from *agros*: "field"; cf. Homer, *Od.* 9.175 and 9.292 ["like a mountain-bred lion"]). The Stranger, likening the Cyclopean community to a "flock of birds" (680e2–3), asks whether their way of paternal rule is not "kingship that is the most just of all kingships" (680e3–4).[38] It would seem to follow by necessity that this "flock," living together in a single dwelling, would be one in which men, women, children, and property were held in common, like the "community between the limbs of an animal's body and the rest of the body" (Averroes, *On Plato's Republic* 1. 57.5–58.15; 2005, 64–66).

The difference between the soul's practices in the Cyclopean regime and the unwritten law against incest is difficult to discern, when experienced only from within one or the other, though its behavior differs dramatically enormously and points to a willingly anonymous (i.e., completely non-honor loving) responsibility taken to give the law. The ability to give the law is in principle accessible in all times and all places, though in practice it is exceptionally rare. As human beings—not animals, and not divine, but partaking somehow in both—we can only experience this in taking responsibility for good and bad, right and wrong. This is the only difference, but it is a great difference, between humans and animals. It goes without saying that animals too—all animals—decide between good and bad, but they cannot take responsibility for it. They cannot know the conditions of such responsibility— conditions that necessarily mean living without blame and indignation, and therefore *do* suggest that there is something we can *learn* from "animal nature"[39] —in order to attain the freedom to say and do Yes and No, right and wrong, true and false—which is to say, to *know* the good. Only a human being has the potential for this, and it is truly the greatest test of human excellence, in and as the quest for the greatest human achievement.

The awareness in Plato's *Laws* of the permanent need for safeguards of the law and of education, and the problems that need permanently entails, means that the city must attempt to educate some in the city to assume the grave responsibility for the images of Just and Unjust. But this means that that it must educate some to be aware—that is, to never forget—that they are images (867a–c; cf. again Megillos's very careful response at 838c8–d2 with the Stranger's question at 838b10–c7), whereas for those images to function this fact must in general be forgotten or unnoticed. Those images must be vigorously and indeed sometimes murderously defended (*Republic* 517a). The prohibition against incest, to take just one example, is almost universally obeyed (in the breach as in the observance) not because human beings are conscious of that prohibition as an image of justice, but because it is sacred (838a–e, 839c, 840b, 841b–c): it is held to be just *simpliciter*, not an image thereof; it seems to be according to nature. And indeed, it *is* natural.

The Stranger of course does not ever directly say that the incest prohibition accords with nature or is natural. He rather lets this be understood implicitly, by turning immediately from the discussion of incest in which not nature but sacred awe based on "hatefulness to the gods" grounds the law (and nature is in fact not mentioned), to the discussion of changing homosexual customs where nature is *the* principle invoked. Nature takes the place of the foundation of the sacred that was before taken by the gods (cf. 838b10–c1 with 838e6). When the gods are next mentioned in the dialogue, fear of the gods is no longer the standard, and "revering the gods" is a support for the new standard (841c4–d1).

NOTES

1. One may consider in this regard what can only be called the logical, and especially theological, gymnastics by which the Roman Church invented and codified the abstract "sin of sodomy" beginning in the eleventh century—including the wholesale appropriation of the Biblical account of the divine destruction of Sodom, an appropriation that completely displaced the most obvious (and traditional Jewish) interpretation of that destruction as a punishment of egregiously arrogant and violent antihospitality, in order to ground a supposedly absolute divine condemnation of homosexuality (see Jordan 1997 for a careful and learned discussion). The sheer audacity of this appropriation, and of those gymnastics as a whole, points to just how weak any rational argument—or even any rational argument based on divinely revealed religion—in this respect actually is. As Jordan notes, the inventor of the word "sodomy" (or rather, its original Latin *sodomia*), Peter Damian, deployed precisely the argument against homosexuality that in the *Laws* is deployed by the Stranger: that homosexuality is against nature, as can be seen from the behavior of animals: "The 'miserable' Sodomite is so blinded by the fury of his self-indulgence (*luxuriae rabies*) that he does what no buck, ram, stallion, bull, or even ass would do" (Jordan 1997, 55 and n 50, citing Peter Damian, *Liber Gomorrhianus*, Reindel ed., 1:313.5–13). The fundamental incoherence of such an argument, as Jordan further notes, was in fact recognized and illustrated by the twelfth century theologian Alain de Lille, in his *De planctu naturae* (*The Plaint of Nature*). While ostensibly (and most often interpreted as) a

condemnation of sexual vices, and homosexuality in particular, as perversions or violations of nature, De Lille's work is at a deeper level a deliberate (though also deliberately subtle) illustration of how untenable any such argument about nature and what is "against nature" actually is: what appears on the surface as a complaint *by* nature about sexual sins is in fact a complaint *about* nature, "a complaint against Nature's failure to speak satisfactorily about those sins" (Jordan 1997, 67–91; quote at 87).

2. Finnis (1994) stresses that the point he wishes to make is that two spouses' *"real common good"* is *"their marriage* with the two goods, parenthood and friendship" (1066; emphases in original). But since his premise is that this is good *because* it is "common" in the very specific way that he describes—that is, at least potentially productive of a concrete biological unity of the two spouses (though with what seems to me to be a totally illogical— illogical on Finnis's own terms, that is—exception made for sterile heterosexual married couples)—it is hard to see how this is not a simply circular argument (Finnis makes the identical point about the "common good" of a political community: the fact of commonality is itself the only thing he suggests is necessary for the existence of such a "common good": "To say that a community has a common good is simply to say that communication and cooperation have a point which the members more or less concur in understanding, valuing and pursuing" [1070]: on such an understanding, the commonly concurred-upon extermination of the Jews, gypsies, homosexuals, and Communists was, in Nazi Germany, a "common good," and indeed, one could not even reasonably assert the possibility of anything commonly held to be of value being less than good). He writes: "Sexual acts cannot *in reality* be self-giving unless they are acts by which a man and a woman actualize and experience sexually the real giving of themselves to each other—in biological, affective and volitional union in mutual commitment, both open-ended and exclusive—which like Plato and Aristotle and most peoples we call marriage" (Finnis 1994, 1067; emphasis in original). But even if this is so (and it can hardly be said to be demonstrated by Finnis), why is this more-or-less undefined "self-giving" with a fantasy of concrete physical unity (not completely unlike the fantasy in Aristophanes's poetic description of *eros* in Plato's *Symposium*, incidentally) the desideratum that alone can lay claim to validity in a relationship between two people? And on what meager definition of philosophy could this fantasy stand as the basis for a "philosophical" promotion of the moral worth—let alone the *exclusive* moral worth—of indulging the desire for copulation in this way? That fantasy, after all, quite explicitly valorizes the most unreflective sense of what is "one's own" *as the only morally acceptable criterion* by which to assess "the good," and therefore despises the philosophic principle of the worthiness of attempting to take only what actually *is* the good *as* "one's own." It is worth noting that, on Finnis's own terms, the Socratic spiritualization of desire into nonsexual *eros* of the highest friendship—a spiritualization that truly does transcend what Finnis calls "the instinctive coupling of beasts" and "merely animal" erotic behavior (1067)—is as threatening to Finnis's conception of marriage (which is marriage of conception) as he perceives homosexuality and bestiality to be. For Finnis's description of the "common good" of marriage does not merely legitimate or authorize "bodily union" within the confines he insists upon. It demands it.

3. The dative *thêriôi* has troubled some editors, with Stephanus, followed by Ast, emending to accusative *thêrion* (England 1921, *ad loc.*), which yields "power to eat and drink every kind of thing, like an animal," with sexual voraciousness not specifically included in the animal analogy. This is a possibility, but I side with England in retaining the manuscript reading. As England points out, "the dat[ive] looks forward to *paraschein*" (ibid.)—which I have translated as "allow himself," above. Eating, drinking, *and* sexual gratification are thus comprehended within the animal analogy. We may add to England's comments that the Stranger thus uses an almost Thucydidean hyperbaton, whereby what the Stranger believes "power" means, to such people, is finally only supplied at the end of the long sentence: *pasan plêsmonê*—complete satiety. Power, so imagined, is delusional: the fulfillment *per impossibile* of the unfulfillable, the satisfaction within the bounds of finite human capacity of boundless or infinite human desire. Note how the Stranger here appeals to Kleinias's predilection for imagining categories as total—all or nothing—and that predilection's similarity with (and impact on) law. Not *most* men, or all but a very few men, but *"every* man" (*panta andra*) is said here to be driven by this complete lust for moneyed wealth (the word *pas*—"all" or "every"—and its derivatives appear

six times in rapid succession in this single sentence). What of the speaker of this accusation, the Stranger himself?

4. There are certainly animals that are possessed of frenzied desire for food (though not alcohol), and seem to be possessed of such a desire even for sex, of which ancient Greeks were aware: rats are an example. But rats are not "beasts" (*thêria*) on Greek terms. The actual or potential ferocity of beasts does not extend to their appetites for these things.

5. The epic of *Gilgamesh* beautifully relates, in part, the travails entailed in overcoming the longing for such an image of oneself. After the death of his friend and lover, Enkidu, Gilgamesh goes into the wilderness "in the skin of a lion," searching for the immortality of Utnapishtim, the everlasting man. After superhuman struggles, he finds and loses the chance for immortality in that sense, sheds his lion's skin, and returns to Urdu as the poet of his own epic—he repeats at the end of the poem the words that began it. Consider as well, in this respect, the seventh Book of the *Ramayana* of Valmiki, in which the character Valmiki teaches Rama's sons the story of Rama, which they then sing to Rama, and which is the *Ramayana* of Valmiki. Borges relates this to the six hundred and second night of the *Thousand Nights and a Night*, in which Scheherazade begins to relate the Sultan's own story to the Sultan, which would inevitably contain that six hundred and second night ("Partial Magic in the *Quixote*").

6. Hobbs (2000, 217n55) directs our attention as well to *Symposium* 211d8–e3, and "Diotima's" description there of "the flesh and colors of human things, and much other mortal nonsense" (*Symp*. 211e2–3; my translation—Hobbs refers to "mortal trash").

7. Lutz (2012, 108) insightfully draws our attention as well to Maimonides, *Guide* 1.54 here. Twice in that chapter, Maimonides claims to have "gone beyond the limits/subject of this chapter" (1963, 124, 127). The first time is with respect to the grace of God and His nearness as a relationship of knowing—like Moses—His ways; the second is with respect to ignorance of God and His ways as distance from and destruction by God. Maimonides thus suggests that the example of Moses—here called not the "master of the prophets" (as he is, e.g., at 2.19), but the "master of those who know" (also at 3.12, 3.54)—illustrates the opposite of Hobbs' assumption. Cf. also *Guide* 2.32, 33. Strauss (2013, 482) mentions that the phrase "master of those who know" (*sayyid al-'ālimīn*) is, as Muhsin Mahdi pointed out to him, a modification of the Qur'anic expression *sayyid al-'ālamīn*—"a master of the *worlds*, of men and angels"—and is "said of Muhammad." This is from a transcription of a postlecture discussion (I have corrected the editor's Arabic transliteration), and Strauss mistakenly attributes this phrase to the Qur'an rather than the Hadith as he speaks off the cuff. In the Qur'an, Allah—and only Allah—is called *Rabb' al-'ālamīn* ("Lord of the worlds"—cf., e.g., Surah 1.2, 6.45, etc. [seventy-three times]). The Hebrew רַבִּי (Maimonides was one of the most prominent of his time) would therefore translate into Arabic as *sayyid*, rather than *rabbi,* in these circumstances.

8. *Anapnein*: Bury's translation, "breathe a word" fits neatly into modern English usage, but completely misses and indeed obscures the point. There is no "breathing" of words in Greek—that is a modern English colloquialism (in Greek, the basic sense of what is conveyed by this English phrase would be expressed by, e.g., *mimnêskein*, as in *oude mnêsthênai*—"to not even mention"—at 781b7). Megillos's point here is that we breathe the *law*, that the unwritten law is something we *do* in the same way that we breathe: it is precisely his point, and his realization, that words and other actions "against" the law do not necessarily mean that one does not breathe the law. We do not breathe the *words* of the law, or words against the law; we breathe the *law* or against it. Cf. *Cratylus* 399d8–e1 (I believe this is the only other use of the active form of *anapnein* in Plato's dialogues).

9. Saxonhouse (2005) articulates the unspoken evocation in Jocaste's condemnation of her son Polyneices's marriage to a foreigner, without family involvement, very well: "The xenophobic standpoint articulated by Jocasta in her interchange with Polyneices reflects the inclinations of the audience to whom Euripides speaks. But the audience, knowing well the myth of Oedipus or at least having just heard Jocasta recall it in her prologue, must also be aware that the insularity she craves for her city underscores the insularity of her own family's impieties and the offenses against the gods it expresses. Insensitive to the too-narrow frame of the familial relations that mark her own incestuous family, she bemoans the foreignness of Polyneices' marriage alliance" (481).

10. When Socrates speaks to those who have condemned him to die (*Apol.* 38c1–5), he of course notes that others will indignantly blame (*oneidizein*) them—but this is merely acknowledging what others are bound to do, and in no way means that Socrates himself blames those jurists. Socrates uses reproach (*oneidizein*) only as instructive—as exhortative to self-reflection (*Apol.* 41e1–42a2). There is an obvious correlation here between punishment as retribution (*timê*) and punishment as correction (*to kolazein*).

Despite his very good insights into the importance of the problem of indignation for both Plato and Al-Farabi, Parens (1995, 105) is, I think, on one hand incorrect to see *thumos* only as "indignation," and on the other, incorrect to look only to the word *thumos* for representations of "indignation." What is characteristic about indignation is not merely "spiritedness" (*thumos*) in general, nor is all spiritedness indignation (both acute fear and noble generosity are spirited, without being—or at least without necessarily being—indignant as well). What is characteristic of indignation is spirited *blame* (*psexis, memphesthein, epitiman, nemesis*; and depending on context, *loidorein* and *oneidizein*). Cf. 935c8–e2, 936a2–5.

11. One could consider the importance of such free consideration with other examples, of course. For example, while it may or may not be a beneficial thing for political communities to have the opinion that everyone naturally fears death, it is very difficult to see what unconditional knowledge could be experienced within a "political science" that assumes that this is simply true. Likewise it would be a foolish general indeed who did not attend to the significant variance in human beings with respect to their comportments toward death (cf. 830d–831b; and Benardete 2000, 235). One may also think, in this regard, of the opinion that all suicidal attacks are "cowardly," the opinion that women are naturally inferior to men with respect to politics, the opinion that a leader or general who has an adulterous affair is unfit to rule or command, and so on.

12. The Stranger at the same time abbreviates a phrase that Megillos uses, an abbreviation that introduces an ambiguity and perhaps an invitation. Megillos had spoken of the Stranger holding as worthless "our human race"—*to tôn anthrôpôn genos hêmin* (804b5). Responding, the Stranger speaks of letting "our race"—*to genos hêmôn* (b9)—not be worthless. To be very clear: this does *not* refer to anything like a modern "ethnic" opinion about "race."

13. This list, incidentally, highlights another "error" that the Stranger seems to make in his description of the incest engaged in by the three characters he mentions. Only one, Macareus, has incest with his sister, not all three, as the Stranger seems to imply (838c6). As usual, the Stranger's speech, while—or because—ambiguous, was also quite precise: his use of the plural seems to suggest that all three characters had incestuous relations with their sisters, but in fact is grammatically compatible with being limited to only "certain Macareus-types."

14. Consider that the Stranger's exhortation to moderation appeals to *honor*—the honor of being "superior to oneself," of besting the "animal" drives within. Whereas the unwritten law against incest depends on *shame*—incest itself is hateful to the gods and therefore simply shameful. We see here that while honor and shame appear to be two sides of the same coin, they are not necessarily symmetrical or even proportionate. Depending on the erotic regime valorized, they *can* be proportionately involved: honor may accrue to, say, chastity, and shame to lack thereof (for Roman Catholic priests, for example, and for the unmarried young—especially women—in many parts of the modern world). But *no* honor accrues to the man or woman who successfully makes it through an entire lifetime without any incestuous activity. The unwritten law—and one may fruitfully consider to what extent this is true of *any* unwritten law—allows only the possibility of massive shame in the breach, and absence of shame in the observance. A case in which honor *needed* to be appealed to would by that very fact be shameful, and the honor false (i.e., a lie told to someone considered particularly degenerate). As the examples of Thyestes and Oedipus indicate, even breaching this law completely unawares does not mitigate the attending shame. We may additionally note that the Stranger's discussion of Socratic or spiritual eros appeals to neither honor nor shame.

15. Recall that it was precisely in the conversation about the "devices" of the Spartan legislator that Megillos first added his own voice emphatically to what "the Lacedaimonians" say (*egôge* at 633b1–2; cf. the specific question to which Megillos is here directly responding—633a7–9, especially the pointed mention of *tês allês aretês* at a8). Even more specifically, the device that he there discusses is hunting, which, as the Stranger's "legislation" thereof at the

end of Book 7 indicates, is deeply bound up in erotics (822d–24a; cf. *Sophist* 222d–223c, *Symposium* 203d; Barringer 2001, 125–28). In Book 7, the Stranger calls hunting—in an almost exact mirror of what he later says of friendship, in Book 8 (837a)—"a very many-sided (*pampolu*) thing, despite it being now mostly (*schedon*) embraced by one name" (823b1–2).

16. As Strauss (1975) notes, "[t]he law enjoining all these restrictions is *almost* said to *be* according to nature" (121; my emphases). Strauss is alerting us to the fact that the Stranger says this law "is, first, laid down (*keitai*) according to nature." Nota bene.

17. I am here working from the general impression that the Stranger wants to give. In fact, the Stranger leaves his statements open to much broader interpretation (cf. *schedon* at 679b8, and the generality of the assertion there). The most specific statement he makes is that these people "believed that what[ever] was said about both gods and human beings was true" (699c5–7). It would not be at all surprising, in the cataclysmic circumstances in which these people were supposedly living, if what was said about the gods were not entirely pious, nor celebrating their good works and benevolence toward human beings. One can imagine the possibility that piety was, in the "naïveté" (*euêtheia*) of these human beings, simply irrelevant, and therefore irrelevant to what "they heard was noble or shameful" (c3–4). Consider, in this respect, *Od.* 9. 273–79; Euripides, *Cyclops* 328–47. One may consider as well that a very great deal of people, a great deal of the time, believe what they hear about God or the gods and human beings (see Kleinias's list of six inventors of the arts at 677d1–6, as well as his slide from accepting a flood as one hypothetical destructive event among several over the course of the immeasurable past [677a], to accepting it as an actual event from which his own epoch emerged; also 782d2–3; and Rousseau (2003), *Discours sur l'origine de l'inégalité* I: "ce n'est pas chez lui qu'il faut chercher la Philosophie dont l'homme a besoin, pour savoir observer une fois ce qu'il a vû tous les jours" [144]). And *from whom* do these naïve believers hear about the gods?

18. While it should be remembered that the Stranger's myth of the Cyclopean families is not one of linear "evolution" since the "dawn of man," but of repeated cycles of political and technological development and natural destruction thereof, we can nevertheless say that modern genetic research supports the spirit of the conclusions he draws from his inquiry. Read (2014, 10) notes that recent studies of DNA data demonstrate high rates of inbreeding in, for example, Siberian Neanderthal groups (citing Prüfer et al. 2013); neurocranial studies demonstrate the same in Late Pleistocene Homo groups in China (citing Wu et al. 2013); as does research on genetic relatedness in some Upper Paleolithic burials (ibid.).

19. When Vico, for his own purposes which are almost entirely beyond the scope of this inquiry, wishes to interpret this Platonic myth in a nonincestuous way, he understands that he must introduce "historical" interpretations and additions that are completely absent from Plato (and Homer and Strabo), and he indeed seems to go so far as to initially establish Strabo's commentary on this "*luogo d'oro di Platone*" ("golden sentence of Plato") as the focus of his inquiry, thereby averting the immediate need to engage that "golden sentence" and its full implications directly (*Scienza nuova* §296 [Nicolini numbering]; Vico 1959, 117—cf. with §338, 502–3, and the order of Varro and Augustine in §88 ["*un luogo d'oro di Varrone (appo sant'Agostino*, etc.)," as opposed to "*Appresso Strabone è un luogo d'oro di Platone*, etc." in §296]; as well as the attribution of "golden sentences" without intermediary to Lactantius, Iamblichus, and Aristotle, etc., in §188, 207, 269, 271, 273, *inter alia*). As might be imagined or understood, Vico never uses the phrase "golden sentence" carelessly. When he turns to what "family" means in this "state of nature of the philosophers," Vico insists that its definition derives primarily from the *famuli*—the many refugees protected by a hero who had fame (*fama*)—in the age of "Cyclopean paternal *potestà*," or "Cyclopean family discipline," and that "family" includes both the immediate "blood" family of the hero, *and* the many "families" of refugees under his protection (ibid., §523, 552, 555–56, 582, 584, 670). There is no necessary incest involved in these original or postpolitical communities, per Vico. But Vico is well aware that Plato and Homer tell a different story—a story of "wives and children"—and he is ultimately unable, as he well knows, to escape from this story himself (ibid, §547, 576, 644, 996, 1013, 1098).

20. As Lerner remarks, "The general common nomos is something like a natural standard, a set of rules common to all times and places, without which any kind of lasting human associa-

tion would be impossible. It does not aim high" (in Averroës 2005, 75n). Lerner cites Al-Farabi, *Summary* 7.14; we may add 3.2 (end) and 6.13.

21. It may be wondered whether an awareness of this problem was not involved in the mediaeval Christian classification of the "sin of Sodomy"—the "sin against nature"—as quite specifically a greater sin than even mother-son incest (see Jordan 1997, 95–97, 105, 110–12; citing the thirteenth-century penitentials of Paul of Hungary, Robert of Sorbonne, and William Peraldus).

22. Thucydides writes, in his own voice, at 3.84.2: *Xuntarachtentos te tou biou es ton kairon touton têi polei kai tôn nomôn kratêsasa hê anthrôpeia phusis, eiôthuia kai para tous nomous adikein . . .*—"And the way of life having been thrown into confusion, human nature, both because it had overpowered the laws in this particular critical moment for the city, and because its habitual custom is to wrong the laws..." [Note on editing the Greek text: *kai . . . kai . . .* construction is postpositive: *es ton kairon touton têi polei* should not be taken as part of the absolute—Steup's suggestion (Thucydides 1966, *ad loc.*) that a *prin* has been lost after the initial *kai* is therefore unnecessary; participles outside of absolute are in typical Thucydidean concentric symmetry (cf. *inter alia* 1.6.6, 1.37.5) around their single referent, therefore strike comma after *phusis*]. "Human nature" here picks up on Thucydides's comment on "the same nature of human beings" at 3.82.2. Chapter 3.84 has been a consistent target for authenticity-denial during what I term the *Schriftenablehnung* period of the *Strohhalmgreifen* school of nineteenth- and twentieth-century German philology, beginning with Classen (Thucydides 1966 [originally edited by Classen, 1863], vol. 3, *ad loc.*), who elevates one ancient commentator's difficulty with Thucydides's text to an authoritative pronouncement on the chapter's inauthenticity. See Christ 1989 for an incisive and thorough refutation. As Christ notes: "What should be regarded as a shortcoming of ancient scholarship—the confident rejection of a Thucydidean passage on aesthetic and philological grounds—has given rise instead to a variety of unreasonable attacks on Chapter 84. Few genuine Thucydidean passages could survive such an onslaught" (147).

23. *Oligon chronon* and *polun chronon* translate as "a little time" and "much time," respectively, but the adjectives *oligon* and *polun* are most widely used to describe "few" versus "many." The ways in which Socrates discusses the value of and desire for "a little time" versus "much time"—not to mention "all time" (*ho pas chromos*) and "the rest of time" (*ton loipon chronon*), especially—paint a picture of how Socrates sees the philosophic "few" valuing "time" and time of life, as against the "many's" desire for "much time" *simpliciter*. Cf. *Timaeus* 37d5 and 7; *Gorgias* 512d–e; *Menexenus* 247e–248c, and dramatic context of Socrates "repeating" this as a speech of Aspasia, long after both Aspasia's death, and Socrates's; Aristotle, *Physics* 218a10, 219b1–23, 220a20, 220b14–15, 222a10–12. Consider also the "aporetic" agreement between Zeno and the young Socrates, in the *Parmenides*, that "the one," in changing, must change in "no time" (*en oudeni chronôi*—156e); with the double-framing of the dialogue in time. Kephalos remembers meeting Antiphon "a long time ago" (126b), and when they meet again, Antiphon relates the story he had heard from Pythodorus about a conversation between Parmenides, who was "very near 65 years old," Zeno, who was "just about 40," and Socrates, who was "very young" (127b–c; cf. 136d, twice stressing the advanced age of Parmenides). Zeno, when seconding Socrates's request that Parmenides go through his "way through all [things]," says that he is eager to hear it again, for he has not heard it "for a long time" (136e). Shakespeare offers us a beautiful meditation on what is at stake here with his *Romeo and Juliet*, though in terms of "life" rather than time. By way of entry into that meditation, he gives us "a pair of star-cross'd lovers take their *life*" (Prologue, 6; note the singular, as also in "with their *death*" two lines later), to be compared with "your *lives* shall pay the forfeit of the peace" in the next scene (I. i, 84). Cf. Louis Macneice, "Selva Oscura" (". . . all the life my days allow").

24. Note, again, the language of agriculture employed by the Stranger here. Cf. Benardete (2000, 244–45).

25. In his introduction of the two basic kinds of friendship—of equals and of opposites—the Stranger had emphasized *philia*, and in fact had couched his remarks as an attempt to draw out the meanings and confusions of that word, noting that "when either of the kinds becomes vehement (*sphodron*), we name it *erôs*" (837a8–9). In the sequel, he begins by noting that the

"friendship of opposites is terrible and savage and rarely mutual among us, whereas that of equals is gentle and mutual throughout life" (837b2–4). The "friendship" of opposites—of need and hunger—seems always to be "vehement," whether in its pure form or mixed with the other (837b4–6). In the remainder of his exposition, the Stranger drops the word *philia* altogether and speaks exclusively of *erôs* (five times, 837b4–d7)—until he turns to Megillos, calling him "friend" (837d8).

26. Consider especially 838e4–6: "For this was what I was talking about, that I had an art (*technê*), [*directed*] *toward* (*pros*) this law (*touton ton nomon*), for the need according to nature for child-producing intercourse." With apologies for the jarringly literal translation, two points are in order: First, the *art* and the *law* discussed here are not the same thing—the art spoken of is subsidiary to and serves the law spoken of. A careless listener such as Kleinias, who has understood none of the conversation between the Stranger and Megillos, or rather has understood what he wanted to hear, will miss this. Clark (2003, 135–36) and Schöpsdau (2003, 255–56) both interpret Kleinias's interpretation as what the Stranger means, and miss the distinction (Schöpsdau, at least, should know better than to ignore the accusative case structure of *touton ton nomon* with *pros* here); second, the *need* for (or *demand* for, or *infliction of*) [*tou . . . chrêsthai*] "child-producing intercourse" is what the Stranger says is "according to nature" here, *not* "child-producing intercourse" itself. The Greek is remarkably unambiguous about this. Need that accords with nature, to say nothing of other need, does not automatically mean that what is needed is naturally *produced*. If it did, no animal would ever starve, no plant would ever die for want of water, and no species would ever go extinct. Conventions laid down to meet the *needs* that accord with nature of the human species or individuals, and that took such needs as the natural standard, would by that fact alone not take what is naturally *produced* as *the* standard (though any convention that ignored this very grave consideration, or marginalized it, would almost certainly be suicidal), and vice versa (including parenthetical comment). This point cannot be overstressed. Cf. endnote 25 on friendship, above.

27. That the Stranger and Plato do not believe the establishment of such laws in his time and place is possible, does not mean that either believes such establishment to be impossible *tout court*. At the same time, as I have discussed in chapter 5, possibility is not the only question with respect to desirability.

28. It is important to understand that what looks like, and is, *askêsis* in the friendship described here does *not* indicate the frigid and lifeless image that Nietzsche so criticized as the "ascetic *ideal*," and which he associated with Pauline practice of "mortification of the flesh" (e.g., Romans 8:13, Colossians 3:5)—which in Nietzsche's view betrayed Christ to the core. As the Stranger puts it, the friend and lover that he valorizes "holds desire for the body to be *subordinate* (*parergon*)," not something to "mortify"—that is, kill or let die (837c4). The philosopher, as Plato presents him or her, is not immune to the typical erotic and thumotic desires (to preserve, provisionally, a Platonic distinction that may or may not be a genuine one), but as it were experiences a stronger or superior erotic wonder and compulsion to understand those desires as connections between parts within the whole. Socrates could learn nothing of such connections if he did not himself experience, for example, real sexual desire for Alcibiades and Charmides, and indeed find beautiful "almost everyone of that age" (*Charmides* 154b; cf. 155d and *Lovers* 133a). He does not "transform" those desires into a supposedly higher desire for friendship—he experiences a higher desire to understand, rather than immediately gratify, those desires. That wonder and desire to understand extends also to other erotic and thumotic connections between parts of the whole, including envy, resentment, longing for revenge, and devotion to justice—at least some of which are in fact disposed of by the very existence of the desire to understand them (which is why the Greek word *sungnomê* really does mean just "understand," contains no "intuition" of the modern English word "forgiveness," and should never be translated as this word), and can therefore only be observed in others.

29. The grammar used by the Stranger in fact indicates homosexual eros—*eromenou* (masculine "beloved") at 837d1.

30. "Form" and "Idea"—*eidos* and *idea*—are not identical. There is, for example, no *idea* of justice mentioned in the *Republic*.

31. Cf. 875b–c; Aristotle, *Politics* 1253a26–29, 1284a3–15 and b32–34,1288a24–29; *Nicomachean Ethics* 1113a29–33, 1127b34–1128a32, 1143b11–14, 1144b32–1145a2, Book 7 as a whole; *Protrepticus* fr. 5.

32. We are reminded of the discussion in the *Minos*, and Socrates's conclusion (which, in the midst of a long series of questions for the comrade, is not phrased as a question) that worthless law is not law (317a–c)—just as the worthless statesman is not a statesman (*Statesman* 291a–b) and the worthless philosopher is not a philosopher (*Republic* 487c–d, 489c–d). Cf. 693a.

33. I refer here to the logic of gradual human progress as an historical process, not to any particular writer who presents him- or herself as an adherent of this doctrine. Barring a divine revelation, the only way that such a doctrine could logically allow an ultimate or principled (i.e., not simply wishful or sentimental) separation between nature and law or convention is—not coincidentally—also the only way in which such a doctrine would not simply be logically self-confounding in every respect, including any and all assumptions of "progress": the belief in, or demonstration of, the historian's own moment as an absolute moment outside or as the culmination of that process. This is of course Hegel's "end of history," and I exclude any modern liberalism that accepts this Hegelian (ab)solution from my assessment of progressive gradualism here (though it is to be wondered to what extent this historical absolution would, on principle, render such a liberalism nonliberal in the modern sense of the term). Plato was well aware of the peculiar hold that the doctrine of progress has on the imagination, even in the face of being unable to justify itself. The *Hippias Major* recounts the hold that doctrine has on Hippias "the beautiful and wise" (281d–286c in particular, but the theme is constant throughout the dialogue). Cf. *Laws* 888b6–8.

34. Note that the power here is "*of* money" (*hê tôn chrêmatôn dunamis*), not of human beings who *have* money. This power is said by the Stranger to "produce insatiable and limitless desires for acquisition"—these desires are *not* the product of the human beings who are in their grip. And this not by human "will," but "because of *nature* and also the evil that is lack of education" (*dia phusin te kai apaideusian tên kakên*).

35. Cf. also Strauss 1965, 92; and 1988b, 175–79, on "the problem which Hobbes has to solve": "Man's activity may appear as the conquest of nature or as a revolt against nature; but what takes place in fact is that a part of nature revolts by natural necessity against all other parts of nature" (176; it is unlikely to be accidental that the title of Strauss's [1965] *Natural Right and History* is ambiguous, and can be read as meaning "natural right and natural history"). Strauss here capitalizes on a distinction made by Hobbes when the latter presents his "definition" of science in the *Leviathan* (1.5.17), which is in fact (or rather, in speech, and thereby in fact), two definitions: the first, what "men *call* Science," being "knowledge of all the consequences of *names* appertaining to the subject at hand"; the second, what "Science *is*," being "knowledge of consequences, and dependence of one *fact* upon another" (Hobbes 1994, 25, my emphases).

36. Consider *Protagoras* 355a–b: Socrates leads "the people"—answered for by Protagoras—(353e) through an argument challenging their assumptions that one can do bad things knowing they are bad, and not want to do good things knowing they are good. Socrates, of course, holds that such "knowing" is evidently *not* knowing. But the way he illustrates this is by introducing something into the argument that had not been mentioned by him up to this point, and that he can slip in unnoticed only because it is such a basic assumption of "the people" (and perhaps Protagoras). What he slips in are the phrases: "it being *possible* [for the person] to not do [what he knows is bad]" (*exon mê prattein*); and "knowing what is good, a human being is *unwilling* to do them" (*prattein ouk ethelei*). It is the aspect of *voluntariness* in this respect that makes the people's argument, as constructed by Socrates, simply "laughable" (*geloion*). Cf. *Laws* 902a8–b2 (Mayhew [2008, 56] ignores the import of *legontai*—"are *said* to"—at a9, and therefore misconstrues the sentence as showing that Plato allows here for someone to *know* what is good, and not choose it). Cf. Hume (2007, 305), *Treatise* 3.1.2.9, second and third sentence.

37. My attention was originally drawn to this important article by a note in Strauss 1978 (333–4n68). Strauss cites Savonarola as holding this interpretation of Averroism, and indeed of

Thomism, Scotism, and various ancient schools including the Stoics and the Peripatetics (citing Savonarola, *Prediche sopra l'Esodo* XX; cf. also 175). I see no reason to disagree.

38. There are two subtle points to note here: (1) the Stranger asks this as a question, though a leading one to be sure—it is Kleinias who affirms that this is true, not the Stranger (Kleinias: "Definitely"—680e5); (2) the Stranger's leading question concerns kingship (*basileia*), and only kingship, and the criterion considered is justice, and only justice. Needless to say, the particular kingship considered here is "artless" (cf. *Statesman* 259b–c), and preserves proportion as such. There is no possibility of producing better people or citizens, just as there is no possibility of producing worse (678a–b, 721b–c, especially *phusei tini*, "a *certain* nature," at b8 and England's note, 1921, *ad loc.* [Rowe—2010, 48—notes the importance of this phrase, but translates the remainder of this sentence as: "immortality—something at which in fact every desire of every human being is by its nature aimed." Rowe thus contends that "Plato" means that all desire is for immortality (49–50). This translation ignores the Greek grammar, and is incorrect. It also ignores the context, in which the Stranger is precisely speaking to those with desires that conflict with a desire for a share in immortality. The Stranger is *not* saying here that every human desire is aimed at immortality, but that "everyone naturally holds a desire to share in immortality in every way" [*meteilêphen athanasias, hou kai pephuken epithumian ischein pas pasan*]; cf. *Statesman* 297a–b, *Timaeus* 35a1–4; and the anonymous *Prolegomena philosophiae platonicae* 27.76–83 and 22.15–18, on Plato's use of history [*historikon*] to demonstrate that the human is a "mediation" between divine beings and "generative beings" [*genêtoi*]; and Al-Farabi, *Summary* Introduction 1, and 3.2 on the initial development of arts for the sake of necessities versus their later development "for the sake of noble and fair things").

39. With respect to this, and to "learning from nature" in general, we may be reminded of Socrates's statement to Phaedrus, in most English translations, about the countryside and the trees not teaching him anything (*Phaedrus* 230d). This is not what he says. He says that the countryside (*chôra*) and trees have nothing they *want* (*ethelei*) to teach him. Cf. *Minos* 315a.

Chapter Seven

Concluding Remarks

Methinks I hear him now; his plausive words
He scattered not in ears, but grafted them,
To grow there, and to bear . . .

—King of France in Shakespeare's *All's Well That Ends Well* I.ii.53–5

In deference to the way of Megillos that has preoccupied this book, it is fitting to close with an economy of words (cf. 721e–722b and 683b–c).

The highest of all high offices in Magnesia is the supervisor of education. No other magistracy or office of any kind attains the level of official responsibility and nobility that the man (765d7) in charge of maintaining the city's education attains (765e–766c). The importance of this office is matched by the quandaries involved in filling it. A person like Kleinias would likely often occupy the position, as it is essential that the officeholder command the respect of everyone in the city. Yet the supervisor of education is not specifically included in the predawn assembly / nocturnal council (961a–b), though this is clearly, as Pangle (1988, 508) rightly notes, the site of the "highest education" in the city. Kleinias's own love of fame and honor is appealed to in order to inspire him to establish or see the benefit of such a council, but no official honors are said to accrue to its members for anything they do with respect to the council. The conversations between the three characters regarding sexual moderation and the unwritten laws cautiously reveal why this must be so.

Kleinias, as we have seen, really is a marvel to behold. He is pulled in different directions by two mutually exclusive images of animal nature, each of which is false. On the one hand, he takes pleasure in imagining the "freedom" of animals who, because they have no laws, are free to indulge every desire, and to the extent that they wish—and he is pained by having such an image held up to him as contemptuous for a human being. On the other hand, he just as easily imagines the complete moderation of animals, who live in a stable equilibrium of moderate desire and moderate satisfaction, and who have no laws because they need no laws to survive (as individuals and as species), since they are ruled by the absolute laws of instinct. Kleinias is Hegel's "Unhappy Consciousness" without the self-recognition of contradiction (*Ph.desG.* §126). The falseness of each image, and their contradiction, are resolved in and for (and concealed from) Kleinias because, taken together, they allow him the compelling dream of the possibility of—indeed the *natural* tendency toward—a stable life of guaranteed survival and security, as well as ease and indulgence of the desires he experiences without hindrance or shame (and perhaps, indeed, with honor).[1] It is easy to see how such a delusion could end in the political delusion of a city, or state, in which a maximum of law and government is imagined not only as compatible with, but indeed the key to, a maximum of freedom as Kleinias understands it (cf. Averroës, *Pl. Rep.* pp. 83–84 [Rosenthal]). We may add in this respect that the alluring quality of the image of the tyrant is in a way inherent in this delusion, as the image of the person who could live this dreamed-of life without contradiction. We speak this allure in our hearts, and sometimes with our tongues.

Setting the delusion and its subsidiary delusions aside, we are then left to wonder if the human desires that lie beneath the simple, false, and contradictory images of nature are subject to any natural right, according with which laws might be discovered or developed, and laid down. Natural right says: natural desire, properly understood, points in *this* direction (cf., e.g., 721b–c with 966a–b). It may not be readily understandable to everyone, but as *right*, and not simply "what is natural," it must make sense of the basic desires of everyone. As *right*, it cannot be "the advantage of the stronger," in the sense of dividing people "naturally" into predators and prey, for this is exactly the relativism that leads us to inquire into natural right to begin with. And it cannot say that most of the desire experienced by most people is simply wrong, and remain *natural* right, for such a dispensation of right would require a divinity (and human interpretations of that divine dispensation, which eventually brings us full circle back to the original search). Finally, the *need* for a natural right standard does not mean that there is natural right. While demonstrative proofs of that need may themselves indicate a great deal about what natural right would necessarily entail, equating the need of something with its existence is false *by nature*: however much the presence of food may provoke my hunger, or direct it, my hunger itself does not demonstrate that "therefore there is food available" (cf. Rousseau's three notes on "natural man" as a frugivore, *Discours sur l'origine de l'inégalité* n. 4, 6, 10 [Rousseau's original numbering; later editors' posthumous numbering: 5, 8, 12]).

Setting aside, for the moment, the desire for order, we must say at least this much concerning the desire for freedom before we conclude. The desire for true freedom necessarily points to the desire for truth—for knowledge of the whole in which freedom might be freedom. No one ever says that they want false freedom—everyone yearning for freedom always and everywhere would openly declare that they want true freedom (provided they are not compelled to say otherwise or to be silent). Properly understood, the desire for freedom requires the step of, or is subsidiary to, the desire for truth (cf. 730c1–2 with *Rep.* 379c2–7). The way of the Stranger, and Megillos, is drawn by and pursues this encompassing goal, without disposing of the essential character of Kleinias's desires, and indeed while amplifying the affinities between the two.

To put this more concretely, in terms of the *Laws*, it is very easy to illustrate that while Kleinias represents the only real political opportunity for founding new laws, he is nevertheless the chief obstacle thereto inasmuch as his mind is narrow and closed, nor can he be overcome by main force (nor would the latter be effective even if possible, given the project of laws that is undertaken is not only for now, but for a posterity that must equally be persuaded). But such an illustration on its own would overlook that the responsibility that the Stranger has (that he *is*) and that Megillos learns (to *be*) cannot blame Kleinias for this because it does not *know* blame. And not only is it not resentful of the meagerness of Kleinias's character, but it is *grateful* for it. This is responsibility in the broadest (or, from this point of view, the only) possible sense (*Laws* 727b4–c1, 744a).

I have attempted in this book to demonstrate, or to suggest, that this sense of responsibility is the philosophical core of Plato's *Laws*, and is accessible in the *Laws* only once we attend carefully to the seemingly negligible, but on closer examination massive and essential, differences between the characters of Megillos and Kleinias the Cretan. To this end, while I have situated my focuses within a global reading of the *Laws*, I have concentrated especially on two of its most puzzling sections, the "history" in Book 3, and the nature of sexuality and erotics in Book 8. In doing so, I have to some extent inevitably betrayed the harmony that I intended to examine therein, just by examining its parts in isolation from each other. I have, for example, inevitably held Kleinias up for ridicule precisely in illustrating why he ought not be ridiculed, and why and how he is not ridiculed by Megillos and the Stranger. I would submit that this failure on my part—and this separately from my own personal shortcomings as a commentator and author, which are considerable—is an indication that an art of writing that is, like Plato's own, more elusive (and allusive) is in fact more appropriate to addressing some matters of fundamental importance than is a purely explicative or expository manner of writing. And this not in order to keep dark truths concealed from those whom Kleinias calls "the mindless many," but because if "nature loves to hide herself," then an art that balances evocation and concealment in order to not sunder her inseparable parts in fact has a much closer correspondence to reality than any attempt to spell everything out clearly and forthrightly once and for all.

If this is so with history and sexual erotics (to use a misleading anachronism), it is doubly so with what I have discussed as responsibility. What von Clausewitz (2016) notes with respect to "determination" applies in spades to my discussion of responsibility:

> Those who speak of "determination" unconscientiously mean by this name a mere inclination toward daring, nerve, audacity, or reckless pursuit of something. But when there are sufficient motives within a person . . . there is no basis to speak of "determination" [in this way], for to do so is to put ourselves in his place, and weigh in the balance doubts that he did not have (1.3, 41; my translation).[2]

So too with "responsibility." To say nothing of other distinctions, where those who speak of responsibility unconscientiously might generally mean by that name a "choice" to own up to one's deeds, or a response to the indignation of injustice, or even the compulsion to accept criminal "responsibility" in the form of a judicial sentence; to experience responsibility in its true sense is to experience neither choice nor indignation, nor is (or can be) the compulsion thereof in any way something that can be assigned by another. In many ways, the unconscientious meaning of "responsibility" and the experience of true responsibility are so at odds with one another that if such a thing as "opposites" existed in human nature, we would call them opposites. In the drama of the *Laws*, these opposing positions on or of responsibility lead to what initially appears to be confusion as to what responsibility is, an appearance that led us to carefully consider just who the characters are in that drama, and why such confusion might arise.

In observing the three characters, and reflecting carefully on their words and deeds, we saw that such consideration was not only our own concern, but was dramatized within the *Laws* itself: the Stranger and Megillos are deeply concerned to conduct their own investigations into the character of their fellow interlocutors from the outset of the dialogue, whereas Kleinias's assumption that he already knows everything he needs to know about the Athenian and the Spartan precludes any such investigation on his part. Plato does not simply rely on his reader importing a concern for character that might not have been Plato's own. He demonstrates the importance of that concern by showing the impact of its presence or absence (and the quality of its presence or absence) on his own characters' understanding within the drama of the *Laws*. Thus, for example, it remains permanently unimaginable to Kleinias that a Spartan might be extraordinary, or have opinions subversive to Kleinias's own, though he is of course on his guard about just such a possibility with Athenians. Kleinias's concern is with reputation (*doxa*), whether of a person or a group of people, and he cannot ascend from this to a "second sailing" that entails close reflection on the "speeches," because he is unable to imagine the need to do so. Plato warns his reader against reading the *Laws* with a similar heedlessness by illustrating the consequences that heedlessness has for Kleinias within the *Laws*.

Kleinias, believing he is leading Megillos, is unaware of how much and in what ways he is being influenced by Megillos.[3] Relying on what he sees as the Spartan's traditionalism, Kleinias cannot imagine that Megillos's true traditionalism transcends patriotism and devotion to ancestral custom, and reaches not only toward the old but toward what precedes the old in time and in dignity: toward first things. My own investigation of Megillos's character suggests that his nature is philosophic, that he is a profoundly reflective thinker and a careful and thoughtful speaker. A great deal of the interpretation of the *Laws* that I have offered here depends on the legitimacy of this unusual interpretation of Megillos's character, for which reason I began by defending that interpretation in considerable detail.

The ways in which Megillos leads Kleinias while appearing to follow him is strikingly illustrated in Book 3 of the *Laws* with the "history" of the world laid out by the Stranger, and abetted by Megillos. Far from being "Plato's" historicism, this is Kleinias's historicism—an imagination of his own time and its history on terms—on the only terms—in which Kleinias can see the world and himself. That the Stranger designs his inquiry into the past to rely absolutely on Megillos's support—it is a history that culminates in a factually imaginative though spiritually true account of Sparta (and politically dominant powers in general), about which Megillos quite obviously has an authoritative opinion in Kleinias's eyes—is intended by Plato to provoke reflection. If the Stranger can count on Megillos's authoritative confirmation of what would in our time be called "revisionist history," then he must either have already understood the latter to be at least sympathetic to his pursuits (such that he could rely on Megillos lying to Kleinias for reasons understood by the Stranger but, obviously, not Kleinias), or else privilege testing Megillos in this respect above pursuing whatever political program he might be interested in with Kleinias (such that if Megillos failed to support his version of Spartan history, and thus prevented whatever he needed to do with that version with Kleinias, the consequence for the Kleinian project would be of secondary or tertiary importance at most). Whatever the Stranger's motivations might be, Megillos supports his account to Kleinias, and thereby authorizes Kleinias to see the history of the world played out on Kleinias's own terms. As with most human desires, this fulfillment of Kleinias's ardent desire does not please him, and what he might have imagined as a culmination is in fact a dismay that provokes him to turn, reluctantly to be sure, to the Stranger for assistance.

Within the scope of the history the Stranger lays out, with Megillos's assistance, both the focus on the Cyclopes as "heroes" and the affirmation of Kleinias's limited imagination of justice is surprising. To neither of these circumstances does the Stranger react with any indignation. With respect to both the mythical cannibal of flesh, and the contemporary cannibal of spirit, the Stranger speaks with equanimity and understanding, blaming neither the one nor the other. His apparent concern is justice, yet he seems and is incapable of blaming others for even the worst transgressions of justice. This lack of indignation, together with the incorporation of all antecedent events known and unknown into his actions, emerged as part and parcel of his responsibility.

At the same time, two examples of what seemed to be strongly expressed indignation posed challenges to this reading: in Book 7 of the *Laws*, Megillos indignantly comes to the defense of the human species as a whole, and in Book 8 the Stranger is accused by Kleinias of outright hatred of certain human beings. Understanding these challenges required detailed consideration of the context in which they emerged, the discussion of erotic desire for moneyed wealth and sex, and in particular the strange image of animal desire and self-control that is presented by the Stranger to Kleinias, throughout the *Laws*, as a seeming standard of natural right. Upon closer consideration, that image turned out to be at odds not only with "the nature of beasts," and not only with the very human psychology to which it seemed intended to appeal (through a sense of honor), but also—indeed especially—with the philosophical "Socratic" eros that the Stranger and Megillos (though not Kleinias) agreed was the highest human eros, and even presented as the most desirable eros politically. The Stranger's hesitancy or refusal to speak of that image as simply true emerged as a pregnant hesitancy, as a deliberate and successful attempt to speak separately with Megillos about the severe limits of human voluntariness even as he urged Kleinias to celebrate voluntariness as a capacity that only the dishonorable would fail to exercise. Put another way, the Stranger and Megillos illustrate in deed what it means to *take* responsibility, which entails accepting that Kleinias is unable to do so or even to imagine what such responsibility might be, and therefore also entails depending politically on the limits of Kleinias's imagination—honor and shame, reward and retribution, blame and evasion—if the notion of responsibility is to have any political bearing at all.

The true standard of natural right presented by Plato in the *Laws* is thus responsibility as it is lived by the Stranger and Megillos, a responsibility that by its nature entails the adoption of images of responsibility that point toward true responsibility in terms that may be actively imagined and enacted by those who are not by nature responsible. The drama of the *Laws* illustrates the ways in which such images, properly laid down according to nature, may at once satisfy such a human being as Kleinias, and provoke someone like

Megillos toward understanding that the image is an image. Careful consideration of the Stranger's proposals for the erotic regime of Magnesia—which seem to unequivocally condemn homosexuality and extramarital sexual relations, but in fact rely on both fundamentally—reveals the ways in which this is so, and why. At issue here is the quandary of the difference between nature and convention or law, a quandary that, to Plato's mind, is itself an image that both conceals and reveals the true difference: between what is natural and what is voluntary (which should not be equated or confused with "freedom"). And the only possibility of acting voluntarily is to take responsibility for every circumstance of one's life, the entire history of one's becoming, the whole of one's company: for human nature. Such people as take this responsibility, and only such people, are worthy of the name Lawgiver, though it would by their own standards be irresponsible to deny that title to Kleinias.

NOTES

1. And yet the two sit uneasily together, even in Kleinias's dream, and maintain their contradiction in, among other things (762e), separate images of gender. One may wonder to what extent the images of gender affect the contradictory desires, and to what extent the contradiction of desires affects the images of gender. Cf. 802e8–803a1 with 681b1–4, 814e–815d (n.b. 815c8–d5), and 770c7–e5.

2. It is worth noting, for our purposes, that what von Clausewitz means by "determination" is the absence of what the Stranger says is called "the greatest ignorance."

3. To what extent Plato's readers are in the same manner influenced by him is worthy of reflection. It does not seem impossible to me that Plato anticipated Kleinian readers.

Bibliography

Adam, J. 1902. *The* Republic *of Plato*. Cambridge: Cambridge University Press.

Adam, J. 1911. *The Vitality of Platonism and Other Essays*. Ed., A. M. Adams. Cambridge: Cambridge University Press.

Al-Farabi. [No date]. *Summary of Plato's* Laws. Trans. M. Mahdi. Unpublished, on file with the author.

Al-Farabi. 2001. *Philosophy of Plato and Aristotle*. Trans. M. Mahdi. Ithaca, NY: Cornell University Press.

Al-Farabi. 2011. "The Political Regime." In *Medieval Political Philosophy*, 2nd Edition, eds. J. Parens and J. C. Macfarland. Trans. C. E. Butterworth, 36–55. Ithaca, NY: Cornell University Press. 36–55.

Allen, D. 2001. "Democratic Dis-ease: Of Anger and the Troubling Nature of Punishment." In *The Passions of Law*. Ed., S. A. Bandes. New York: New York University Press. 191–214.

Annas, J. 1981. *An Introduction to Plato's* Republic. New York and London: Oxford University Press.

Anonymous 2003. [*Prolegomena philosophiae platonicae*] *Prolégomènes à la philosophie de platon*. Ed., L. G. Westerlink. Trans. J. Trouillard. Paris: Société de l'édition Les Belles Lettres.

Arendt, H. 1998. *The Human Condition*. Chicago: University of Chicago Press.

Ast, G. A. F. 1816. *Platons Leben und Schriften*. Leipzig: Weidmann.

Averroës. 2005. *Averroes on Plato's* Republic. Trans., with Introduction and Notes, R. Lerner. Ithaca and London: Cornell University Press.

Averroës. 2011. "The Decisive Treatise." In *Medieval Political Philosophy*, 2nd Edition. Eds., J. Parens and J. C. Macfarland, trans. F. M. Najjar, 123–40. Ithaca, NY: Cornell University Press.

Barringer, J. M. 2001. *The Hunt in Ancient Greece*. Baltimore: Johns Hopkins University Press.

Belge, C. 2011. State Building and the Limits of Legibility: Kinship Networks and Kurdish Resistance in Turkey. *International Journal of Middle East Studies* 43: 95–114.

Benardete, S. 2000. *Plato's* Laws*: The Discovery of Being*. Chicago and London: University of Chicago Press.

Benardete, S. 1991. *The Rhetoric of Morality and Philosophy: Plato's* Gorgias *and* Phaedrus. Chicago and London: University of Chicago Press.

Bloom, H. 1998. *Shakespeare: The Invention of the Human*. New York: Penguin Riverhead Books.

Blondell, R. 2006. *The Play of Character in Plato's Dialogues*. Cambridge: Cambridge University Press.

Bobonich, C. 2010. "Images of Irrationality." In *Plato's* Laws*: A Critical Guide*. Ed., C. Bobonich, 149–71. Cambridge: Cambridge University Press.

Bobonich, C. (ed.) 2010. *Plato's* Laws*: A Critical Guide*. Cambridge: Cambridge University Press.

Bowen, A. C. 1988. "On Interpreting Plato." In *Platonic Writings, Platonic Readings*. Ed., C. L. Griswold, Jr., 49–65. New York: Routledge.

Brann, E. 2004. *The Music of the* Republic*: Essays on Socrates' Conversations and Plato's Writings*. With P. Kalkavage and E. Salem. Philadelphia: Paul Dry Books.

Burger, R. 2008. *Aristotle's Dialogue with Socrates: On the* Nicomachean Ethics. Chicago and London: University of Chicago Press.

Burkert, W. 1983. *Homo Necans: The Anthropology of Ancient Greek Sacrificial Ritual and Myth*. Trans. P. Bing. Berkeley: University of California Press.

Christ, M. R. 1989. The Authenticity of Thucydides 3.84. *Transactions of the American Philological Association (1974–)* 119: 137–48.

Cicero, M. T. 1994. *De officiis*. Ed., M. Winterbottom. Oxford: Clarendon Press.

Cicero, M. T. 2006. *De re publica, De legibus, Cato maior de senectute, Laelius de amicitia*. Ed., J. G. F. Powell. Oxford: Clarendon Press.

Clark, R. B. 2003. *The Law Most Beautiful and Best: Medical Argument and Magical Rhetoric in Plato's* Laws. Lanham, MD: Lexington Books.

Clausewitz, C. von. 2016. *Vom Kriege*. Altenmünster: Jazzybee Verlag.

Cusher, B. E. 2011. From Natural Catastrophe to the Human Catastrophe: Plato on the Origins of Written Law. *Law, Culture, and the Humanities* 9 (2): 275–94.

Dihle, A. 1982. *The Theory of Will in Classical Antiquity*. Berkeley and Los Angeles: University of California Press.

Dunshirn, A. 2010. *Logos bei Platon als Spiel und Ereignis*. Würzburg: Königshausen & Neumann.

England, E. B. 1921. *The* Laws *of Plato: The Text Ed. with Introduction, Notes, etc*., 2 vols. Manchester: Manchester University Press.

Erez, E., and P. Tontodonato. 1992. Victim Participation in Sentencing and Satisfaction with Justice. *Justice Quarterly* 9 (3): 393–415.

Ficino, M. 1588 [Imprint]. *Divini Platonis Opera Omnia*. Lyon: Nathaniel Vincent.

Ficino, M. 2006. *Gardens of Philosophy: Ficino on Plato*. [Ficino's commentaries on 25 dialogues of Plato, and the Letters.] Trans. A. Farndell. London: Shepheard-Walwyn.

Ficino, M. 2009. *When Philosophers Rule: Ficino on Plato's* Republic, Laws, *and* Epinomis. Trans. A. Farndell. London: Shepheard-Walwyn.

Finnis, J. M. 1997. Good of Marriage and the Morality of Sexual Relations. *American Journal of Jurisprudence* 42: 97–134.

Finnis, J. M. 1994. Law, Morality, and Sexual Orientation. *Notre Dame Journal of Law Review* 69 (5): 1049–1076.

Follon, J. 2003. "Note sur l'idée d'amitié dans les *Lois*." In *Plato's* Laws*: From Theory into Practice, Proceedings of the VI Symposium Platonicum*. Eds., S. Scolnicov and L. Brisson, 186–190. Sankt Augustin: Academia.

Friedland, E. 2013. "Not to Destroy but to Fulfill" in *Nietzsche's Therapeutic Teaching*. Eds., H. Hutter and E. Friedland, 235–245. London: Bloomsbury.

Gaca, K. 2003. *The Making of Fornication: Eros, Ethics, and Political Reform in Greek Philosophy and Early Christianity*. Berkeley: University of California Press.

Gomperz, T. 1902. *Griechische Denker: Eine Geschichte der antiken Philosophie*, vol. 2. Leipzig: Velt.

Gonzalez, F. 2013. "No Country for Young Men: Eros as Outlaw in Plato's *Laws*." In *Plato's* Laws*: Force and Truth in Politics*. Eds., G. Recco and E. Sanday, 154–168. Bloomington: Indiana University Press.

Görgemanns, H. 1960. *Beiträge zur Interpretation von Platons* Nomoi. Munchen: C. H. Beck Verlag.

Gray, J. G. 1998. *The Warriors: Reflections on Men in Battle*. London: Bison Books.

Grote, G. 1888. *Plato, and the Other Companions of Sokrates*, New Edition, 4 vols. London: John Murray.

Hadot, I. 1996. "Introduction générale." In *Simplicius. Commentaire sur le Manuel d'Epictète.* Introduction et édition critique du text grec. Ed., I. Hadot, 1–182. Leiden, New York, and Köln: E. J. Brill.

Hadot, P. 2002. *Exercices spirituel et philosophie antique.* Paris: Albin Michel.

Hadot, P. 2001. *La philosophie comme manière de vivre.* Paris: Albin Michel.

Haveli, Y. 2009. *The Kuzari: In Defense of the Despised Faith.* Bilingual Edition. Trans. N. Daniel Korobkin. New York: Feldheim Publishers.

Havelock, E. A. 1982. *Preface to Plato.* Cambridge, MA: Harvard University Press.

Hobbes, T. 1994. *Leviathan.* Ed., E. Curley. Indianapolis: Hackett.

Hobbs, A. 2000. *Plato and the Hero: Courage, Manliness, and the Impersonal Good.* Cambridge: Cambridge University Press.

Howse, R. 2015. *Leo Strauss: Man of Peace.* New York: Cambridge University Press.

Hume, D. 2007. *A Treatise of Human Nature: A Critical Edition.* Eds., D. F. Norton and M. J. Norton. Oxford: Oxford University Press.

John of Salisbury. 1991. *Metalogicon.* Eds., J. B. Hall and K. S. B. Keats-Rohan. (Corpus Christianorum Continuatio Medievalis, vol. 98). Turnhout: Brepols.

Jordan, M. D. 1997. *The Invention of Sodomy in Christian Theology.* Chicago and London: University of Chicago Press.

Kahn, C. H. 1988. "Discovering the Will: From Aristotle to Augustine." In *The Question of "Eclecticism": Studies in Later Greek Philosophy.* Eds., J. M. Dillon and A. A. Long. Berkeley and Los Angeles: University of California Press.

Kahn, C. H. 1998. "Pre-Platonic Ethics." In *Companions to Ancient Thought 4: Ethics.* Ed., S. Everson, 27–48. Cambridge: Cambridge University Press.

Kang, J. M. 2003. The Uses of Insincerity: Thomas Hobbes' Theory of Law and Society. *Law and Literature* 15 (3): 371–93.

Klosko, G. 1988. The Nocturnal Council in Plato's *Laws. Political Studies* 36: 74–88.

Kochin, M. S. 2002. *Gender and Rhetoric in Plato's Political Thought.* Cambridge: Cambridge University Press.

Krämer, H-J. 1972. *Platonismus und Hellenistiche Philosophie.* Germany: de Gruyter.

Lampert, L. 2010. *How Philosophy Became Socratic: A Study of Plato's* Protagoras, Charmides, *and* Republic. Chicago: University of Chicago Press.

Lampert, L. 2002. Socrates' Defense of Polytropic Odysseus: Lying and Wrong-Doing in Plato's *Lesser Hippias. The Review of Politics* 64 (2): 231–59.

Lenzner, S. 1999. The Problem of Happiness Today. *The Good Society* 9(2): 52–54.

Lewis, G. C. 1845. "The Hellenics of Xenophon, and Their Division into Books." In *The Classical Museum: A Journal of Philology, and of Ancient History and Literature*, vol. 2. Ed., L. Schmitz, 1–44. London: Taylor and Walton.

Lewis, V. B. 1998. The Nocturnal Council and Platonic Political Philosophy. *History of Political Thought* 19 (1): 1–20.

Locke, J. 1996. *Some Thoughts Concerning Education and of the Conduct of the Understanding.* Eds., R. W. Grant and N. Tarcov. Indianapolis: Hackett.

Locke, J. 2005. "The Second Treatise of Government. An Essay Concerning the True Original, Extent, and End of Civil Government." In *The Selected Political Writings of John Locke.* Ed., P. S. Sigmund, 17–124. New York: Norton.

Loomis, W. T. 1972. The Nature of Premeditation in Athenian Homicide Law. *The Journal of Hellenic Studies* 92: 86–95.

Lord, C. 1981. The Character and Composition of Aristotle's *Politics. Political Theory* 9 (4): 459–478.

Lutz, M. J. 2012. *Divine Law and Political Philosophy in Plato's* Laws. DeKalb, IL: Northern Illinois University Press.

Maffi, A. 2007. Quarant'anni di studi sul processo greco, I. *Dike* 10: 185–267.

Maimonides, M. 1963. *The Guide of the Perplexed*, 2 vols. Trans. S. Pines. Chicago: University of Chicago Press.

Maimonides, M. 1997. *Mishneh Torah*, 18 vols. Trans. E. Touger. Brooklyn: Moznaim.

Mathie, W. 1986. Reason and Rhetoric in Hobbes's *Leviathan. Interpretation* 14 (2 and 3): 281–98.

Manning, K. E. 2005. Marxist Maternalism, Memory, and the Mobilization of Women in the Great Leap Forward. *China Review* 5(1): 83–110.

Mayhew, R. 2008. *Plato: Laws 10, Translated with an Introduction and Commentary.* Oxford: Clarendon Press.

Meyer, S. S. 2015. *Plato: Laws 1 and 2, Translated with an Introduction and Commentary.* Oxford: Clarendon Press.

Minow, M. 2001. "Institutions and Emotions: Redressing Mass Violence." In *The Passions of Law.* Ed., S. A. Bandes, 265–81. New York: New York University Press.

More, Thomas. 2003. *Utopia.* Trans. R. M. Adams. Cambridge: Cambridge University Press.

Morgan, K., and B. L. Smith. 2005. Victims, Punishment, and Parole: The Effect of Victim Participation on Parole Hearings. *Criminology and Public Policy* 4 (2): 333–60.

Morrow, G. 1960. *Plato's Cretan City.* Princeton: Princeton University Press.

Müller, G. 1951. *Studien zu den platonischen* Nomoi. *Zetemata: Monographien zur klassischen Altertumswissenschaft,* vol. 3. Munich: C. H. Beck.

Munn, M. 2013. "*Erôs* and the *Laws* in Historical Context" in *Plato's Laws: Force and Truth in Politics.* Eds., G. Recco and E. Sanday, 31–47. Bloomington: Indiana University Press.

Nails, D. 1993. Problems with Vlastos' Platonic Developmentalism. *Ancient Philosophy* 13 (2): 273–305.

Nietzsche, F. 1966. *Werke in Drei Bänden,* 4 vols. Ed., Karl Schlechta. München: Carl Hanser

Nietzsche, F. 2005. *Thus Spoke Zarathustra: A Book for Everyone and Nobody.* Trans. G. Parkes. New York: Oxford University Press.

Nightingale, A. W. 1999a. Historiography and Cosmology in Plato's *Laws. Ancient Philosophy* 19 (2): 299–326.

Nightingale, A. W. 1999b. Plato's Lawcode in Context: Rule by Written Law in Athens and Magnesia. *The Classical Quarterly* 49 (1): 100–122.

Nightingale, A. W. 1993. Writing/Reading a Sacred Text: A Literary Interpretation of Plato's *Laws. Classical Philology* 88 (4): 279–300.

Nussbaum, M. 1994. Platonic Love and Colorado Law: The Relevance of Ancient Greek Norms to Modern Sexual Controversies. *Virginia Law Review* 80 (7): 1515–1651.

Okin, S. 1977. Philosopher Queens and Private Wives: Plato on Women and the Family. *Philosophy and Public Affairs* 6 (4): 345–69.

Pangle, L. S. 2009. Moral and Criminal Responsibility in Plato's *Laws. American Political Science Review* 203 (3): 456–73.

Pangle, T. L. 1976. The Political Psychology of Religion in Plato's *Laws. The American Political Science Review* 70: 1059–77.

Pangle, T. L. 1987. "Editor's Introduction." In *The Roots of Political Philosophy: Ten Forgotten Socratic Dialogues.* Ed., T. L. Pangle, 1–20. Ithaca and London: Cornell University Press.

Pangle, T. L. 1988 = Plato 1988.

Parens, J. 1995. *Metaphysics as Rhetoric: Alfarabi's* Summary of Plato's "Laws." New York: SUNY Press.

París Albert, S. 2013. Philosophy, Recognition, and Indignation. *Peace Review: A Journal of Social Justice* 25 (3): 336–42.

Picht, G. 1990. *Platons Dialoge "Nomoi" und "Symposion."* Ed., C. Eisenbart. Stuttgart: Klett-Cotta.

Plato. 1988. *The* Laws *of Plato.* Trans. with Notes and an Interpretive Essay, T. L. Pangle. Chicago: Chicago University Press.

Plato. 1956–1968. *Les Lois* in *Plato, Oeuvres complètes,* vols. 11–12. Eds. and trad., E. des Places & A. Diès. Paris: Société d'Édition "Les Belles Lettres."

Plato. 1994–2011. *Nomoi* in *Platon Werke* IX.2 (3 Bänden). Übersetzung und Kommentar von K. Schöpsdau. Göttingen: Vandenhoeck & Ruprecht.

Plato. 1995. *Opera,* vol. 1. Eds., E. A. Duke, W. F. Hicken, W. S. Nicoll, D. B. Robinson, and J. C. G. Strachan. Oxford: Clarendon Press.

Plato. 1960–1962. *Opera,* vols. 2–5. Ed., J. Burnet. Oxford: Clarendon Press.

Plato. 2003. *Rempublicam.* Ed., S. R. Slings. Oxford: Clarendon Press.

Plato. 1991. *The* Republic *of Plato,* 2nd Edition. Trans. A. Bloom. New York: Basic Books.

Plato 2009. *The Tragedy and Comedy of Life: Plato's* Philebus. Trans. with Commentary by S. Benardete. Chicago: University of Chicago Press.

Pocock, J. G. A. 1972. *The Machiavellian Moment: Florentine Political Thought and the Atlantic Republican Tradition*. Princeton: Princeton University Press.

Post, L. A. 1939. Notes on Plato's *Laws*. *American Journal of Philology* 60 (1): 93–105.

Post, L. A. 1930. Some Emendations of Plato's *Laws*. *Transactions and Proceedings of the American Philological Association* 61: 29–42.

Proust, M. 1999. *À la recherche du temps perdu*. Paris: Gallimard.

Read, D. W. 2014. Incest Taboos and Kinship: A Biological or Cultural Story? *Reviews in Anthropology* 43 (2): 1–23.

Reeve, C. D. C. 2006. "Plato on *Eros* and Friendship." In *A Companion to Plato*. Ed., H. H. Benson, 294–307. Malden, MA: Blackwell Publishing.

Rilke, R. M. 1997. *The Rose Window and Other Verse from New Poems*. Bilingual edition with various translators. New York: Bullfinch Press.

Roberts, J. 1987. Plato on the Causes of Wrongdoing in the *Laws*. *Ancient Philosophy* 7: 23–37.

Ross, M. H. 2009. "Culture in Comparative Political Analysis." In *Comparative Politics: Rationality, Culture, and Structure*, 134–61. Cambridge: Cambridge University Press.

Ross, M. H. 2004. "Ritual and the Politics of Reconciliation." In *From Conflict Resolution to Reconciliation*. Ed., Y. Bar-Siman-Tov, 197–223. Oxford: Oxford University Press.

Rothschild, Z. K., and L. A. Keefer. 2017. A Cleansing Fire: Moral Outrage Alleviates Guilt and Buffers Threats to One's Moral Identity. *Motivation and Emotion* 41 (2): 209–29.

Rousseau, J. J. 2003. *Oeuvres complètes*, vol. 3. France: Bibliothèque de la Pléiade, Éditions Gallimard.

Rowe, C. 2010. "The Relationship of the *Laws* to the Other Dialogues: A Proposal." In *Plato's* Laws*: A Critical Guide*. Ed., Bobonich, C. New York: Cambridge University Press. 29–50.

Russon, J. 2013. "Education in Plato's *Laws*" in *Plato's* Laws*: Force and Truth in Politics*. Eds., G. Recco and E. Sanday. Bloomington: Indiana University Press. 60–74.

Salem, E. 2013. "The Long and Winding Road: Impediments to Inquiry in Book 1 of the *Laws*" in *Plato's* Laws*: Force and Truth in Politics*. Eds., G. Recco and E. Sanday, 48–59. Bloomington: Indiana University Press.

Sallis, J. 2013. "On Beginning after the Beginning" in *Plato's* Laws*: Force and Truth in Politics*. Eds., G. Recco and E. Sanday, 75–85. Bloomington: Indiana University Press.

Sanday, E. 2013. "Propriety and Impropriety in Plato's *Laws*: Books 11 and 12." In *Plato's* Laws*: Force and Truth in Politics*. Eds., G. Recco and E. Sanday, 215–236. Bloomington: Indiana University Press.

Saunders, T. J. 1972. *Notes on the* Laws *of Plato*. London: Institute of Classical Studies.

Saunders, T. J. 1994. *Plato's Penal Code: Tradition, Controversy and Reform in Greek Penology*. Oxford: Clarendon Press.

Saunders, T. J. 1976. Review of *The Argument and the Action of Plato's* Laws, by Leo Strauss. *Political Theory* 4(2): 239–42.

Saunders, T. J. 1968. The Socratic Paradoxes in Plato's *Laws*: A Commentary. *Hermes* 96 (3): 421–34.

Saxonhouse, A. 2005. Another Antigone: The Emergence of the Female Political Actor in Euripides' *Phoenician Women*. *Political Theory* 33 (4): 472–494.

Sayre, K. M. 1988. "Plato's Dialogues in Light of the *Seventh Letter*." In *Platonic Writings, Platonic Readings*. Ed., C. L. Griswold, Jr. New York: Routledge. 93–109.

Schlabach, G. W. 1994. Augustine's Hermeneutic of Humility: An Alternative to Moral Imperialism and Moral Relativism. *The Journal of Religious Ethics* 22 (2): 299–330.

Schleiermacher, F. 1833. *Introductions to the Dialogues of Plato*. Trans. W. Dobson. Cambridge and London: J. J. Deighton and J. W. Parker.

Schmidt, V. A. 2008. Discursive Institutionalism: The Explanatory Power of Ideas and Discourse. *Annual Review of Political Science* 11: 303–26.

Schneider, L. 2014. *Government of Development: Peasants and Politicians in Postcolonial Tanzania*. Bloomington, IN: Indiana University Press.

Schöpsdau, K. 2003. "Syssitien für Frauen: eine platonische Utopie." In *Plato's Laws: From Theory to Practice; Proceedings of the VI Symposium Platonicum*. Eds., S. Scolnicov and L. Brisson. Sankt Augustin: Academia. 243–56.

Schöpsdau, K. 1994–2011. *See* Plato. 1994–2011.

Sewell-Rutter, N. J. 2007. *Guilt by Descent: Moral Inheritance and Decision Making in Greek Tragedy*. Oxford: Oxford University Press.

Shorey, P. 1903. *The Unity of Plato's Thought*. Chicago: University of Chicago Press.

Skinner, Q. 2002. *Visions of Politics, Volume 1: Regarding Method*. Cambridge: Cambridge University Press.

Stalley, R. F. 1983. *An Introduction to Plato's Laws*. Indianapolis: Hackett Publishing.

Strauss, L. 1975. *The Argument and the Action of Plato's Laws*. Chicago: University of Chicago Press.

Strauss, L. 2013. *Leo Strauss on Maimonides: The Complete Writings*. Ed., K. H. Green. Chicago: University of Chicago Press.

Strauss, L. 1968. *Liberalism Ancient and Modern*. New York: Basic Books.

Strauss, L. 1965. *Natural Right and History*. Chicago: University of Chicago Press.

Strauss, L. 1987. "On the *Minos*." In *The Roots of Political Philosophy: Ten Forgotten Socratic Dialogues*. Ed., T. L. Pangle, 67–79. Ithaca and London: Cornell University Press.

Strauss, L. 1991. *On Tyranny* (revised and expanded edition). New York: Free Press.

Strauss, L. 1988a. *Persecution and the Art of Writing*. Chicago: University of Chicago Press.

Strauss, L. 1966. *Socrates and Aristophanes*. New York and London: Basic Books.

Strauss, L. 1978. *Thoughts on Machiavelli*. Chicago: University of Chicago Press.

Strauss, L. 1988b. *What Is Political Philosophy? And Other Essays*. Chicago: University of Chicago Press.

Sweet, D. R. 1987. "On the Greater Hippias." In *The Roots of Political Philosophy: Ten Forgotten Socratic Dialogues*. Ed., T. L. Pangle, 340–55. Ithaca and London: Cornell University Press.

Taki, A. 2003. "The Origin of the Lengthy Digression in Plato's *Laws*, Books I and II." In *Plato's Laws: From Theory to Practice; Proceedings of the VI Symposium Platonicum*. Eds., S. Scolnicov and L. Brisson, 48–53. Sankt Augustin: Academia.

Taplin, O. 2001. "Spreading the Word through Performance." In *Performance Culture and Athenian Democracy*. Eds., S. Goldhill and R. Osborne, 33–57. Cambridge: Cambridge University Press.

Tarnopolsky, C. 2011. Plato's Politics of Distributing and Disrupting the Sensible. *Theory and Event* 13 (4).

Tarnopolsky, C. 2010. *Prudes, Perverts, and Tyrants: Plato's* Gorgias *and the Politics of Shame*. Princeton: Princeton University Press.

Thucydides. 1966. *Thukydides*, 8 vols. Ed., J. Classen, Rev. J. Steup. Berlin/Zürich/Dublin: Weidmann.

Treantafelles, J. S. 2013. Socratic Testing: *Protagoras* 310a–314b. *Interpretation* 40 (2): 147–73.

Valiquette, N. 2013. *Musical Judgment: Aesthetics and Jurisprudence in Plato*. PhD Book, McGill University. On file with the author.

Vico, G. 1959. *Principj di scienza nuova d'intorno alla comune natura delle nazioni*. In *Opere*. Ed., P. Rossi. Milan: Biblioteca Universale Rizzoli.

Vlastos, G. 1991. *Socrates: Ironist and Moral Philosopher*. Ithaca, NY: Cornell University Press.

Voegelin, E. 1977. *Order and History*, vol. 3. Baton Rouge: Louisiana State University Press.

Wallace, R. 1996. "Amaze Your Friends!" Lucretius on Magnets. *Greece & Rome* 43 (2): 178–87.

Walser, R. 2015. *Looking at Pictures*. Trans. S. Bernofsky, L. Davis, and C. Middleton. New York: Christine Burgin and New Directions.

Wedeen, L. 1999. *Ambiguities of Domination*. Chicago: University of Chicago Press.

Wedeen, L. 2002. Conceptualizing Culture: Possibilities for Political Science. *American Political Science Review* 96 (4): 713–28.

Weil, R. 1959. *L'"archéologie" de Platon*. Paris: Klincksieck.

Whitaker, A. 2004. *A Journey into Platonic Politics: Plato's* Laws. Lanham, MD: University Press of America.

Wieland, W. 1982. *Platon und die Formen des Wissens*. Göttingen: Vandenhoeck und Ruprecht.

Wilamowitz-Möllendorff, U. von. 1920. *Platon* (2nd ed.), Band 2. Berlin: deGruyter.

Wilamowitz-Möllendorff, U. von. 1982. *History of Classical Scholarship*. Ed. (and Introduction), H. Lloyd-Jones. Trans. A. Harris. Baltimore: Johns Hopkins Press.

Winch, P. 1959. Nature and Convention. *Proceedings of the Aristotelian Society*, New Series 60: 231–52.

Wolfson, H. A. 1950–1951. Averroes' Lost-Treatise on the Prime Mover. *Hebrew Union College Annual*. 23 (1): 683–710.

Zuckert, C. H. 2004. Plato's *Laws*: Postlude or Prelude to Socratic Political Philosophy? *The Journal of Politics* 66 (2): 374–95.

Zuckert, C. H. 2009. *Plato's Philosophers: The Coherence of the Dialogues*. Chicago: University of Chicago Press.

A Note on the Index

In the interest of avoiding a Borgesian map the size of the territory it is intended to chart, I have been selective rather than exhaustive, both in terms of the headings and the page references listed for those headings. Many of the headings are revisited so often throughout the text that citing every instance would defeat the purpose of an index. Characters from the *Laws* are not listed here, nor are their cities/territories of origin, as they each appear on the majority of the text's pages. "Nature" and "law" are likewise omitted, as is "justice."

Index

About the Author

Eli Friedland holds a PhD in political science from Concordia University. He is an independent scholar in Montréal.

www.ingramcontent.com/pod-product-compliance
Lightning Source LLC
Chambersburg PA
CBHW022314280326
41932CB00010B/1096